How to Live Well

How to Live Well

ETHICS IN THE
WORLD RELIGIONS

Denise Lardner Carmody
John Tully Carmody

UNIVERSITY OF TULSA

Wadsworth Publishing Company
Belmont, California
A Division of Wadsworth, Inc.

Religion Editor: Sheryl Fullerton
Editorial Assistant: Cynthia Haus
Production Editor: Lisa Danchi
Managing Designer: Donna Davis
Print Buyer: Barbara Britton
Designers: Lisa Mirski and Donna Davis
Copy Editor: Greg Gullickson
Compositor: G & S Typesetters, Inc.
Cover: Mark McGeoch

Printed in the United States of America   19
    2   3   4   5   6   7   8   9   10——91

Library of Congress Cataloging-in-Publication
Data

Carmody, Denise Lardner, 1935 –
    How to live well.
    Bibliography: p.
    Includes index.
    1. Religion and ethics.   I. Carmody, John,
1939 –
II. Title.
BJ47.C33   1988   291.5   87-15964
ISBN 0-534-08472-9 #16094165

For
Jim and Margie
Haines

Contents

Preface

This text is a simple, consistent treatment of the ethical convictions of the major world religions. It presupposes no special background and claims only to be a first survey or general overview. In each chapter the format is the same: orientations to the history and world view of the tradition, and then concise treatments of family life, work, social justice, nature, and models of the ethical ideal. We define our main terms and explain our main assumptions in the introductory chapter, and in the concluding chapter we attempt a sustained contrast between the traditional ethical systems that have emerged in the major world religions and modern Western ethical assumptions.

In our Introduction, we describe the generalist approach we have thought suitable for undergraduates and briefly allude to the more technical distinctions favored by specialists when they deal with ethical theory, theory of religion, and analysis of such central issues as evil. Here perhaps we should situate our text regarding the emerging speciality called "comparative ethics." The state of this speciality is suggested by the following description by Ronald L. Green, one of its aspirant practitioners: "Unfortunately, while there are a number of good specific discussions of Christian, Jewish, Hindu, or Buddhist ethics, relatively little work has been done on the comparative analysis of religious traditions in a way comprising not just their specific normative teachings but also their doctrines of retribution and their fundamental ways of relating ethics to other features of the religious life." ("Morality and Religion," *The Encyclopedia of Religion*, ed. Mircea Eliade [New York: Macmillan 1987], vol. 10, p. 105).

To Green's own work (*Religious Reason*, [New York: Oxford University Press, 1978]) and that of David Little and Sumner Twiss (*Comparative Religious Ethics: A New Method*, [San Francisco: Harper & Row, 1978]), one should now add *Cosmogony and Ethical Order: New Studies in Comparative Ethics*, ed. Robin W. Lovin and Frank E. Reynolds (Chicago: University of Chicago Press, 1985). Certainly all three of these works shed valuable light on an enterprise like our own, but none of the three is appropriate for undergraduates. Each is a work by specialists for specialists, which means that the language is technical and the authors generally assume their readers know the rudiments of the history and doctrine of the religious tradition in question. Properly enough, the authors are chary of risking comparative generalizations, with the result that readers have to go other places if they are to secure a summary, synoptic sense of what living well has meant to Hindus and Jews or a rough indication of how Muslims and Japanese have differed in their views of marriage or social justice.

Since we have been so venturous as to try to offer undergraduates this sort of sense and indication, perhaps here we should provide a brief explanation of why we think the traditions can be treated in a generalist or holistic fashion. The essential explanation is twofold. First, on their own terms all of the traditions we treat are viewed as wholes—ways of life, organic cultural entities. Their own analysts of course make distinctions, because that is how any analytical mind works, but the common members of the communities in question, who are not scholarly analysts, sense that such distinctions are matters of convenience rather than ironclad differences found in either nature or the self. So, for example, most ordinary people in traditional cultures find it hard to separate law from custom. Equally, they think of their ethics as a compound of things encoded in reality (as a result of the way the world was born), things done by their ancestors to keep harmony with nature and within the tribe, and things that the self "knows" are right and just.

Of course, this commonsensical tendency is finally proven right by the silence into which the best scholarship heads. At the end of any analysis going deeply enough to contact the mystery of existence, the mind realizes that reason is unequal to the task of mapping the infinity of details. When this realization is allowed to bear its proper fruit, scholarship gains the wider contexts of wisdom and mysticism necessary if it is to be a helpful servant rather than a misleading lord.

Living well is a matter of the heart and the will as much as a matter of the mind. It depends on the constraints of nature, the pressures of one's social group, and the grace of God—all matters out of any actor's or analyst's hands. Unless one is able to make one's peace with these ways that (by the testimony of both the religious traditions and common sense) things are and forge some conclusions general enough to honor the mysteriousness of one's situation yet specific enough to catalyze the decisions one has to make, one will be unrealistic, unhappy, and either precipitous or paralyzed.

The second reason we have felt licensed to launch our venture is the sameness of human nature, which underlies the great variety of the religious cultures. All of the people we treat, and all of the people we address, are mortal, ignorant, capable of goodness, capable of evil, aware of beauty, troubled by ugliness, in need of guidance, aware (or soon to be made aware) that no guidance is infallible. Everywhere, therefore, ethics is a groping, tentative, evolving, corrigible affair—perhaps most poignantly where, in their anxiety or their straitened views of human nature and divinity, theologians, lawyers, and ethicists resort to fundamentalist absolutes and try to position themselves as the mouthpieces of a Power that escapes ignorance, error, and change.

Consequently, ethics is something done everywhere by people like ourselves, people from whom we can learn and to whom we might offer a word of advice. Seen in this way, the religious traditions about wisdom, living well, right behavior, and the like are not just matters for specialists. They are matters for any of us with the wit to realize that insight knows no cultural boundaries and with the gumption to exercise our imaginations and see how what others have found might brighten our own day. In this spirit, we almost rejoice that comparative ethics is a fledgling enterprise, and we hope that it will always retain the modesty becoming any exploration of a whole as mysterious as world religion. Long after specialists have pored over the relations of the contributions made by ritual, doctrine, economics, sociology, environment, and the dozen other influences on the ethical life, people having to find enough light to keep them from total confusion, enough love to keep them from total despair, will still be asking for brief advice about how to live well. Knowing this, each of the traditions we treat has come up with its own version of the final word uttered by Augustine: love and do what you will. That's pretty much the last of our own prefatory sentiments: get on with it—time is short and there's a lot to do.

We owe thanks to friends such as Jerry and Renée Unterman and Jim and Margie Haines, who have stimulated us to reflect on the ethical strata of the world religions; to Sheryl Fullerton of Wadsworth Publishing Company for sponsoring the project; and to the following readers who have offered helpful criticism and advice: Robert Ellwood, University of Southern California; Stephen Sapp, University of Miami; and Stephen Snyder, Linfield College.

Introduction

Ethics
World Religions
Evil
Preview
Summary, Study Questions, Notes

Ethics

The first notion we have to clarify is *ethics*. The word derives from the Greek *ethos*, which means the customs, mores, or traditional values of one's group. In terms of etymology or original usage, therefore, *ethics* implies "doing things as our kind have thought they should be done." For example, if the tradition of one's tribe was hospitality to strangers, then to refuse to share one's tent or one's food with a wayfarer who came knocking or calling was unethical. This seems simple enough, but only a little reflection is necessary to suggest how easily it could become complicated. Suppose, for example, that the person who came along was an enemy. Suppose that in a battle several years ago he had killed the eldest son of one's family. Did the tradition of hospitality to strangers still hold in such a case, or was it supplanted by a stronger instinct that one who killed a member of one's tribe ought ever after to be unwelcome in one's home?

One can see, therefore, that even in relatively simple cultures ethics quickly becomes complicated and supple. Traditions grew rather informally, as people met new circumstances and sought by trial and error to handle them wisely. Often, conflicting values brought people down on different sides of an issue. So frequently the custody of the community's ethics came to repose in the elders, who had been around long enough to have witnessed many different occasions when decisions had had to be forged. It is against this background that we should hear the Greek phi-

losopher Aristotle's opinion that one should start to discourse on ethics
only when one has reached fifty years of age. Prior to fifty, one would not
have had sufficient experience to discourse wisely.

Over time, of course, Aristotle's opinion was both respected and
disregarded. Over time, many communities did in fact look to their
elders to supply wisdom about public affairs, but younger tribal members frequently broke away to act on their own. Indeed, when civilization reached the stage where schooling was formalized and an academy
of people who professed expertise in different areas grew up, ethics could
become a subject with a supposedly objective body of data and principles
that students could master. In recent times it could develop subspecialties, such as the ethics of business or the ethics of medicine. It could
even subdivide these subspecialties, so that one could concentrate on
the ethics of investing or the ethics of abortion.

People who discourse on ethics today introduce several distinctions
that we should acknowledge and explain. First, there is a difference between **prescriptive ethics,** which deals with what ought to be done, and
descriptive ethics, which deals with what in fact is done. At the historical roots of ethical theory, where small-scale societies sought to order
themselves in the world successfully, these two aspects overlapped. Usually a tribe lacked a detached, analytical treatment of human nature by
which it could judge whether prospective actions fit the needs for which
human beings had been made, and so the tribe's ethics blended what traditionally had been done with what the tribe sensed to be fitting. Thus,
we might say that before the rise of modern **critical intelligence,** prescription and description were not adequately distinguished.

One may also speak of **metaethics,** meaning by this the world view
that grounds an ethical system. Even though small-scale societies frequently have not articulated their view of reality clearly and systemati-
cally, they usually have finally appealed to their sense of how the gods
made the world and where human beings fitted in. The societies informed by the great world religions have had available quite full meta-
ethical visions, since Hinduism, Buddhism, Christianity, and Islam have
all articulated their beliefs regarding human origins and human destiny
in considerable detail. For such societies, both what one ought to do and
what one's society in fact was doing could be set in the bigger framework
of how nature, society, and the self were thought to have been structured
by greater powers.

Nonetheless, only relatively recently has ethics become a separate
field of intellectual inquiry mapped by such distinctions as prescriptive
ethics, descriptive ethics, and metaethics. Moreover, these are not the
only distinctions that impinge on studies of ethics in the world religions. Thus even a brief article by David Little, who with Sumner Twiss
wrote one of the first American studies of comparative religious ethics,
distinguishes three main types of ethical systems.[1] The first is struc-

tured by a concern for the **ends** for which proposed actions are under-taken. Here the critical question is why one is attempting the given action, what good one hopes to achieve. An example would be President Harry Truman's decision that dropping atomic bombs on Japan would shorten the war and in the end save human lives. Frequently, therefore, an ethics focused on ends becomes **utilitarian.** The means that one is taking can be justified by the usefulness, the end result, that they intend. Joseph Fletcher, an American ethicist often considered the leading exponent of "situation ethics" (the view that what is right varies considerably depending on the circumstances, so that one's intentions or ends are the crucial determinant), represents this point of view.

A second type of ethical system that Little describes is structured by a sense of duty or obligation. In such a system certain principles always obtain and so block the sort of **relativism** and utilitarianism to which a system structured by ends is liable. An example of one such principle would be what the Christian ethicist Paul Ramsey calls "nonmaleficence." According to this principle, one may never directly seek to injure an innocent person for the sake of some supposedly greater good. If such a principle is granted full force, the action of dropping the atomic bombs on Japan was immoral, since it was bound directly to injure innocent people.

A third type of ethical system, often associated with H. Richard Niebuhr, a very influential American Protestant theologian of the past generation, stresses neither ends nor duty but responsibility. For Niebuhr, responsibility involves a sense of what is most fitting or appropriate—what best responds to the situation (including the people involved) with which one is concretely confronted. This third type places great weight on the character of the person making the ethical decision, since that person must both discern what is going on in the given situation and sense what response would be most fitting.

These three types of ethical systems that have evolved in recent American Protestant thought by no means exhaust the field, but they do illustrate the sort of refined analysis, replete with many conceptual distinctions and terminological fine-tunings, that has developed in modern times. Were we to continue this description and deal with Roman Catholic ethical theory, we would have to speak of "natural law": the notion that God has encoded in creatures, including human beings, basic patterns that they are either physically or morally bound to follow. Similarly, were we to extend our survey of ethics as a scholarly discipline so that it covered what Jewish, Muslim, Hindu, Buddhist, and other great religious systems have thought, more descriptions and definitions would be necessary. For our present introductory purposes, it will be sufficient that most of our treatments of given religious traditions stress prescription: what the given tradition says *ought* to be done. We will also indicate from time to time how the given tradition measured up to its ideals (description), and both in our introductions to the given traditions and in our treatments of their prescriptions under certain key headings, we shall regularly allude to the underpinnings on which a given ethical ideal depends (metaethics). But those seeking a full correlation of the ethics of the world religions with such current American Protestant interests as ends, duty, and responsibility will have to go to more specialized treatments. These are some of the technical aspects of current ethical theory that one can find displayed in any comprehensive handbook.[2]

One can find the practical aspects displayed quite grandly in any Sunday edition of the *New York Times*. The most personal aspects play in smaller theaters called private consciences. For while the newspapers and national legislatures and academic organizations are bound to keep agitating the complexity and enormity of social ethics, individuals have day by day to make specific choices, many of them almost cruelly narrowed to either/or. Either Mary Jane aborts this child with which she is four months pregnant or she carries it to term and then has to decide about the disposition of a new human being. At this point her other choices—the variant possibilities—seem shunted to the sidelines. Either Sean Joseph takes the job with the international conglomerate and works on laser weaponry or he turns it down. Tomorrow he may have a new job offer, of course, and with it a new set of decisions to make. Similarly, two years from now Mary Jane may be in quite different circumstances and so may view possible motherhood quite differently. But day after day individual human beings face here-and-now decisions that seem likely to color their lives ever after.

The burdens of ethical living therefore can seem crushing, and it is no wonder that hordes of people try to escape them. Still, the traditional wisdom of many different peoples has implied that one becomes fully human only by trying to shoulder precisely these ethical or moral responsibilities. Indeed, many peoples have defined wisdom itself as the capacity to balance the many demands of human responsibility with a simple love of human life. Primary among these people have been the most respected teachers of the great traditions of the world religions, to which we now turn.

World Religions

We understand **religion** as the dimension of human life or the sort of human activity that deals with the ultimate or biggest questions: Where did we come from? Where are we going? What is most important in life? The linguistic roots of the word *religion* are Latin, and most commentators point to a central figure of "binding" or "tying." Religion, then, would be the way that one ties oneself into reality, the binding stance that one takes toward the mysteriousness of sunrise and sunset, of death and life.

Just as there are various understandings of ethics and various approaches to ethical theory, so there are various understandings of religion and various theories of how to study religion. For some scholars, religion is completely a human enterprise. For other scholars, religion is a compound of both human and divine actions. Where some analysts of religion find it to be purely emotional, to the point of irrationality, other analysts deal with religion as centrally shaped by coherent ideas. A balanced approach to the comparison of different religious traditions, such as the approach of Joachim Wach, an influential scholar of the past generation, tends to give each of these factors its due.[3] Thus Wach accepted the view of his teacher Rudolf Otto that religion deals with a mystery that can be both fearsome and fascinating, whereas in his sketches of how religion ought to be studied he provided for religious thought, religious action, and religious communities.

Hans H. Penner, a more recent analyst of methodology in the study of religion, has distinguished at least six different approaches that have been influential in recent generations.[4] First, many scholars have been interested mainly in detailing the historical development of a given religious tradition. Thus we find many studies of particular epochs of Jewish history, of particular Hindu thinkers and statesmen, of Iranian Islam at a given time, and so forth. A second approach has been psychological. Indeed, such influential thinkers as Sigmund Freud, C. G. Jung, and William James have all proposed explanations of religious behavior, and many scholars continue to work in their wake, seeing religion largely in terms of the mechanisms that individuals develop for coping with death, disease, injustice, and life's mysteriousness.

A third approach to religion has been sociological. Here the pioneer figures were Émile Durkheim and Max Weber, who in their different ways laid open for further study the strong interaction between a society's self-conception and its ideas about God or the ultimate shapers and sanctioners of human behavior. Fourth, numerous scholars, especially in Europe, have approached religion **phenomenologically,** interesting themselves mainly in describing what religious people do in their ceremonies, assemblies, storytelling, and the like. Such phenomenologists tend to leave the further probing of the significance of such activities to philosophers or theologians, either because description seems to them sufficiently useful work in its own right or because they are not confident that "further significance" can be secured.

Penner's fifth and sixth approaches to the study of religion are **structuralist** and **semantic.** These are more recent methods that owe a great deal to developments in linguistics and studies of how people communicate meaning. It remains to be seen what long-lasting influence these latter approaches will have, but insofar as one may group them with other literary and philosophical methods that focus on meaning (such as **hermeneutics**), it is clear that presently they are much in vogue.

No doubt one could add to Penner's list, but his six approaches should be enough to suggest that religion can be approached in a great variety of ways. One could also make clearer than his brief article does that few of these methods are rigorous to the point that one could call them scientific, and that many good scholars employ several of the methods conjointly—for example, by analyzing both the history and the sociology of a given religious phenomenon or by providing both a description and a hermeneutical analysis. Our own approach will be mainly phenomenological, in the sense that we will be offering descriptions of how the tradition in question has considered its ideals for family life, social justice, and the like.

The world religions are those traditional ways of facing the mystery of life that have grown to the point where they embrace huge numbers of human beings. Most such traditions arose in the period between 2000 B.C.E. (before the historical era that Christians share with other peoples) and 650 C.E. Today the major religious traditions of the world enroll perhaps two-thirds of the world's five billion people. It is hard to obtain precise figures on this matter for several reasons (for example, the identification of religion and national tradition in such areas as East Asia and the lack of figures for most Communist countries), but it is clear that more people in the world today situate themselves in terms of a world religious tradition such as Hinduism or Islam than those who situate themselves without reference to a world religious tradition. Moreover, if one had raised the question of religiousness in periods prior to **modernity** (say, before the seventeenth century), the answer would have been even clearer. Prior to modernity, it was the rare individual indeed who did not subscribe to a religious orientation in the world.

For our purposes in this book, it is important to note the connection between ethics and religion in most traditional cultures. Almost without exception, peoples of the past have gained their sense of how they ought to act in the world, of what was right and what was wrong, from their Buddhist or Christian or other religious world view. So Buddhists have spoken of morality as one of the three principal concerns of the Buddha's teaching (meditation, morality, and wisdom), while Christians have placed "moral theology" alongside their theology that deals with doctrine, or what they believe. Moral theology is the study of how Christian doctrine applies to practical life, and Christians can point back to Jesus' own preaching (indeed, to the commandments that Jesus inherited from the Hebrew Bible) to authenticate its legitimacy.

This book deals with seven religious traditions that have shaped the lives of billions of human beings. Even today they shape the lives of the majority of the hundreds of millions of East Asians and Indians, of Europeans, Latin Americans, and Africans. In China, for example, the ancient teachings of Confucius, Lao Tzu, and the Buddha probably continue to be as influential (at least indirectly) as the more recent views of Karl Marx and Mao Tse-tung. In Japan the influence of Shinto and Buddhist traditions is at least as significant as the influence of the **agnosticism** that has come along with Western technology. The nations of the Middle East and of Africa would be markedly different it if were not for the deep imprint of Islam. Europe, North America, and Latin America all have been shaped in their present foundations by Christianity, and all continue to house vigorous Christian churches today. Hinduism continues to be the national culture of India. Judaism, finally, has both played the parent to Christianity and Islam (as an impartial history would see those traditions) and fostered a small but significant presence in a great many areas dominated by other religious traditions. Recently, of course, it has also gained dominance in the state of Israel.

None of these traditions teaches exactly the same ethics as any other, but all of them differ from ethical systems that do not claim religious roots. Judaism, Christianity, and Islam, for instance, all relate their ethical views to the **revelation** of a **monotheistic** divinity that they hold to be the creator of the universe. Hinduism and Buddhism are more complicated than the others on the question of divinity, but each speaks of an **unconditioned** state or goal by reference to which worldly actions may be transformed. For the East Asians who have been shaped by Confucius and Lao Tzu, a "way" come down from the venerable past offers guidance on how to gain harmony in both social affairs and one's relations with nature. So the ultimacy that we have associated with religion is quite prominent in all of these traditions.

By comparison, the ethical systems that divorce themselves from these traditions (or from less influential religious traditions that on this point are quite like these seven) both deal with ultimacy differently and generate a different tone. Marxism, for example, does not like to consider questions of first origin and final destiny. It is loathe to speak of mystery, sin, grace, revelation, yoga, enlightenment, ritual, and tradition with the reverence and docility that the religious traditions manifest. Similarly, the other **humanistic** ethical systems that have come to exert considerable influence in the modern West are more comfortable with economic, political, psychological, and scientific questions than they are with origins, destinies, and mysteries. So the religious ethical systems constitute a distinctive group. Even when the lines between them and nonreligious ethical outlooks blur on some points, their central concern with the ultimate or with big questions gives them a different configuration and feel.

Our focus in this book is the religious ethical systems, so we leave the nonreligious systems to the side. In making this choice we don't at all mean to imply that there is no wisdom in Marxism or other humanistic systems. Our exclusion is mainly pragmatic: we have only limited space at our disposal here, and it makes a neater package to handle only one portion of the already overwhelming reams of data. Indeed, any one of these seven traditions could be the subject of several full volumes of ethical investigations.

Evil

One of the central tensions and concerns in any ethical system is the relation between evil and good. People everywhere have felt themselves torn between experiences of things going badly and causing pain and experiences of things going smoothly and giving pleasure. Such terms as *badly, pain, smoothly,* and *pleasure* of course admit of different interpretations and significances. Ultimately any given ethical system has to define such terms in relation to one another. Indeed, the interlocking of its definitions of such terms is what makes an ethical perspective systematic. But for the moment let us leave such terms undefined, taking them in their rough, commonsensical significance. The only point we want to make right now is that all the different ethical systems, religious and nonreligious, refer to the common human experience that life is ambivalent: sometimes good and sometimes bad or evil. As a result, we can identify somewhat with any of them.

As we have expanded briefly on the notions of ethics and religion to suggest the complexity of current scholarly approaches to such notions, let us now expand briefly on the notion of evil. James P. Carse has described at least five different ways in which the religious and intellectual traditions of the world cultures have dealt with the problem of evil.[5]

First, there is the view that human freedom is an illusion and that human beings are not responsible for the human desires that lead to evil consequences. The ancient Greek philosophers called Epicureans tended to this view and many recent scientists, both natural and behavioral, in effect espouse it. Second, there is the view that human desire is the reason people suffer, a view that usually leads to a program that would have people use their freedom to eliminate human desire. Buddhists and Stoics are among the most famous groups that have advanced this position.

Third, there is the view that a single agent ultimately is unifying all of the actions in creation, with the result that what appears to be evil on our level is but part of an overall pattern of greater good. In effect, therefore, this third position denies the ultimate significance of what is evil according to the human perspective. Vedanta, a leading school of Hindu philosophy, is one of the Eastern examples of this position, while in the West, Plato and Leibniz stand out as its proponents. In the fourth view that Carse describes, a single agent will secure a final victory of good over evil. Judaism, Christianity, and Islam all fit this profile, inasmuch as all three both acknowledge the existence of evil and claim that God will finally triumph over evil.

Fifth, there is the dualistic position that makes evil and good coexist ineradicably. Zoroastrianism is a partial exponent of this position, as is Manicheanism, insofar as both religious traditions envision a time when forces of good and evil battle on fairly equal footing, before the final victory of good. Such modern Western thinkers as Jakob Böhme and William Blake espoused a more radical dualism, apparently thinking that evil and good were always equal possibilities because of divine and human freedom. Certain schools of Hindu theology approach this position, inasmuch as they find destruction and evil to be essential strands of the fabric of creation. One sees, therefore, that evil is far from a simple notion. Throughout history, different groups have taken quite different stances toward it.

What the religious traditions we shall deal with think about evil should emerge in the course of our exposition of their ethical views. At the moment, however, we want to secure the connection between what a Buddhist or a Christian of perhaps 1500 years ago experienced and what we experience today. We run into the evils known in the past whenever we take up an ancient text, and many such evils appear quite familiar. Theft, lying, infidelity, murder, prejudice, laziness, and the other individual vices, small or great, can seem a monotonous chant linking reports from the past with reports of today. But there are significant differences in the technologies of different ages, and sometimes there are significant differences in the social perceptions as well.

For example, the word *war* takes on a different meaning when one introduces nuclear power that has the capacity to destroy a local biosphere. The meaning of *lying* changes significantly if a political power acquires the capacity virtually to determine the news. And, relatedly, *justice* shifts its meaning significantly when changes in communications and travel make people part of an international economic and political system. *Violence* can undergo a parallel shift, leading to such perceptions as that of the Latin American "liberation theologians" who speak of a "white violence" (*violencia blanca*) that expresses itself in systematic poverty, hunger, ignorance, poor health care, and deprivation of political rights. Much of what we perceive to be "reality" or "actuality" depends on the range of our experience and the interpretive categories we use. Since these have shifted markedly in modern times, our educational encounters with the past usually need considerable cross-cultural translation.

The evil that plays at the center of so much of the world's literature takes many different forms, but most of them reduce to the instinctive assertion "This should not be." Sophocles, for example, examined the evil of disobeying one's conscience, setting it alongside the evil of disobeying the legitimate authority of one's city-state. The two evils crisscrossed when the dead person was both a sibling and an accused traitor. On a more abstract level, the Buddha set off in search of enlightenment because he had witnessed old age, sickness, and death. In each case the suffering the Buddha saw struck him as something that ought not to exist, something that he should try to outwit or escape. As he thought more about human existence in the light of this triple suffering or evil, he came to think that what we call life or creaturely existence is marked to the core by suffering. Thus, if we could outwit or escape suffering we would be capable of transforming the human condition as we first know it.

The biblical traditions, too, have devoted much ethical energy to evil, and in their case *salvation* or *righteousness* have served as the counter-terms to signify what things would be like if evil were overcome. So we may see their ethical systems, like the ethical systems of the ancient Greeks and the traditional Buddhists, as expressing their convictions about the nature of evil and the way that evil can be overcome.

As people who are now going to encounter such ethical systems, you will be well served by clarifying at least to some extent what you your-selves think or assume about evil. For example, do you tend to think that evil is a force like radiation or magnetism, working everywhere to shape personal and social situations? Do you think there is a mastermind be-hind the wars, tortures, frauds, and even natural disasters that pepper the weekly headlines? Or do you think that *evil* is just a vague name for hu-man stupidity or weakness, that it is caused either by bad heredity or bad environment? One way of making this kind of question specific is to ask yourselves whether you think people should be held accountable for their crimes or evildoing. Do you, for instance, hold yourselves account-able when you distort the truth or take what is not yours or fail to fulfill your promises?

One cannot think very long about such questions without starting to get a headache. They entail so many further questions and assump-tions that they make idiots of us all, even those of us who may claim the title of professional ethicist. The fact is that evil, and thus ethical think-ing, takes place in the midst of such complexity and ultimate mystery that we can never work out an airtight system. Ethics therefore is quite unlike mathematics or statistics. That is at the same time both its bur-den and its consolation.

Preview

How, then, do we plan to study the basic ethical advice that the major world religious traditions have offered? First, we shall take an essen-tialist or centrist approach, meaning by this an effort to stress what the mainstream or majority outlook has tended to be. Without denying the creativity or significant influence of dissident or minority positions, we shall emphasize what Jewish or Christian or Muslim **orthodoxy** has taught, both in the distant past and in recent times. Accepting the dictum "First things first," we have decided to concentrate on what most members of a given tradition would have been counseled in most ages. From time to time we shall point out alternative views that the given tradition has spawned or tolerated, but our usual treatment will not pay great heed to **sectarian** or idiosyncratic positions.

Second, we have adopted a rough-and-ready division of the world religious traditions into two parts, Western and Eastern. We shall introduce each part briefly, offering some suggestions about how the various traditions hold together and what the reader should look for, and then we shall develop the chapters on the seven different traditions that we are treating according to the same format or rhythm. The division of these traditions into Western and Eastern units can be challenged, of course, because Judaism, Christianity, and Islam all arose in the Middle or Near East, and because Indians and East Asians have taken their native traditions with them as they have emigrated around the world. So we are not suggesting that this division into two parts has great explanatory power. On the other hand, it makes some theoretical as well as practical sense, because Hinduism and Buddhism are sibling religions, while Buddhism interacted intimately with the native traditions of both China and Japan. Moreover, the emphasis of the Western traditions on a personal God distinguishes them from the less personalist and theistic Eastern traditions, at least on the gross level. But we counsel the reader not to make too much of this West-East distinction, since many personal and social dynamics cut across such distinctions and allow us to compare traditions more individually.

We begin with the Western traditions, thinking that these will be more familiar to most of our readers and so will make a less demanding start. This assumption also has its perils, however, because almost all teachers of world religions soon find that most students do not know their own religious traditions with the kind of detachment and academic sophistication that the most profitable comparative study requires. For example, one often meets Christian students who know very little about the faith of fellow-Christians brought up in a different one of the three major family groupings (Protestant, Catholic, and Eastern Orthodox). Even more frequently, Christians know virtually nothing about Judaism (as contrasted to the religion of the Old Testament) and often assume that with the coming of Jesus Judaism ceased to have any significance. Islam is an unknown continent to the majority of both Christians and Jews, and the recent tensions between Israelis and Palestinians regularly create a huge obstacle to mutual understanding. The majority of Muslims, for their part, are not familiar with the academic study of religion and find it very hard to approach their own tradition in a detached fashion. The same is true for many Christians brought up in fundamentalist churches. Thus it frequently turns out that the Western religions are not at all well-known even to Westerners, and that the Eastern traditions prove easier for Westerners to study. (It will be interesting to observe whether the reverse proves true for the many Hindus, Buddhists, and adherents of the native ways of East Asia who become Americans.)

A point that we cannot make too forcefully at the outset, therefore, is that we are trying to deal with all seven of these traditions in a detached or nonconfessional way. In dealing with Christianity, for instance, we are trying not to be unduly influenced by our own upbringing in Roman Catholicism. In dealing with the other traditions, we are trying to muster a steady blend of sympathy and objectivity. None of the world religious traditions has a monopoly on wisdom or virtue. For our purposes here, none of them merits a privileged position as expressing an exclusive revelation. All are very human entities, with much to be proud of but also much to be ashamed of.

We should also say, once and for all, that even after one has divided ethical systems or traditions into the religious and the nonreligious, there are significant religious statements or ways of life that we have no space to handle. Thus Jains, Bahais, Sikhs, and Zoroastrians will get virtually no attention. The traditions of ancient civilizations now gone to rest, such as those of classical Greece, Rome, Egypt, and Mesopotamia, will be similarly absent. We shall say nothing about the traditions of pre-Christian Europe and nothing about the rich ethical views of the shamanic traditions, ancient and contemporary, that were at the center of American Indian, traditional African, traditional Australian, and Eskimo cultures. Our book is but a small beginning, a brief introduction.

Finally, a word about the order of presentation that we shall follow in each chapter. To facilitate comparisons among the seven traditions that we do treat, we shall proceed in the same order for each tradition. First, we shall sketch the history of the given tradition, so that the reader has some sense of its chronological unfolding. Second, we shall give an abstract of the world view that such a brief history suggests: the basic outlook and sense of what is most important. Our third and fourth considerations will be what individuals in the given tradition have been counseled in the two areas that Freud thought most crucial for personal mental health and happiness: love (or family life) and work. The fifth topic will be social justice: how the tradition has spoken about economic, class, racial, sexual, and other sorts of equality and discrimination. Our sixth topic will be ecological matters (views of nature), and here, as in our consideration of social justice, we shall frequently be thinking about war. The final consideration in each chapter will be the models that the tradition has offered its adherents: how the saint, prophet, or sage who was proposed as a personal epitome of ethical success was supposed to look, think, and act.

At the end of each chapter we shall provide a brief summary. If the reader will link this summary with the outline that we provide at the outset of each chapter, the old advice given to public speakers may come to mind: tell them what you are going to do, do it, and then tell them what you have done. The study questions, which are usually review questions, are not principally queries for factual information. From time to time they will merely ask for a fact or a definition, but more frequently they will require the use of one's understanding to show, through performance or application, that one has indeed gotten the point. Many of the questions, no doubt to students' occasional irritation, do not have a right or wrong answer in any simple sense. Rather, they provide opportunities to manifest a good or a poor understanding, a creative or an uninspired use, of what one has been studying. The notes, finally, briefly indicate either our sources or further primary sources,[6] succinct treatments by other scholars,[7] or the fuller context that a more comprehensive textbook can provide.[8]

Summary

We began with a definition of ethics, so that our subject matter could immediately come into view. Thus we noted the etymological significance of *ethos* and the way in which the etymology implies trial-and-error experience and the role of tribal elders. We then surveyed the several sorts of ethics that scholars discuss and looked at three representative modern ethical emphases.

Our next introductory clarification concerned world religions. We noted the connations of "binding" that the word *religion* seems to bear and our particular interest in the traditions that have enrolled immense numbers of people and now span the globe. We also considered several different ingredients in religion and the variety of methods that modern scholars of religion employ.

Our third section, on evil, focused on the conflict between good and evil that helps to make all the ethical systems comparable. We also noted the sorts of changes that modern technology and modern social awareness have introduced, and we considered the variety of different approaches to evil that the world religions and philosophies have developed. We then discussed the reader's own sense of evil and human responsibility.

By way of preview, we discussed the distinction between Western and Eastern traditions that we are using, noted the limitations of our presentations (their focus on mainstream positions and their neglect of many smaller religious systems with interesting ethical viewpoints), and described the detached or academic viewpoint that we are attempting. We explained why students may be less familiar with Western traditions than they initially think, and concluded by sketching the seven considerations that we shall take up in each chapter.

———————————————— STUDY QUESTIONS ————————————————

1. What are the advantages and the drawbacks in the ethical attitude expressed in the saying "An eye for an eye and a tooth for a tooth"?

2. According to traditional etymology, to what is the religious person "bound" or "tied"?

3. What is constant in peoples' experience of evil through the centuries?

4. What are the advantages and disadvantages in taking an expository stance that grants none of the world religions' ethical systems privileged status as revealed (by either God or ultimate wisdom)?

———————————————————— NOTES ————————————————————

[1] See David Little, "Ethics, Types and Theories," in *Abingdon Dictionary of Living Religions,* ed. Keith Crim (Nashville: Abingdon, 1981), pp. 240–42.

[2] See, for example, *The Westminster Dictionary of Christian Ethics,* ed. J. Childress and J. Macquarrie (Philadelphia: Westminster, 1986).

[3] See Joachim Wach, *The Comparative Study of Religion* (New York: Columbia University Press, 1958).

[4] See Hans H. Penner, "Religion, the Study of," in *Abingdon Dictionary of Living Religions,* pp. 610–13.

[5] See James P. Carse, "Evil," in *Abingdon Dictionary of Living Religions,* pp. 244–47.

[6] A good collection of representative selections from the sacred texts of the world religions is *Sacred Texts of the World: A Universal Anthology,* ed. N. Smart and R. Hecht (New York: Crossroad, 1982).

[7] Many of the leading scholars of the past generation contributed to *The Concise Encyclopedia of Living Faiths,* ed. R. C. Zaehner (Boston: Beacon Press, 1967).

[8] Our own comprehensive textbook in world religions is *Ways to the Center,* rev. ed. (Belmont, Calif.: Wadsworth, 1984). See also *World Religions: From Ancient History to the Present,* ed. G. Parrinder (New York: Facts on File, 1983).

PART
ONE

Western
Religious
Ethics

As explained, we have divided the traditions we are treating into Western and Eastern religions. The Western religions—Judaism, Christianity, and Islam—do in fact comprise a discernible family. For Jews, Christians, and Muslims all speak of themselves, at least from time to time, as children of Abraham.[1] Christians began, in a sense, as dissident or sectarian Jews, and Muslims honor both Abraham and Jesus as prophetic forerunners of Muhammad. Despite all the enmity and slaughter that have occurred among these three religious peoples, therefore, they have grounds for considering one another kin.

The mention of Abraham calls to mind the stance toward life called **faith,** while the mention of Muhammad calls to mind the religious phenomenon of **prophecy.** Both of these notions are useful when it comes to reflecting on the peculiar character of what we are calling Western religion. For, first of all, all three of our traditions claim that human beings best situate themselves in the world when they take to heart a revelation from a God who is beyond the limitations of the world. This taking-to-heart is what theologians mean by the word *faith.* The implication is that God, the creative mystery at the origin and the destiny of the uni-

verse, is trustworthy and should be made the treasure or central reference of one's whole moral life. This God is thought to have revealed or
disclosed himself (all three of the Western traditions have usually depicted God as masculine: a lord or father) to particular people or in particular events that thereafter become the paradigms around which the
religious tradition organizes itself.

For example, Abraham becomes the "father of the Jews" and the exemplar of faith by trusting that the Lord, Yahweh, will make him the
progenitor of a people who will finally be more numerous than the stars
in the heavens or the grains of sand along the seashore (we accept the
biblical hyperbole for what it is). The key notion is that Abraham situ-
ates himself, and his family and later descendents, through a conviction
that surpasses sensible data or sure human inference. Abraham has no
"proof," no "evidence," weighty enough to afford him confidence on human grounds that the destiny for which he longs is reasonable or likely
to come about. It is true enough that Abraham, as we meet him in the
biblical book of Genesis, is the literary product of many centuries of
memory and reflective analysis. We have no sure way of knowing what
actually happened to Abraham or what prompted the biblical accounts
of God's revealed promises to him. But for our purposes here neither of
these considerations matters very much. What matters is that Jews (and
Christians and Muslims) have looked upon Abraham as the father of the
way that they should situate themselves in the world. After Abraham—
and because of Abraham and on the model of Abraham—Jews, Christians, and Muslims all have been brought up to place their final hopes in
a divinity whom ordinary human experience or understanding never
could contain or adequately explain.

Jesus of Nazareth, who is most crucially depicted in the four Gospels
of the New Testament (all of which mention Abraham), certainly seems
to have placed great importance in faith, so much so that frequently he
correlates his ability to work cures with the faith that people offer him.
But to understand Jesus or get him in historical focus, we also have to
employ the notion of prophecy. After Abraham and the other figures who
dominate the first five books of the Hebrew Bible (Moses is the standout
figure), a group of personalities and writers called the prophets comes to
center stage. As a group, they are characterized by a conviction that the
God of Abraham and the other patriarchs, Isaac and Jacob, has commissioned them to speak forth his directive Word. Sometimes this Word, like
the divine Spirit, is depicted as a semi-independent entity, but in the
final analysis the ties between the prophets and the biblical God are
plain enough. As Isaiah and Jeremiah, especially, describe their vocation,
the Word of God seized them and they had no choice except to obey.

The main work that the Word of God asked of the biblical prophets
was not so much a prediction of future events as a proclaiming of God's
judgment on present times. By and large, the message of the prophets

is that the people of Israel, and occasionally those of the Gentile nations, are not living out the relationship with God that was established through Abraham, Moses, David, and the other formative figures. This relationship, called the covenant, requires that the people offer God a pure worship and render one another social justice. Specifically, the prophets usually criticize the people for adulterating their worship by honoring gods other than Yahweh, as well as for neglecting the poor and unfortunate members of society and allowing the rich and powerful to ride roughshod over them.

Jesus of Nazareth comes on the scene recorded in the New Testament as a prophetic personality. He announces that the Reign or Kingdom of God (the time when God will directly establish a sociocultural situation worthy of God's own holiness and goodness) is at hand, and that people should repent, should turn away from their present faithlessness. Jesus depicts God as a loving and intimate parent. He sketches a communal life in which people are to love others as dearly as they love themselves. So one finds in his preaching and person both the monotheism at the core of Israelite religion and the concern for social justice that was a hallmark of the classical prophets.

To be sure, this message changes somewhat, especially when, after Jesus' death, Jesus' followers represent him as a unique, even divine, expression of the Word in human flesh. But, as one would expect from Jesus' own Jewish roots, the main motifs of the religion of the Hebrew Bible are very much present. Indeed, the motifs of the prophet known as Second Isaiah (whom we consider the author of chapters 40–55 of the Book of Isaiah), which stress the consolations that God will bring to an Israel suffering captivity in Babylon, stand front and center in the early Christian interpretations of Jesus. Jesus becomes the more-than-prophetic Suffering Servant in whom, Christians claim, all human beings can find redemption.

Muslims claim both Abraham and Jesus as servants of God's revelation to humanity, but for Muslims Muhammad is the greatest channel of revelation: the "seal" or consummation of prophecy. The keystone of Islam, the religion derived from the revelations to Muhammad, is the uniqueness (the strict monotheism) of the God Allah and the privileged authority of the disclosures that God made to Muhammad. Allah is the God of Abraham and Jesus, now more fully clarified, and the Qur'an is the written collection of what Allah revealed to Muhammad, in which one can find the straightest path to pleasing God. If one pleases God one will avoid hellfire and gain the complete fulfillment of the paradisal Garden. Through faith one submits one's whole life to Allah, who is the splendid Lord of the Worlds and is worthy of absolute submission.

We shall consider more fully the ethical prescriptions that the three Western traditions derived from their prophetic faith, but right now we should stress their common foundation. For each of the traditions, human beings are rightly ordered (realistic and wise) only when they make God their sole treasure. Because God is God—the unique and mysterious Creator—one's relationship to God is like no other relationship one could fashion. Indeed, all of one's other relationships should be set so that they radiate from and honor one's central relationship to God. If we use the word *faith* to designate this central relationship, we can say that for all three of the Western religions faith sets the agenda. How one ought to correlate faith with human reason (growth in knowledge) is a difficult and important question, very much at the heart of each Western religion's ethical probings. But faith in God and justice towards one's neighbor are, at least for the orthodox, always paramount.[2]

NOTES

[1] See F. E. Peters, *Children of Abraham* (Princeton, N.J.: Princeton University Press, 1982).

[2] We have dealt more comprehensively with Judaism, Christianity, and Islam in our *Western Ways to the Center* (Belmont, Calif.: Wadsworth, 1983).

1

Jewish Ethics

Historical Orientation
World View
Family Life
Work
Social Justice
Nature
Models
Summary, Study Questions, Notes

Historical Orientation

If Jewish life begins with Abraham, who is usually said to have flourished around 1800 B.C.E., the historical period that we have now to summarize extends for about four thousand years. Before Abraham, the culture of Canaan (the best name for the general area of Palestine, Israel, and parts east), was **polytheistic.** Michael Grant speaks for the mainstream of historians in describing Canaanite polytheism as follows: "In polytheistic Canaan, as in many other countries, each locality and settlement and craft and aspect of life had its own deities. They included minor gods, to whom ordinary men and women liked to attach themselves, as protectors of their interests. But there were also high gods, with universal aspects, although their omnipotence and domination over humankind seemed diminished by the rival existence of their fellow divinities. This was a doctrine which mirrored the inter-state and inter-city wars people saw raging around them. It scarcely made for psychological security. Yet it did satisfactorily account for the diversity of phenomena. Moreover, the essentially agricultural basis of Canaanite life, as of the life of Mesopotamia and Egypt, involved a close view of nature's manifold, varied expressions, which prompted the assumption of a divine division of labour."[1]

The new stance of Abraham, which called for faith in a sole sovereign God, therefore was quite a radical departure from Canaanite custom. By 1200 B.C.E. or so, when Moses led an exodus of Hebrews or proto-Jews out of Egypt, where they had been slaves for perhaps four hundred years, the religion of the children of Abraham included a passionate desire that the God of Abraham should liberate them from bondage. The accounts of Moses and the exodus from Egypt that we find in the biblical books of Exodus and Deuteronomy were composed many centuries after the events, but they show that the covenant between the Jews and their God was rooted in a conviction that God had acted decisively on their behalf. The laws that the Jews thought God had given to Moses on Mount Sinai became the most important legislation in Western history. As many commentators note, the burden of the centerpiece of these laws, the Ten Commandments, is to rectify such simple and basic human relationships as those between parent and child and neighbor and neighbor.

After Moses, the next great biblical figure is David, the prototypical king, who ruled Israel around 1000 B.C.E.. David's kingdom broke apart into a northern and a southern portion after the death of his son Solomon, and the northern portion fell captive to the Assyrians in 722. The southern portion fell to Babylon in 586, prompting the consoling prophecies of Second Isaiah that we have mentioned.

The Jews were free to return to their native land after 538 B.C.E., and the remainder of the pre-Common Era was, with a few exceptions (most notably the period of sovereignty won by the Maccabean revolt of 168), spent under foreign rule: first Persian, then Greek, and finally Roman. By the end of the pre-Common Era the materials now assembled into the Hebrew Bible had all been written, edited, and largely accepted as instructive for Jewish faith. This collection, called the **Tanak,** has traditionally been divided into three groups of writings: the Torah (first five books), the Prophets, and the Writings. Each has been an important source of Jewish ethics, although in terms of prestige the Torah has outranked the Prophets and the Prophets have outranked the Writings.

In 70 C.E. the Romans destroyed Jerusalem, and in the second century C.E. they in effect dispersed Judaism from its homeland. With the destruction of the Temple in Jerusalem that had been the ceremonial center of Jewish life, study and commentary on **Torah** or divinely given teaching became the new Jewish center. The traditional view was that there had been an authoritative oral teaching, to complement the written teaching available in the Hebrew Bible, and the task of the rabbis who became the strongest authorities in Judaism was to gather, comprehend, and apply Torah in its fullness (both written and oral sources). The collections of the rabbis' teachings, many of which were cast in the form of opinions about how Torah applied in given moral situations, thus became both a supplement to the original Torah and a guide to its full implications. Such collections as the **Mishnah** and the **Talmud** touched on virtually every aspect of Jewish life and so were the basic ethical texts for most of the Common Era. We may see them as forming in the pre-Common Era, becoming relatively complete around 500 C.E., and reigning virtually unchallenged until modernity, which came to most of Judaism in the nineteenth century.

In dispersion from its native land, Judaism naturally adapted to the various local cultures where it took root. This meant that customs varied from northern to southern Europe, from North Africa to eastern Europe and Asia Minor. Jews experienced many fluctuations in their fortunes, sometimes being allowed by the local Gentile political powers to live pretty much as they wished and sometimes being subjected to outright persecution. Overall, however, the many centuries of minority status served to reinforce Jews' sense of singularity or chosenness. In other words, their differences from their Muslim or Christian fellow-citizens was always very prominent in Jews' consciousnesses. In the Roman world, Jews had won a grudging respect because their ethical lives had stood apart from pagan licentiousness. The orthodox Muslim view was that Jews and Christians both deserved special status as "peoples of the book" who shared some biblical foundations with followers of Islam. Christians tended to believe that they had superseded the Jews, and at times they regarded Jews as cursed by God for having killed Jesus of Nazareth.

In modern times Christendom itself came apart, and from the debris of the religious wars that followed in the wake of the Protestant Reformation there arose among intellectuals a hunger for a nonsectarian tolerance. Some Jews took this prospect of tolerance as a stimulus to rethink Judaism in almost purely ethical terms, and we find much of their heritage in today's **Reformed Judaism.** The majority of Jews, however, continued to live under the sway of either the Talmudic traditions or of **Hasidic** devotional movements (which themselves had many Talmudic elements). What today is called **Orthodox Judaism** is the least-changed successor of traditional Talmudic Judaism, while **Conservative Judaism** stands somewhere in the middle between Orthodoxy and Reform. Hasidism maintains an intriguing presence, both in Israel and in the United States,[2] and large numbers of Jews now consider themselves nonreligious or **secular.**

The experience of Nazism and the concentration camps of the Second World War has deeply affected the current generations of Jews, and the "Holocaust," as the death of about six million Jews (perhaps 40 percent of the total Jewish population) in the Nazi camps often is called, frames almost all Jewish religious and cultural reflection nowadays. The creation of the state of Israel in 1948 was the fulfillment of the movement known as **Zionism,** which worked for a return of Jews to their homeland in the Near East, and Israel too has become a strong force in

Jewish consciousness. In the state of Israel one probably finds the greatest variety of current Jewish life and thought, for secularists and religionists, Europeans and Orientals, hawks and doves all battle constantly about the political and ethical courses that Judaism now ought to take.[3]

World View

Faith, prophecy, monotheism, creation, the covenant, and social justice—to speak only of concepts that we have already mentioned—together wove an outlook or sense of reality that greatly shaped the ethical lives of most Jews. To be sure, none of these notions was static. All changed, however imperceptibly, as Jews experienced now this and now that historical vicissitude or cultural success. Regularly, however, faith in the God of the fathers Abraham, Isaac, and Jacob meant viewing the world as the free work of a sovereign Creator. As well, it meant assuming that God would be present to Jewish experience as it unfolded over time, somehow standing by the implicit promises he had given in the Exodus and the explicit promises he had given in fashioning the covenant with Moses. Let us consider these two elementary assumptions and symbols, creation and covenant, for they have greatly colored the Jewish sense of reality, wisdom, evil, and goodness.

Creation, as the biblical book of Genesis above all represented it to countless generations of Jews, was the formation of the world by God's simple fiat. God took what had been unorganized primal matter and gave it the shape of contemporary nature. This may seem unsophisticated by today's scientific standards, and so it is if we read it as an attempt to compete with current astrophysical work on the big bang that got the universe going. But Genesis exerted most of its influence symbolically (which is not to deny that most Jews probably took it literally), presenting images that took hold in the subconscious and made Jews feel relatively at home in the world.

For example, the little note that God rested on the seventh day dovetailed with the Jewish tradition of observing a sabbath. Similarly, the depiction of the creation of human beings as a special act of God, and the further depiction of God's giving Adam and Eve a special jurisdiction over nonhuman creation, tended to make Jews think that nature and the animal kingdom were congenial and revolved around human beings' welfare. Even the story of the fall of the first human beings and their expulsion from Eden had its consoling notes, for God clothed the reduced couple and implied that their subsequent life of toil and child-rearing would be acceptable, if penitential, in his sight.

The result of all such symbolism was the strong Jewish conviction that creation and the human situation were essentially very good. Judaism has not been a world-fearing religion or ethical system. It has not thought of nature, either that of the physical world or of human beings, as illusory or wicked or unsubstantial. Even when Judaism has recognized very profoundly that many things are wrong in history and society, it has instinctively defended God and creation from the charge of being essentially or intrinsically evil. God may permit the evils that come about, or they may serve God's desire to chasten an unfaithful humankind, but neither God nor creation is to be thought of as dualistic—as much evil as good. Even when Judaism came up with the figure of Satan, late in the **pre-Common Era,** it never made Satan the equal of God. This is clear in the Book of Job, where Satan must get God's permission to test Job and Job remains free to preserve his moral integrity.

The symbol of the **Exodus** and the covenant gave Jews a second powerful motivation to accept the burdens of historical existence wholeheartedly. Not only had God made the world, and so guaranteed the goodness of the situation in which human beings found themselves, God had also acted decisively in the past to liberate his people, the children of Abraham, from oppression. Under Moses he had performed as a champion of the people and had served ever after as their great cause for trusting that the future could be good for them. As God had overthrown the wicked Pharaoh of ancient Egypt, so he could certainly overthrow the current king, prince, or politician who was making life difficult. More broadly, a liberating or redeeming God provided Judaism with the basis for considering here-and-now existence worth improving. The notion of heaven or an afterlife has not had in Judaism the full effect that it has had in Christianity and Islam, where frequently it has taken many people's minds away from their worldly responsibilities and troubles. Judaism did finally develop a notion of afterlife (again late in the pre-Common Era); but even after this notion arose, probably as many Jews had doubts about heaven as used it to console themselves for this-worldly troubles. As often as not, the ideas of immortality or an afterlife conjured up the continuing existence of the Jewish people, or the next generation represented by a new round of children. Personal immortality was not an all-absorbing concern, and heaven did not determine Jews' ethical evaluations, though of course it had some influence.

If creation was essentially good, and history could prove redemptive, Jews found themselves quite positively situated in reality. A third significant positioning came in the wake of the covenant and its Torah. Because they considered themselves to be God's people, Jews felt an obligation to keep to the compact that God had made with them. Because this compact had taken a rather fully developed legal form, first in the laws one finds in the Bible (especially in the first five books) and then in the rabbis' refinements, literacy became a commonplace assumption and learning became a high cultural ideal. Indeed, one can argue that the learned rabbi was the most honored figure in traditional Judaism, to be preferred to the person of wealth or secular power when one was contemplating the careers of one's male children. (Until very recently, women could not be rabbis and so usually did not get much formal training in Torah.)

The further consequences of this high esteem of learning ramify almost beyond calculation. Although religious learning clearly took pride of place, Jews could employ their strong intellectual inclinations in scientific and humanistic learning as well. Thus, Jews became leading physicians and musicians, and as new fields of knowledge opened up, they assumed leading roles in such disciplines as physics and psychology. There was a powerful, if often only tacit, belief that understanding itself was a great good. (Since the Holocaust and the phenomenon of many cultured Germans agreeing to the Nazi program of genocide for the Jewish people, this belief has come in for considerable criticism.)

Balancing the intellectualism that was, on the whole, a male preserve stood a concern for good deeds—acts of civic service and neighborly helpfulness—that Jewish women especially spearheaded. So there were burial societies to care for the bodies of the deceased and also for their bereaved families. There were both formal and informal networks to look out for the poor, the sick, and the elderly. The traditional Jewish community was abuzz with information about what was happening in all parts of its realm (which in both medieval and modern times has often been a ghetto). The sense that material prosperity was a good thing, fitting in with the goodness of creation, matched up with the further sense that one's wealth brought social obligations. High among these obligations were both almsgiving to help the poor and support for the community's religiocultural activities (Jewish religion and culture have traditionally been difficult to separate).

This last notion brings us to the final element of the Jewish world view that we shall consider. Being a Jew meant being a person who belonged to a community that worshiped regularly. Not only was one to study God's laws; one was also to worship the Lord with word and song and whole heart. Indeed, study and **worship** came virtually to overlap, insofar as concentrating on divine things was regarded as the highest human activity. So in the **shul** or prayer/study house one moved back and forth between praising God and trying to understand better the divine will. The laws that one strove to keep also fitted into this conception of the religious center, because their purpose was to make people pure or fit for communicating with God, for being God's chosen people.[4]

Family Life

We shall now focus on several specific ethical areas, assuming the historical and philosophical orientations that we have laid out. The first of these ethical areas is family life, which has seemed the best context in which to consider the personal love so important to mental health and happiness. From the outset one must realize that the biblical traditions pertaining to family life are resolutely patriarchal. Abraham, Moses, David, and the other paradigmatic figures all were the unquestioned (official) leaders of their extended family or clan. Polygamy was permitted, and one of David's perquisites as king was the royal harem. Since the time of David, of course, many of these ancient customs have been altered. Still, virtually until the present, Jews have accepted almost without question that a male should be head and official authority figure of the family.

The biblical injunction to "be fruitful and multiply" (Genesis 1:28) further shaped the life of the traditional Jewish family. Having children was both the first end of marriage and the greatest blessing. Such procreation certainly promoted the fulfillment of the individual spouses, but it also served the primary need of the Jewish community as a whole, which was to ensure its own survival—something the many periods of persecution regularly placed in doubt.

Individuals therefore did not marry in a spirit of romantic pursuit of individual happiness. No doubt romance frequently was present, but most marriages were arranged by the young people's parents (frequently through a "matchmaker," who was a person of some significance in the typical Jewish town). Marriage was considered the ordinary human estate, and Judaism never sponsored a celibate clergy or a monastic religious life (one might have to make an exception for the Essenes, a separatist group that lived near the Dead Sea at the end of the pre-Common Era and appears to have had both married and celibate members). A man who did not marry was considered both strange and pitiable, while a spinster was nearly certain to be lamented. Similarly, a wife who proved barren was in many periods considered disfavored or even cursed by God, and the poor woman usually would examine her conscience to try to discover where she had gone wrong.

From biblical times a man had the right to divorce his wife virtually at will, though the rabbis devised ways of keeping this from being a sheer license. Women's rights to divorce were much more circumscribed, so frequently their way out of an intolerable marriage was through exerting less formal or official social pressures on their husbands. The wedding ceremony entailed signing a formal contract, which in some periods included dower rights and responsibilities, and the ceremony itself was a high point in the community's ritual life. Significantly, the prayers made as much of the woman's fruitfulness in children as they did of the couple's prospective happiness. Indeed, the two were linked, fruitfulness in children being assumed to be the greatest blessing the couple could share.

In this context, the somewhat qualified right to abortion that Judaism has allowed serves as a good example of the sophistication that the rabbinic mind brought to most ethical questions. By the injunction to be fruitful and multiply, a couple naturally was warned away from any easy abortion. Killing a child even one day old (infanticide) was equated with murder. However, the abortion of an unborn child, although prohibited, was not the same as murder. There was some ambiguity in all of this, because much hinged on the question of whether the unborn was viable. During many periods viability was equated with actual emergence from the womb, so prior to birth it could be questioned. Moreover, a fetus considered to endanger the mother's life could be aborted, unless it had started to emerge from the womb. One recent popular Jewish publication puts this whole matter in almost too vivid detail: "Abortion is definitely permitted in Jewish law if the fetus endangers the mother's life. Thus, 'if a woman is in labor (and it is feared she may die), one may sever the fetus from her womb and extract it, member by member, for her life takes precedence over his.' This is the case only as long as the fetus has not emerged into the world, and is thus not yet viable—'it may be killed and the mother saved.' However, once either the head or the greater part of the child's body emerges into the world, it is considered to be viable and, as such, has the same right to life as the mother, and killing it is no longer permitted."[5]

Going back to the Jewish wedding, the assumption tended to be that both bride and groom would come to their wedding day as virgins (especially the bride), and folklore played humorously with the trials and delights of gaining sexual expertise. The rabbis tended to be quite reserved, at times even prudish, about sexual matters, and their counsel followed the path of many male-dominated religious traditions in stressing the seductive powers of women. The blood taboos that one finds in the biblical legislation continued right through to the present era, with the result that a woman who was menstruating or who had recently given birth was considered ritually unclean. In the same vein, the **priestly legislation** from the time when biblical priests performed ritual sacrifices made seminal emission a cause of ritual unfitness, though this was a lesser impurity than menstruation. Psychologically, women's association with blood was a main reason that they were not allowed into the priesthood, and this later meant that they were not considered apt for the rabbinate.

The three commandments especially directed to Jewish women included the obligation to visit the ritual bath each month. Leo Trepp has placed this in context as follows: "Another Jewish law may have added to the permanence of the home. Jewish law based on Torah prohibits intercourse during the period of menstruation and seven days thereafter; for about twelve days every month, husband and wife may not even touch each other. She is *Niddah*, ritually 'Separated.' Then the wife has to immerse herself in a ritual bath of purification, a *Mikveh*, before intercourse can again be permitted. As a matter of cleanliness and hygiene, this immersion was of great value, especially in the Middle Ages, when bathing was very rare in most other cultures. This commandment is strictly observed by Orthodox women to this day. Thus husband and wife can hardly get tired of each other physically, a factor greatly contributing to the stability of the home."[6] Trepp also points out that contraception usually was permitted.

In Jewish ethics, the question of intermarriage (between a Jew and a non-Jew) took on rather grim overtones. Blu Greenberg, whose recent article in an issue of the *Journal of Ecumenical Studies* dealing with marriage in all the major world religious traditions is a good source on how feminism is changing orthodox conceptions of Jewish marriage, puts the question of intermarriage as follows: "From earliest times, intermarriage was explicitly forbidden to Jews (Dt. 7 : 3–4, Av. Zar. 36B). Because Judaism, the religion, took root in a family, the concept of Jewish peoplehood was perhaps more central than for most other religions. But it was not purity of bloodlines that was the issue; rather, it was the integrity of the faith community. One could join the faith community through conversion; one could not enter Judaism simply through the act of marrying a Jew. For Jews, exogamy represented not only a violation of halacha [religious law] but also a dilution of Jewishness of the community. Throughout Jewish history, intermarriage was kept to a minimum. Several forces were at work. Aside from the laws—which were made very clear—the response that followed such a marriage was an even more powerful preventive. If a Jew married out of the faith, he or she knew what to expect: total banishment from family and community. Parents and siblings would rend their garments and observe the *shiva* mourning period, as if the child were no longer alive."[7]

One can see, then, that faith or theology or religious law was supposed to prevail over personal sentiment in matters of Jewish family life. The same has held, as we shall see, in most other religious traditions. To a modern or postmodern mentality this can raise the question of how ethical the religious traditions themselves sometimes have been. If a religious law turns out to be very cruel, can it have truly been sanctioned by God, or is it rather more likely the self-defensive legislation of a community that can grow sinful and heartless? All traditional religionists—Jews, Christians, Muslims, Hindus, Buddhists, Confucians, Taoists, Shintoists, and others—need to hear this counterethicial probe that modernity often presses.

Work

Human beings derive a great deal of their health and happiness from the love that ideally fills their homes. A second primary source of personal satisfaction is people's work. If it is merely a matter of assuring physical survival, work certainly has a bare sort of dignity. The ideal, however, is for work to be a way for the worker to create something significant, beautiful, and useful to the wider human community. Traditional Jewish views of work embraced this whole range of concerns.

In *Life Is with People*, a fascinating study of small-town eastern European Jewish life prior to World War II, one finds that financial success or a good livelihood was coupled with good health in the most common toast. When one wanted to wish someone well, "Health and prosperity" sprang to one's lips. The assumption was that God himself wanted both health and good livelihood for all his people. Indeed, people considered God a partner in their shops and businesses. They themselves were to work hard, but they could expect the Lord God, praised be He, to approve of their hard labors.

Among the different sorts of work that one might choose, scholarship had the highest status. This depended upon native talent, of course, but on the whole the proudest hopes of a Jewish parent were to raise a brilliant young rabbi. Still, this esteem for Talmudic scholarship did not mean that people downgraded the business professions. As we have mentioned, Jews usually have looked upon creation as thoroughly good, and as a consequence have considered wealth and worldly success blessings for which to praise God. A scholar might in fact be quite poor, and virtue did not demand that one gain wealth; but on the other hand wealth was less ambiguous in Judaism than it often was in Christianity, where **vowed poverty** was part of the highest religious ideal.

Where the father of a household was a scholar, the wife took primary responsibility for the material and financial well-being of the family. If the father was not a scholar, the two spouses often shared the shopkeeping or trading equally. Idleness was considered a sin, so even small children would be pressed into service. How this conception of prosperity or livelihood (*parnosseh*) might foster a zeal for business is suggested in the following reminiscence about small-town Jewish life: "Neither time, space nor weather interferes with the pursuit of parnosseh. You go long distances through the storm to earn a penny. You freeze in winter and bake in summer in order to 'have for the Sabbath' and to live as befits a 'mentsh' [man]. And you will do anything that is not directly forbidden, no matter how difficult, how strenuous, how unfamiliar."[8] The underlying notion is that one is responsible for one's family, and that no labor is too great to assure their decent living.

As the quotation shows, the Sabbath helped to structure the traditional Jewish conception of work, serving both to limit any tendency to idolize work and to give people a goal for their labors. The laws for the Sabbath forbade any work, since the time was supposed to be given over to God and to one's family. The rabbis glossed these laws endlessly, spinning out finer and finer understandings of what constituted work. For the highly observant, it could mean turning on lights or starting fires, so pious Jews would arrange for a Gentile to perform these chores on the

Sabbath. The Sabbath was the high point of the traditional Jewish week, the days after the Sabbath somewhat basking in its glow, and the days from midweek on looking forward to the next Sabbath. The symbolism for the Sabbath represented this holiest of days as a bride of God, and nothing was too good for celebrating it. So the family would have its best meal on the Sabbath, saving for this even when times were hard. The mother would put out the best china and silver, or their equivalents, and hospitality to the less fortunate was the rule. The whole family would go to the synagogue, there would be time for mild recreation and pious study, and husband and wife were encouraged to make love leisurely. Thus the Sabbath often seemed to justify the hard work required during the week, and one has to admire the wisdom of traditional Judaism in hallowing it.

Household work largely devolved upon the wife and daughters, as did taking pains to assure that the family observed the laws for diet (keeping **kosher**) and celebrated the annual religious festivals. These latter, like the Sabbath, helped structure the Jewish sense of time and give the year a certain rhythm. So, for example, all observant Jews would think of the fall as the beginning of the new year and as a time for repentance. The Talmud contained full discussions of how these and the other annual festivals such as Passover were to be observed, but custom educated all members of an observant household in most of the details. Part of the social function of the festivals, of course, was to unify the community, and insofar as one would later be having business dealings with people with whom one had prayed, celebrated, confessed one's sins, and pledged mutual reconciliation, the festivals tended to help keep the competitive aspects of business in perspective.

The rabbis generally praised hard work, including manual labor, and several commentators have noted that this probably was in part because many rabbis themselves had to work with their hands: "In thus eulogizing manual toil, the Rabbis practised what they preached. We read of a few of them belonging to wealthy families, but the majority were humble workmen who earned a precarious livelihood. The story of Hillel's poverty has already been told. Of other Rabbis we learn that Akiba used to collect a bundle of wood daily and exist on the price he received for it (ARN vi); Joshua was a charcoal-burner and lived in a room the walls of which were begrimed by his manner of work (Ber. 28a); Meir was a scribe (Erub. 13a); Jose b. Chalaphta was a worker in leather (Shab. 49b); Jochanan was a maker of sandals (Aboth iv. 14); Judah was a baker (p. Chag. 77b); and Abba Saul held a menial position as a kneader of dough (Pes. 34a), while he mentions that he had also been a grave-digger (Nid. 24b)."[9] These famous names, complete with references to the Talmudic literature upon which the author bases his characterization of their livelihoods, suggest that for those who looked upon the study of Torah as their spiritual food and drink, how they gained a material living was somewhat incidental. But both these rabbis and Jews more absorbed with material success believed strongly that diligence in this-worldly labor was pleasing to God.

The Jewish sense of honesty, of the dignity of work, and of justice in financial matters led the Talmudists to spend considerable amounts of energy on the matter of labor contracts: "In long-term labor contracts, including those relating to the leasing of land, the agreement was recorded in writing. The laws of deeds contained numerous halakhic problems, one relating to the validity of the guarantee to pay a fine for non-fulfillment of the contract. In certain contracts extremely high fines were specified in order to exert pressure on the recalcitrant party, and the query arose as to whether such a document was legally valid."[10] Thus, even in their contractual aspects, business practices were considered subject to the inquiries of the religious teachers into what was just or was in keeping with covenantal Law (Torah). The line between pushing hard to maximize the fruits of one's labors and falling over into sharp or even ruthless business practice may always have been hard to draw exactly, but certainly the rabbis tried to keep work in proper perspective and not let individual ambition become a source of injury to others.

Social Justice

Justice is one of the watchwords of both biblical and rabbinic Judaism. Thus Deuteronomy 16:19–20 enjoins justice upon all who would belong to the community convenanted with God: "You shall not pervert justice; you shall not show partiality; and you shall not take a bribe, for a bribe blinds the eyes of the wise and subverts the cause of the righteous. Justice, and only justice, you shall follow, that you may live and inherit the land which the Lord your God gives you." Genesis 18:25 and Psalms 9:5 both make justice the prime attribute of divine action. God's intent in giving the commandments was to establish justice throughout the world (Psalms 119: 137–44). When the messianic age comes, and things are as God intends them to be, justice will rule universally. In many biblical contexts, *justice* is virtually synonymous with *holiness, mercy,* and *grace.* Thus, some Jewish ethicists go so far as to say that "virtually the entire spectrum of ethical values is comprised in the notion of justice."[11]

One senses in many Jewish writers an irritation that such justice could ever be deemed inferior to Christian love or Buddhist compassion. In the eyes of Leo Baeck, an important theologian of the past generation, such a judgment is dim-witted, since Baeck so admires the "imperative force and urgency" of Jewish justice that he finds Christianity and Buddhism, by comparison, either individualistic or sentimental: ". . . in Christianity the determining factor is to experience the miracle of grace and thereby be redeemed; thus the 'I' of the individual man stands alone at the center of religion, apart from the fellow man. Sometimes Buddhism's love of mankind is contrasted with that of Judaism. Buddhism's doctrine of love fondly preaches mercy and benevolence toward every living thing, but in its inner core this feeling is one of sentimentality and melancholy. It lacks the reverence for the fellow man which distinguishes Jewish teaching; it lacks the emphasis upon positive justice and hence the clear demand of the moral task. It lacks the great 'Thou shalt,' the imperative force and urgency, the social and the messianic elements which are emphasized by Judaism. Beyond mere feeling Buddhist morality does not go. That is what gives it its characteristically passive and negative stamp. . . . And for it, like Christianity, salvation means everything; the question of the 'I' is the sole question of life."[12]

Regardless of the accuracy or inaccuracy of Baeck's descriptions of Christianity and Buddhism, his stress on the solidarity of human beings and on the imperative or commanded quality of social justice is representatively Jewish. The community has bulked larger than the individual throughout Jewish history (for instance, Jewish prayer usually uses plural forms). God made his covenant with the community as a whole, and the community as a whole has been forced to contemplate the relations between Jews and outsiders.

Social justice sometimes runs into the question of forgiveness, and here the attitude of the rabbis seems somewhat complicated. Abraham Joshua Heschel, another leading theologian of the past generation, brings this home with a telling story about the rabbi of Brisk, a great scholar. The rabbi was in a compartment in a train going from Warsaw back to his home. Some salesmen sharing the compartment got up a card game and invited him to join in. When he refused, wanting to think his own thoughts, they became irritated with him and finally pushed him out of the compartment. Back in Brisk, when one of the salesmen found out who it was that he had ejected from the compartment, he went to the rabbi and begged forgiveness. The rabbi refused to forgive him, finally explaining to his own son, when he came to intercede on the salesman's behalf, that because the salesman had offended him as a common man (not knowing his true identity), the salesman would have to find a common man to ask for forgiveness. Applying this to the case of Jews asked to forgive Nazis for the crimes committed against the victims of the Holocaust, Heschel writes: "No one can forgive crimes committed by other people. It is therefore preposterous to assume that anyone alive can extend forgiveness for the suffering of any one of the six million people who perished. According to Jewish tradition, even God Himself can only forgive sins committed against Himself, not against man."[13]

Within Jewish circles this view would not go unchallenged, especially if it were made into a hard-line stance that left no way toward reconciliation with one's enemies. Thus Earl Shorris's book *Jews without Mercy: A Lament*[14] is a call back to the more liberal traditions that

Shorris thinks are the best part of the Jewish heritage. The question of justice, of course, becomes acutely difficult when applied to policy decisions about reprisals against enemies in war or terrorists who work toward one's extermination, and both Jewish tradition and current Jewish opinion seems to be divided or ambivalent on this matter. From biblical times we find a tradition of **holy war** that makes the enemies of Israel the enemies of God and even puts into God's mouth commands to slaughter the enemy ruthlessly. Equally ancient, however, is the longing for peace and the perception that peace is a great blessing. This comes through in the greeting of *shalom*, which Jews often extend to both fellow Jews and outsiders. Generally speaking, however, rabbinic literature devotes surprisingly little space to the question of war. Voluntary war has to be declared by the Sanhedrin, a court of seventy-one, and truth and justice are the preconditions of peace. War ("the sword") comes as divine judgment on human beings' sins, and in times of war one is not bound by the rules of the Sabbath. Apart from these sentiments, the Talmud has little to say about war.[15]

A desire for reconciliation certainly burns in those Jews who oppose a belligerent stance toward the Palestinians who live in Israel and want to incorporate them into a fully democratic state. Arthur Hertzberg, a professor at Dartmouth College, commenting on a book by Bernard Avishai that advocates this more democratic conception of current Israel, summarizes many of the strains that the complex Jewish tradition of social justice now suffers: "Israel can, and should, be criticized for its insensitivity to the pride of its opponents (as, for example, in Golda Meir's assertion that 'there are no Palestinians') and for its policies in the West Bank, especially Menachem Begin's policy of creeping annexation. Nonetheless, through the years, the major obstacle to peace has been the intransigence of the Arabs. This lack of a partner for settlement has helped evoke, as Mr. Avishai acknowledges, the nationalist hard-line emotions now so prominent in Israel."[16]

We mean this example to suggest the very concrete turn that the Jewish ethical tradition takes when it informs discussions about the policies that the current state of Israel ought to pursue. On questions less dramatic than war and reconciliation with military or insurrectionist enemies, the Jewish concern for social justice has put forward principles that would seem to argue for a much more democratic approach to global problems than now tends to prevail in most countries. For the traditional Jewish view has always been that God is the creator of all people and has purposes for them all. Even when Jews were preoccupied with their own special rights and responsibilities as people uniquely covenanted to God, they reflected on the Noachian covenant (Genesis 9), by which God had bound himself to all of creation. After the flood God promised that never again would such waters threaten the earth. And in a beautiful figure, the author has God promise to remember his pledge whenever he sees the rainbow: "When the bow is in the clouds, I will look upon it and remember the everlasting covenant between God and every living creature of all flesh that is upon the earth" (Genesis 9:16).

A strong line of Jewish reflection on the covenants with Abraham, Moses, and David linked them up with the covenant with Noah, leading Jewish theologians to think that Israel had received its privileges not for itself alone but also for the Gentile world. Israel was to be a light to the Gentiles, a revelation of God's purposes for all humankind. The questions of social justice—economic, military, and the rest—therefore go to the heart of Jews' self-conception. As important as their efforts to render one another justice were, Jews could never fail to sense that God also asked them to render justice, and perhaps even mercy, toward their non-Jewish neighbors.

Finally, the Jewish traditions of social justice provided a basis for treating all of one's neighbors well, regardless of their sex, race, or social status. By today's standards the Jewish tradition, like all other traditions of the world religions, may be called sexist, but it did prize women and their gifts. The community was composed of many different ethnic groups; this of course did not completely destroy ethnic and racial prejudice, but it certainly did help to limit it. And even the lowliest member of the community, such as the beggar, had a source of dignity in the traditional conviction that God had purposes for all Jews, whatever their station or role.

Nature

One probably cannot speak of a traditional Jewish sense of justice toward the land or nature, as today's ecologists would desire, but the **promised land,** flowing with milk and honey, certainly figures prominently in Judaism's biblical beginnings.[17] A prophet such as Jeremiah instinctively links desolation of the land with the social misfortunes that infidelity to the covenant brings to Israel, while from the earliest traditions about the Exodus, the wandering in the desert, and finally the long-awaited entry into the promised land under Joshua, a fertile and nourishing nature functions as a potent symbol of the divine blessings. Some commentators have found it significant that Cain, the first murderer, is remembered as the founder of city life. One might link this anti-urban sentiment with the traditional biblical sense that the wandering in the desert, despite all its difficulties and trials, was the time when Israel's faith was especially pristine or robust.

The key texts for both Jewish and Christian traditional views of nature, however, have been the first chapters of Genesis. We have noted the instinct to look on creation as thoroughly good, and one could hardly get stronger biblical confirmation for this than the constant refrain of the creation account: "And God saw that it was good." The charge that the Bible fostered an anthropocentrism that made possible the pollution of nature created by modern technology has received a rather thorough airing. Generally speaking, both biblical scholars and historians of post-biblical Western religion have argued that while the charge has some merit, if stated so baldly it is patently misleading. The biblical scholars point out that the Bible is more **theocentric** than **anthropocentric,** while the historians point to Benedict, Francis, the Celtic monks, and the Rhineland mystics as evidence that the West often sponsored a great reverence for nature.

These names are not Jewish, however, and there is a strain of biblical thought, most prominent in the prophets, that warns against divinizing nature or paying heed to the naturalistic gods of Israel's neighbors. Throughout Jewish history, the tradition of stark monotheism meant a will to consider nature nondivine, and so a hesitancy about sacralizing it (considering it holy, which is not the same as divine). Judaism strikes the comparativist as a religion that placed more emphasis on social values and energies than it did on naturalistic ones. This emphasis was due in part to the historical fact that in many periods Jews were not allowed to own land and had little access to agriculture. In Europe, certainly, Jews made their mark in the professions and through trade, banking, and business. The religious rituals reflected the times when Israel had moved to agricultural rhythms, for several of them were harvest festivals; but what we would call ecological values—a sense of interconnection with nature, and an extension of human concern to the protection of a nature realized to be quite fragile—are hard to find. This is true of all the world's religious traditions, insofar as ecology is very much a twentieth-century movement. Still, one finds in the religious traditions of most nonliterate peoples a strong sense of kinship with animals and nature generally, while in East Asia nature serves as the great symbol of an impersonal divinity. Neither Judaism nor Christianity nor Islam is ecological in these ways.

The rabbis, to be sure, were concerned about animals, and perhaps an ecological sensibility glimmers behind some of their interpretations of the kosher laws. The Bible says that animals should share in the Sabbath rest, and traditionally the way that one treated animals was considered an index of one's character. According to a Talmudic anecdote, when a calf about to be slaughtered put its head in Rabbi Judah's cloak, he commanded it to go forward to the slaughter, since that was the purpose for which it had been created. This lack of compassion displeased Heaven, however, so it allowed sufferings to come upon the rabbi. The sufferings ceased only when the rabbi came to the defense of some young weasels that his maid was preparing to sweep away. The rabbi quoted Psalms 145:9 ("His compassion is over all that he has made"), so Heaven restored him to good fortune.[18] Laws for kosher slaughtering were intended to minimize animals' sufferings, and the most strictly observant Jews frequently have been vegetarians, both to minimize their chances of eating unclean food and from a sense of compassion toward animal life.

In modern times Zionism brought Jews a renewed sense of their native land. Along with this has come a movement to live close to the land, often in **kibbutzim** (collectives), that certainly has ecological overtones. Thus many young people from America and Europe who travel to Israel in search of their roots not only tramp the streets of Jerusalem but also work the fields and pick the fruit. Israeli agronomists have done some pioneering work in irrigation and specialized kinds of farming, while projects to desalinize the Dead Sea have been pondered seriously. How respectful of nature these projects are remains to be seen.

The impression remains, however, that Jewish political liberalism (there is a strong socialistic tradition) has not developed a strongly ecological dimension. The labor movement, which numbered many Jews in its formative years, easily finds itself at odds with environmentalism, while Jewish theology, no less than Christian theology, has been slow to develop its traditional metaphysical appreciations of the divine creativity into a basis for reverencing nature as a solid presence of God.

An interesting juncture of liberal movements that may raise Jewish interest in ecology and Jewish consciousness of nature's key place in future religious reform occurs at the crossroads of feminism and environmentalism. There is now a strong Jewish feminism, born of unblinking reflection on the second-class status that women have held in traditional Judaism. As feminists have gained theological training, they have realized that women's traditional association with nature (most cultures consider women more "natural" and men more "cultural," because of women's periodicity and somewhat involuntary role in childbirth) holds a key to how humanity may reverse the war making, pollution of nature, and social discriminations that keep it from enjoying a proper prosperity and peace. Thus Jewish ecology, theology of nature, and feminism are topics to keep an eye on.

Models

Among the models set before Jewish women through the ages, probably the most significant has been the description of the good wife in Proverbs 31:10–31, which figured in the ceremonies of the Sabbath meal. The first lines of this text set the general theme: "A good wife who can find? She is far more precious than jewels. The heart of her husband trusts in her, and he will have no lack of gain. She does him good, and not harm, all the days of her life." Further verses specify the ways that a good wife brings her husband good and gain, many of them dealing with business transactions. Thus the young Jewish bride could think that a domestic career or orientation to business dealings was quite natural. The ideal also shows the good wife caring for the poor, being provident about the household finances, supporting her husband's rise to prominence in the community, and in general being very industrious. She is pictured as having children who bless her, but she is not made primarily a producer of children. The next to last line of this famous passage suggests the key to Jewish feminine wisdom and success: "Charm is deceitful and beauty is vain, but a woman who fears the Lord is to be praised." Obviously this text could be abused, but it did remind each generation of both wives and husbands that the center of Jewish ethics was faith and hard work.

Job 31 is perhaps the best parallel to Proverbs 31, offering Jewish men a scriptural sketch of the ethical ideal they ought to pursue. Job describes his probity in terms of sexual restraint, truthfulness, justice toward his servants, charity to the poor and widowed, freedom from avarice and love of money, keeping himself from excessive admiration (worship) of nature, not rejoicing in the downfall of his enemies, courage in acting publicly on his convictions, and a proper treatment of his land. This probity represents Job's case against the divine decision that has brought him down into suffering. As Reformed Jews perhaps especially have appreciated, Job shows his religion principally by the high moral standards of his life. The text speaks much less of direct love of God, let alone of mystical absorption in God, than of justice and mercy toward one's neighbors.

No doubt one can find times and places when the rabbi was not the leading figure in the Jewish community, but certainly after the dispersion of the second century c.e. those were few and far between. At times the **Hasid** or holy man predominated, and his mystical ardor or charismatic ability to move people to strong feelings of devotion became important, but this figure is only partially distinguishable from the more sober rabbi. Both figures were rooted in the Talmud, and if the Hasid taught more in the mode of **Haggadah** or pious story than in the traditional rabbi's **Halachic** or legal mode, this again was not a black-and-white distinction. So Hasidism, like the **Sufism** that gave Islam a strong devotional strain, thought of itself more as a supplement to Talmudic Judaism than as a discontinuous reform.

The model of the rabbi stressed learning—mastery of the traditional guidance come from God in Torah. The ideal rabbi would be rapt in Torah, yet able to bring its guidance to bear on concrete problems of daily life. The result, ideally, would be the firm confidence of the rabbi's followers that they were living pure and holy lives, keeping well the Law that God asked his chosen people to keep. When the mystical movement called **Cabalism** developed in Judaism, the image of the rabbi broadened somewhat, and study of Torah gained an interior or even esoteric dimension. Then the ideal student of Torah knew the secret significance of the holy texts and had access to a universe of spiritual meanings. The Hasidim often were Cabalists, and their special badge probably was the joy that they found in Torah. Thus they would dance with the Torah scroll on the Sabbath, at weddings, and on other festivals, and they would stir up the people's hope. Sometimes such hope focused on the Messiah, and large numbers of Jews came to expect that the messianic age was about to dawn. As in both Christianity and Islam, suffering and a desire to move into a better world were the psychological triggers to this messianic expectation.

In the medieval period Judaism developed sectarian movements that in effect divided the world into three social groups. First there were the Christians, or the Gentiles generally. Second there were the average Jews. And third there were the Jews who were especially proficient in their faith. Often these latter Jews, who in their own eyes were the hope of Judaism, went by the name **Pietists.** They would separate themselves from the average or non-Pietist Jews and try to establish a purer religious life centered around one of their own sages. The sage would have great practical influence in the community life. For example, in the choice of a marriage partner his view would tend to prevail over the wishes of both the young people and the parents. The predominant characteristic that the pietistic sage looked for was Pietism itself. Thus for Pietists, a convert to Judaism who was a Pietist was a more desirable marriage partner than a native Jew who was not a Pietist.

Ivan Marcus has described the problems that such Pietism brought to many Jewish communities: "In addition to devising specific ways of insulating themselves as much as possible from non-Pietists, the Pietists persisted in applying their programmatic interpretations of Judaism in sectarian ways. They restricted a number of religious obligations to apply only to fellow Pietists, instead of to all fellow Jews, and this sectarian focus resulted in social tensions with neighbors and even with family. In particular, they demanded that Pietists pray and give charity in such a way that only Pietists and pietism define the applicability of these obligations. Only Pietists' prayers could reach God. Hence, ever practical, the Pietists reasoned that they alone should serve as cantors. True to their principles that pietism is Judaism, they held that only needy Pietists should be supported by the commandment to give charity. Their stipulations about how Pietist Judaism should be lived led to hostility from other Jews who were offended by the Pietists' exclusiveness."[19] Conflict of this sort continues in Israel today, as conservatives and liberals clash over marriage laws and other civic matters.

If one had to summarize traditional Jewish ethics in a very few principles, probably the following would be most important. First, Jews have believed that their way of life was essentially laid out for them in Torah, God's instructive Law. An ethical, religious, or truly Jewish life—the three here would coincide—stems from following Torah closely. Second, the key to religious morality is justice: giving each party to a transaction its due. The elaborate work of the Talmudists spelled out what justice meant for most of the transactions that crisscrossed traditional Jewish life, and faithful Jews felt constrained by this work. Yet Judaism also allowed considerable freedom for individual interpretation, or at least for argument about what the Talmudic prescriptions might mean in particular situations.

Third, Jewish ethics took the goodness of God's creation seriously and sought to honor creation in daily life. Thus the motto of eastern European life was that Torah, marriage, and good deeds were the three treasures by which one could reverence the Master of the universe and serve the divine plan. Torah included strong prohibitions against injuring other human beings, and marriage involved a strong commitment to keep the chosen people strong. Doing good deeds involved the conviction that wealth or good fortune brought an obligation to share, and that poor members of the community had a strong claim on the help of the prosperous. Deuteronomy had told biblical Jews to look upon the Torah as the way to life, in contrast to the deadly way of irreligious living. Jewish ethics sought a life worthy of the covenant that the holy Creator had made with his special people.

Summary

We began with a concise historical orientation, noting the rise of the Jewish people from Abraham, their early distinction from the surrounding Canaanite polytheists, the covenant God made with Moses, the kingdom established by David, and the composition of *Tanak* by the end of the pre-Common Era. We discussed Israel's subjection to foreign rule, the dispersion the Romans caused, and the predominance of rabbinic authority in areas and periods in which Jews fell under Christian and Muslim rule. Modernity challenged traditional rabbinic Judaism, and the Nazi Holocaust was a terrible crisis. Today the state of Israel is the focus of Jewish culture, and Jewish ethicists struggle with the problems of Israel's survival.

For a philosophical orientation to Judaism, we stressed the two notions of creation and exodus/covenant. The first gave Jews a positive orientation in the world and the second made them hopeful of divine aid. The covenant also oriented Jews toward study, to master the law, and worship was always a high Jewish priority, to honor the Lord God.

In the sphere of family life we found Judaism stressing procreation and the goodness of marriage, greatly blessing children, allowing divorce (though not approving of it), insisting on a marriage contract, allowing abortion in some circumstances, tabooing women because of menstruation, forbidding intermarriage under pain of excommunication, and in general subordinating the spouses' emotional desires to the requirements of the law and the common good.

Jewish ethics has encouraged hard work and has promoted the idea that pursuing a good material living is important. Talmudic study was the most praised work, but business and manual labor were also approved. The Sabbath kept people from becoming obsessed with their work, and women took the major responsibility for domestic work. One could drive a hard bargain, but honesty and justice were to keep all dealings fair.

Social justice is a key notion in traditional Jewish ethics, and some commentators make justice the central Jewish value. Behind this value lies the sense of a divine or a prophetic imperative. Forgiveness is important, but it should not be granted lightly. Peace is a great blessing, and war is taken as a punishment for dishonesty and injustice. Today one finds Jews debating about reconciliation, especially with Palestinians. Traditionally, Jewish social ethics has seen the Noachian covenant as a reminder of Jews' connection to the rest of humanity and has considered all Jews dignified in God's sight.

One finds biblical and traditional sources for a Judaism sensitive to ecological issues, but ecology is not prominent in the traditional Jewish ethical profile. The rabbis were concerned about the welfare of animals, and today's Jewish feminists often link women's liberation with a greater sensitivity to nature.

We discussed Proverbs 31 and Job 31 as biblical texts that offered influential ethical models, noting the good wife's industriousness and the ethical man's concern to be fair to all his neighbors. We noted the central authority of the rabbi and so the connection between study and community ethics. We also discussed the emphases brought by Hasidism, Cabalism, and medieval sectarian movements. Finally we summarized the key ethical emphases of traditional Judaism as a reliance on Torah, a love of justice, and a desire to treat God's good creation appreciatively.

STUDY QUESTIONS

1. How has the Jews' minority status tended to shape their history?
2. How does the Exodus color the traditional Jewish world view?
3. How has patriarchy structured Jewish family life?
4. Why have Jews considered study the highest work?
5. What relation does Judaism find between justice and forgiveness?
6. How has the biblical picture of human beings' place in creation influenced the Jewish view of nature?
7. How adequate is the sketch of the ethical person given in Job 31?

─────────────────── **NOTES** ───────────────────

[1] Michael Grant, *The History of Ancient Israel* (New York: Charles Scribner's Sons, 1984), pp. 21–22.

[2] See Lis Harris, *Holy Days* (New York: Summit Books, 1985).

[3] See Leo Trepp, *Judaism: Development and Life*, 3d ed. (Belmont, Calif.: Wadsworth, 1982).

[4] See Barry W. Holtz, ed., *Back to the Sources: Reading the Classic Jewish Texts* (New York: Summit Books, 1984).

[5] Hayyim Schneid, ed., *Family* (Philadelphia: Jewish Publication Society of America, 1973), p. 48.

[6] Trepp, *Judaism*, p. 325.

[7] Blu Greenberg, "Marriage in the Jewish Tradition," *Journal of Ecumenical Studies* (Winter 1985), 15.

[8] Mark Zborowski and Elizabeth Herzog, *Life Is with People* (New York: Schocken, 1962), pp. 241–42.

[9] Abraham Cohen, *Everyman's Talmud* (New York: Schocken, 1975), pp. 193–94.

[10] Adin Steinsaltz, *The Essential Talmud* (New York: Basic Books, 1976), p. 159.

[11] Steven S. Schwarzschild, "Justice," in *Jewish Values*, ed. Geoffrey Wigoder (Jerusalem: Keter, 1974), p. 195.

[12] Leo Baeck, *The Essence of Judaism* (New York: Schocken, 1974), pp. 222–23.

[13] Abraham J. Heschel, "Response," in *The Sunflower*, ed. Simon Wiesenthal (New York: Schocken, 1976), p. 131.

[14] Earl Shorris, *Jews without Mercy: A Lament* (Garden City, N.Y.: Doubleday, 1982).

[15] See, for example, the works referred to in notes 4, 9, and 10.

[16] Arthur Hertzberg, "What Should Israel Be?" *The New York Times Book Review*, October 13, 1985, p. 7.

[17] See Walter Brueggermann, *The Land* (Philadelphia: Fortress, 1977).

[18] See Abraham Cohen, *Everyman's Talmud*, pp. 235–36.

[19] Ivan G. Marcus, "Religious Virtuosi and the Religious Community: The Pietistic Mode in Judaism," in *Take Judaism, for Example*, ed. Jacob Neusner (Chicago: University of Chicago Press, 1983), p. 108.

2

Christian Ethics

Historical Orientation
World View
Family Life
Work
Social Justice
Nature
Models
Summary, Study Questions, Notes

Historical Orientation

Christianity obviously begins with Jesus of Nazareth, whom his followers considered the Christ or anointed **Messiah.** Jesus is best appreciated as a Jew who created a new and prophetic interpretation of the heritage available in the Hebrew Bible. He preached that the Reign of God was at hand, offering all people a chance to make a new beginning. In light of this reign, Jesus overturned many worldly values. Thus the Sermon on the Mount (Matthew 5–7) contains the beatitudes that bless the poor and the people hungering for justice. The summary of the Torah and the Prophets, in Jesus' view, was the Jewish twofold command to love God wholeheartedly and to love one's neighbor as oneself. After the Resurrection Jesus' followers accorded him a unique status and authority, in effect making him divine. Christianity has always borne the stamp of the paradox that a man condemned as a criminal and forced to suffer a complete failure should have been raised and exalted as the Son of God.

By the end of the first century C.E. the writings that now constitute the New Testament were widely circulated, and Christian communities dotted the Mediterranean shore and Asia Minor. We can see in the so-called Pastoral Epistles (1 and 2 Timothy and Titus) that the tradition

established by the apostle Paul had begun to grapple with moral legislation, as the church settled in for a long life in history. Prior to this,
Christians had been expecting the consummation of history in the return of Christ. In fact, the ethical views of both Jesus and Paul assume
the likelihood that the time between the present and the **eschaton** or
final consummation will be short. Thus in 1 Corinthians 7 Paul counsels
Christians to stay in the state, married or single, in which they now find
themselves and not to be concerned to change their state. Indeed, he rel-
ativizes all worldly or present-minded concerns: "I mean, brethren, the
appointed time has grown very short; from now on, let those who have
wives live as though they had none, and those who mourn as though
they were not mourning, and those who rejoice as though they were not
rejoicing, and those who buy as though they had no goods, and those
who deal with the world as though they had no dealings with it. For the
form of this world is passing away" (7:29–31).

Judaism had developed something like this otherworldliness toward
the end of the pre-Common Era, as we find in the apocalyptic literature
that depicts God's coming judgments. And certainly there were periods
and communities in Jewish history of the Common Era where people
fervently awaited the coming of the Messiah and so suspended present
concerns. But it seems fair to say that Jewish Scripture overall, especially
the Torah but also large portions of the Prophets and the Writings, was
less eschatological than was the original, formative New Testament
Christianity. A Gospel such as Mark is quite apocalyptic, and of course
the Book of Revelation greatly influenced later Christianity. Balancing
this, the Gospel of John and the Acts of the Apostles focused religious
living, and thus ethics, on the present.

In the first centuries of the Common Era the church suffered periods
of persecution from secular authorities, and this kept the eschatological
dimension of its ethical outlook strong. The martyrs, and the monks
who went out to the desert, looked to heaven and the fairer judgment of
God as their justification. But when, in the fourth century, Christianity
became acceptable in the Roman Empire and then was made the official
imperial religion, the this-worldly side of Christian ethics got a boost.
Eastern Christianity developed an **iconic** view of Christ, the saints, and
the emperor, giving all human activities a certain gilding. Western Christianity was greatly influenced by the fall of the Roman Empire, and Saint
Augustine, its key teacher, drew the pessimistic moral that the City of
God and the City of Man were quite opposed.

Medieval Christianity worked out a balance of power between temporal and religious rulers, but in many periods the Pope was the dominant authority. In such medieval Christian classics as Chaucer's *Canterbury Tales* and Dante's *Divine Comedy* one finds the full range of
Christian humanism, from pessimism about human nature and great
concern about heaven and hell to a bawdy celebration of the flesh and

God's good creation. Such key medieval figures as Benedict of Nursia and Francis of Assisi suggested that Christians ought to be stewards of creation and to love nature. The greatest medieval theologian, Thomas Aquinas, worked out a fine balance between faith and reason, showing by his confidence in Aristotle that reason and the rest of human beings' natural endowment should be trusted, but not divorced from higher things such as grace.

1054 is the traditional date given for the separation of Eastern and Western Christianity, but in fact the two portions of Christendom had had different religious styles for centuries. The faith of the East centered on creation, while the faith of the West centered on redemption from sin. Up to the present, the East has continued to sense that the world is filled with the divine Spirit, while the West has worried about human twistedness.

The Protestant Reformation of the sixteenth century further divided Christendom and further blurred the Western ethical emphasis. Martin Luther brought a return to biblical ethics, as well as a renewal of Augustinian pessimism about human nature. John Calvin also stressed the scriptural foundations of Christian faith, and he too was rather grim about human nature. Roman Catholicism, by way of reaction, stressed the importance of human freedom, human reason, and good works. So Protestant ethics came to be dominated by the image of an individual conscience trying to escape from slavery to sin by faith in the Christ revealed in the Bible, while Catholic ethics came to be dominated by church authority, which promoted dogmatic teaching and a strong sacramental life, insisted upon good works, and stressed **natural law.**

Protestantism itself divided further, some churches becoming devotional or pietistic and others becoming rather bare, rigorous, and unemotional. Followers of Calvin gained a reputation for industriousness, thrift, and sobriety, and the influential sociologist Max Weber suggested that this "Protestant ethic" was the driving spirit behind the rise of modern capitalism.

On the whole, however, both Protestantism and Catholicism abhorred modernity, the former mainly because modern science seemed to tear down the biblical picture of creation and human nature, the latter mainly because modern intellectual freedom and movements for political reform threatened the established pattern of authority. So Christian faith was on the defensive from the seventeenth century to the present, and many intellectuals searched for a humanistic or secular ethics to replace the Western mores based on the Bible and on Christian tradition. The wars between the churches seemed a good argument for the humanists' distrust of religions and their call for tolerance or pluralism. On this score one can read Thomas Jefferson and Benjamin Franklin as representative moderns. The discoveries of Darwin, Freud, Marx, and Einstein produced a picture of the world that further alienated the Christian churches, while the cry for social justice that intensified from the second half of the eighteenth century often denounced Christian religion as a tool of an oppressive ruling class.

In the nineteenth century Christian colonialism and missionary work started to make the church truly worldwide, and today Christianity faces the crucial question of how to correlate its ethical tradition with many different ethnic heritages. Only after the wars of the first half of the twentieth century and the manifold crises—nuclear, ecological, economic, and cultural—of the second half of the twentieth century did Christian ethics seem to become competitive in the intellectual culture at large. Today Western ethics often appears dominated by areligious secularists and Christian fundamentalists, with only a few religious humanists (people whose faith fosters critical reason and sponsors cultural creativity) holding down the center. On the other hand, it may well be that such religious humanists, both Christian and non-Christian, are generating the most significant developments in contemporary ethical theory.[1]

World View

The Jewish roots of Jesus and Christianity appear clearly in the significance that Christians have accorded the key Jewish notions of **creation** and **covenant.** Christians have read Genesis 1 and 2 much as Jews have, stressing the sovereignty of God and the goodness of creation. They have made more of the fall of Adam and Eve, developing a view of human nature that emphasizes its sinfulness, yet like the Jews they have appreciated that human beings are images of the divinity. The Christian sense of covenant derives from the death and resurrection of Jesus, as does the Christian sense that a new creation has occurred. Reading the Hebrew Bible as full of "types" or anticipatory sketches that Jesus fulfilled, Christians have taken the death and resurrection of Jesus as an atonement for human beings' sins. They have also spoken of faith in Christ as giving people access to a divine life that will continue after death, and they view the church as the new Israel or people of God.

Where Christian wisdom has most dramatically differed from Judaism has been in its focus upon Jesus as the Logos or Word of God become flesh. Through their theology of the "Incarnation," Christians have taken the position that Jesus Christ is the fullest revelation of both divinity and humanity. This has led to the challenging notion that God has entered into history and used human flesh to conquer suffering, death, and sin by experiencing them. The Eastern churches have tended to stress that the Christ is the Lord of Creation, while the Western churches have tended to stress Jesus' gentleness, suffering, and prophetic concern for society's marginal people.

For Eastern Orthodox and Roman Catholic Christianity, the Incarnation has led to a **sacramental** view of both the physical world and human nature. Thus the rituals of these two Christian families have used incense, water, bread, wine, wax, colors, and music to try to engage all the senses and proclaim the nearness of God. The Protestant family of churches has seen dangers of idolatry in this sensate emphasis, noting the hold that veneration of the saints and the Virgin Mary has had on the Eastern Orthodox and Roman Catholics. So the Protestant tendency has been to try to strip worship and stress the transcendence of God. Protestant theology also has emphasized the divine Word that one finds in the Bible. On the one hand, this frequently has fostered a great respect for learning, as it did in Judaism. On the other hand, Protestant churches sometimes have felt that the Bible contains the only important knowledge and so have disparaged secular learning.

Christian theology, in the strict sense of doctrine of God, differed significantly from Jewish and Muslim theology, again because of Jesus. Not only did Christians claim that Jesus was fully divine, as well as fully human, but they went on to depict the divinity as a trinity of three equal "persons." These "persons" are unlimited centers (an apparent contradiction) of knowledge and love, each fully possessing the single divine nature. Thus Father, Son or Logos, and Holy Spirit are all fully divine, yet each can be considered a distinct modality of God. Christians have insisted that this does not violate monotheism—that they do not have three Gods—but Jews and Muslims have been hard to convince.

The final estimate that Christians have made concerning both the Trinity and the Incarnation of the divine Word is that they are mysterious. By this Christians have meant that they are beyond human comprehension. Neither the Trinity nor the Incarnation would ever be understood, because both were too rich or deep for finite human intelligence to handle. Christians also have spoken of sin in this way, calling it a mystery of iniquity. Here, however, the sense has been that sin is irrational to the core and so gives the mind nothing to comprehend. Why, for example, would any rational person reject the offer of divine life that God has made, or refuse to obey the divine commandments? Overwhelmed by the majesty of God and impressed by their lowly status as mere creatures, many Christians have depicted sin as a prideful aversion from God that makes no sense at all. They have tended to link this prideful aversion or revolt with graphic images of hell, so that frequently the Christian masses have heard more about torment and judgment than about God's goodness and love.

In scriptural terms, the notion of Hebrews 13 : 14 that believers have "here," on earth, no lasting city has been very influential. The notion of heaven or "the city which is to come" has had a powerful influence on the Christian imagination and ethical system, as has the complementary notion of hell. Thus one finds in a Christian classic such as the late-medieval work *The Imitation of Christ* a heavy stress on contemplating death and God's judgment. Mainstream Christianity retained the sense that human existence is finally more a comedy than a tragedy because of Christ's victorious resurrection, yet the symbolism of the cross taught generation after generation that they were but pilgrims and were certain to have to suffer.

In early Christianity vigorous pagan cultures charged the followers of Jesus with a sickly pessimism, just as they charged pious Jews with misanthropy because of their separatism. In modern times the charge of pessimism or destructive otherworldliness returned, most powerfully in the atheistic critiques of Feuerbach and Marx. Christians have made their own countercharges, of course, arguing that their doctrines of creation and Incarnation, if properly understood, sponsor a lovely humanism, and claiming that atheistic humanism, for its part, has little useful to say about the twistedness that lies in the background of most human suffering. Without a proper appreciation of God, **transcendence** (more-than-worldly realities), and human sin, Christians argue, one is nearly bound to think that material evolution, money, political power, or class warfare is the key to understanding reality.

On the whole, then, one senses that the Christian world view ideally is very balanced, but that most Christians frequently find themselves erring by either excess or deficiency. For example, Christian monks who have taken vows of poverty, chastity, and obedience have symbolically asserted that the goods most people pursue should not be considered ultimate or highest. Christian laity, on the other hand, have symbolically asserted that one should love and use God's good creation, and that Christ has made human love trustworthy. When monks came to despise the flesh and try to make Christianity a strongly ascetical religion, they ran counter to the example of the biblical Christ. When laity immersed themselves in the pursuit of wealth or pleasure, they too ran counter to the example of the biblical Christ.

Relatedly, when preachers thundered about hellfire almost to the exclusion of recalling Christ's stress on healing and forgiveness, they missed the point of balance. The complementary failure has been the tendency of other preachers to interpret the Gospel as a completely humanistic venture: "I'm ok, you're ok." The hallmark of what many Christian ethicists would call the most mature or ideal Christian action therefore has been balance or proper proportion.[2]

Family Life

Like Judaism, Christianity has been predominantly a patriarchal religious tradition. Recently, feminist scholarship has found indications that at the time of the New Testament, portions of the church favored an egalitarian balance between men and women, but by the end of the New Testament era patriarchy had asserted itself vigorously.[3] Texts that suggest egalitarianism include Paul's Epistle to the Galatians, 3:28: "There is neither Jew nor Greek, there is neither slave nor free, there is neither male nor female; for you are all one in Christ Jesus." Texts that support patriarchy include 1 Timothy 2:11–15: "Let a woman learn in silence with all submissiveness. I permit no woman to teach or to have authority over men; she is to keep silent. For Adam was formed first, then Eve; and Adam was not deceived, but the woman was deceived and became a transgressor. Yet woman will be saved through bearing children, if she continues in faith and love and holiness, with modesty."

As we have noted, the early Christian expectation of the end of history led Paul, and perhaps also Jesus, to spend little attention or praise on marriage. Jesus spoke of celibacy for the sake of the Reign of God, and Paul preferred that Christians remain unmarried. After the church settled down for a long stay in history, this heritage complicated its approval of marriage and family life. Unlike Judaism, Christianity sponsored a corps of solitary and celibate contemplatives, both men and women, and these people came to be considered the Christian elite. Gradually celibacy was legislated for priests, and many official church documents praise virginity as a higher state than marriage. Eastern Orthodoxy joined Roman Catholicism in sponsoring a monastic or "religious" life, though in the East celibacy was not required of ordinary priests (it was required of bishops). Protestantism attacked both monasticism and ministerial celibacy, wanting to return to what it saw as the priesthood of all believers and the primacy of the sacrament of baptism.

As a result of all of this, in most periods of Christian history marriage was seen as a concession to human weakness. Balancing this, however, was a foundational realization that Jesus had accepted the institution of marriage (though he himself apparently had not married), and that marriage was necessary for the proper fulfillment of the command in Genesis to be fruitful. Both theological and sociological factors combined to make procreation the primary end of marriage, but the mutual affection and help of the spouses were also considered important. A family that brought children up in the faith, nourished them on the sacramental life and preaching of the church, and helped them find their Christian vocations sometimes was honored as a "little church" in its own right.

Until modern times, Christian sexual morality generally forbade intercourse outside of marriage, adultery, and contraception or abortion. Roman Catholicism forbade divorce, and while Eastern Orthodoxy and Protestantism were more lenient, a divorced person usually suffered in those traditions as well. The predominant moral judgment was that abortion, contraception, adultery, homosexuality, and even masturbation were serious sins that broke one's intimacy with God and threatened one with hellfire. Spouses with proven incompatibility usually could gain an approved separation, but they could remarry only under pain of being cut off from the sacraments or church fellowship.

More positively, the solemnizing of marriage that most churches developed testified to the Christian conviction that marriage could be a vocation rich in God's grace. Demetrios Constantelos has approached the Greek Orthodox view of marriage from this perspective: "The best way to understand the Orthodox Church's position on marriage is to study and reflect on its service of matrimony. In the first prayer, after a series of petitions, we read that it is God's will that man and woman should be legally married; that marriage should serve as a source of life that is happy, peaceful, and blessed with longevity, mutual love, and offspring, culminating here on earth with a crown of glory. In the third prayer of the service, the celebrant, standing before the bride and groom, adds: 'O Sovereign Lord . . . join together this your servant [man's name] and this your servant [woman's name] for by you is a wife joined to her husband. Unite them in oneness of mind; crown them with wedlock unto one flesh; grant to them through physical union the gain of well-favored children.'"[4]

The biblical ideal was for marital partners to become "one flesh." This, combined with the notion of Genesis that the humanity that is the image of God is both male and female, gave theological support to the biologically obvious coordination of woman and man. Further, however, marriage figured in a rather elaborate analogy based on the union between Christ and the church or Christian people. As Christ is head of the church, so was the husband to be head of the wife. This supported the subordinate status that Christian wives have tended to have in what has generally been a patriarchal surrounding culture. As Ephesians 5 : 22–26 put it: "Wives, be subject to your husbands, as to the Lord. For the husband is the head of the wife as Christ is the head of the church, his body, and is himself its Savior. As the church is subject to Christ, so let wives also be subject in everything to their husbands. Husbands, love your wives, as Christ loved the church and gave himself up for her, having cleansed her by the washing of water with the word. . . ." Taken in isolation from the whole scriptural portrait of God's dispensation for human beings, a text such as this could easily seem to grant husbands complete control over their wives and make the wifely ideal submission in all areas. Indeed, medieval town laws (and modern customs) that allowed husbands to batter their wives for disobedience drew on this imagery of headship. On the other hand, one has only to reflect on the sort of love that Christ lavished upon the church in giving himself up to death on human beings' behalf to see how prejudicial any reading that supported battering of wives or children had to be.

In Protestantism much of the noxious possibility in a highly biblical view of marriage was blocked by the notion that marriage is a holy **cove-**

nant between the partners. Wilson Yates recently has summarized the main features of this covenantal ideal under six headings. First, the partners commit themselves to creating a life of intimate companionship. Second, they pledge themselves to creating a shared life and home in which honesty, trust, openness, and acceptance prevail. Third, they agree to explore together the religious and moral depths of their Christian faith. Fourth, they agree to aim at a wholeness of love that includes romance, justice, freedom, and order. Fifth, they agree to accept or create behavioral boundaries—ethical norms that they will both support. Sixth, they promise not to break their covenant unless their life together has lost its intimacy.

On this last point, which of course conjures up the specter of divorce, Yates writes: "It should be noted that Protestantism has shifted over the centuries on the question of divorce. While John Milton's treatise, *On Divorce*, built a case for divorce as early as the seventeenth century, it was not until the twentieth century that Protestant denominations were willing to acknowledge that divorce could be a morally responsible action. It is also significant that there is a growing attempt to develop church rituals that recognize divorce and offer support and hope to the partners in their search for new beginnings, though no denomination has yet formally adopted such a ritual."[5]

One finds a parallel loosening of the previously rigid prohibitions against contraception, abortion, and homosexuality, so that Christian sexual and family ethics is now far less certain about these matters than it was even a century ago. Love and responsibility continue to predominate in the ideal Christian marriage, but most churches recognize that interpreting love and responsibility can be quite difficult.[6]

Work

From the account of the fall of Adam and Eve in Genesis 3 Christians received the notion that hard physical toil was a punishment for original sin. Many Christians read texts such as this literally, and so labored in the fields with the sense that they were doing penance. Relatedly, women accepted the notion that the pains of childbearing were a fit punishment for their share in humanity's alienation from God. In spite of this literalism, however, the mystery that healthy religion always evokes suggested positive images and symbols that no doubt influenced many Christians more powerfully than the negative ones did. According to these positive images and symbols, work was but one of several ways that a person experienced the grandeur and the misery of the strange estate called humanity. For even hard manual labor on occasion could become a thing of art and integration, and certainly many peasants made their agricultural work a way to harmony with nature's awesome rhythms. Human crafts brought many women and men to appreciate the creativity of human labor, perhaps implicitly suggesting how apt the notion of "image of God" (the original Creator) could be.

Either way, in pain or ecstasy, traditional Christian toil was fitted to a providential scheme. As Jesus perhaps implied in teaching that God numbers every hair on his children's heads, Christians could finally think, when all was said and done, that their works, whether great or small, whether successes or failures, flowed into a great stream of natural and human history that God was directing to a successful outcome. The Pauline notion that all creation is in labor (Romans 8 : 22) had the overtones of both birth and constant toil. It made quite explicit the viewpoint of biblical faith that God will bring history to a successful consummation. Consequently, those who prayed regularly probably often experienced a deep sense of peace or abandonment, thinking that their efforts to make something beautiful, help their community, or fulfill their responsibilities as parents would finally prove to have been worthwhile.

Still, the price of this ultimate vocational security often was a fairly static or restricted view of human possibilities. Prior to modernity a sense of "natural law" constrained most Christians to think that what they could do through their human efforts was quite limited. Natural law not only influenced the specific ethical positions of a large church such as the Roman Catholic; it also inclined all premodern Christians to think of their particular forms of government, sexual roles, divisions of labor, and forms of church authority as encoded in "the way things are." Only in modern times have we come to understand the human construction of reality and appreciate how arbitrary many definitions of what is possible are. This modern sense has greatly expanded human creativity and exploration, not only in the physical sciences and technology but also in the arts, the social sciences, family life, and even church affairs.

The basic virtue that Christians have presumed should prevail in the business world—where work relations are considered as economic forces—has been justice, as it has been for Judaism. (We shall see more of distributive justice—the fairness that ought to obtain in the sharing of the goods of the earth—in the next section.) Christians have considered justice in matters of work to involve such virtues as honesty in negotiations and trade, giving a fair day's work for a fair wage, shouldering one's responsibilities toward one's family and community, and generally making good use of the talents that God has given one.

In the Roman Catholic church, the Second Vatican Council brought many of the traditional elements of Christian labor theory up to date by explicitly defending workers against economic exploitation: "Since economic activity is generally exercised through the combined labors of human beings, any way of organizing and directing that activity which would be detrimental to any worker would be wrong and inhuman. It too often happens, however, even in our day, that in one way or another workers are made slaves of their work. This situation can by no means be justified by so-called economic laws. The entire process of productive work, therefore, must be adapted to the needs of the person and to the requirements of his life, above all his domestic life. Such is especially the case with respect to mothers of families, but due consideration must be given to every person's sex and age."[7]

It took considerable time for this degree of sensitivity to develop, of course, and considerable prodding from such humanistic systems as Marxism. Biblical Judaism and Christianity both tolerated the institution of slavery, and slavery nearly vitiated American Christian aspirations for several centuries. The Industrial Revolution made brutal factory work a possibility for perhaps the majority of Western people, and today one can extend the logic of defending vulnerable workers to concern for those who are exposed to chemicals or radiation. Hazardous work such as mining is hard to defend, while the boredom of many jobs continues to oppress millions. On the other hand, unemployment has become a source of great suffering. So modern work, despite all the freedom that labor-saving devices have brought, has continued to march under the banner of our first parents' fall. Housework is still far from dignified, and the care of children, despite its absolutely crucial status in the evolutionary perspective, often seems undervalued.

Loss of value, of course, is one of the many problems that work has suffered in Christian history. Certainly nowadays money seems to direct most economic transactions (a great many people would not know how to define *economics* apart from money), but from New Testament times Christians have heard that they could not serve both God and mammon. The Gospels report Jesus' figure of a rich man being no more able to enter the kingdom of heaven than a camel is able to pass through the eye of a needle (Matthew 19:24), while the Epistle of James contains a savage attack on riches: "Has not God chosen those who are poor in the world to be rich in faith and heirs of the kingdom which he has promised to those who love him? But you have dishonored the poor man. Is it not the rich who drag you into court? Is it not they who blaspheme the honorable name which was invoked over you?" (James 2:5–7).

Medieval Christianity limited the depredations of work by celebrating many holy days, and traditionally Christians honored Sunday somewhat as Jews honored the Sabbath. However, neither ecologically nor in their view of work did many Christians take to heart the notion (from Leviticus 25) of a sabbatical year, when the land would lie fallow, or a jubilee year after seven sabbatical years (that is, every fifty years), when landholding and slaveholding would come to an end: "And you shall hallow the fiftieth year, and proclaim liberty throughout the land to all of its inhabitants; it shall be a jubilee for you, when each of you shall return to his property and each of you shall return to his family" (25:10).

Still, the obsession with work, whether for financial profit or for per-

sonal development, that we find developing in the twentieth century has
had few precedents in Christian history. In most periods it would have
been called idolatrous. Prayer so counterbalanced work, and spiritual
standing so counterbalanced financial standing, that in most times and
places Christians were effectively living according to Jesus' question:
"For what will it profit a man, if he gains the whole world and forfeits his
life? Or what shall a man give in return for his life?" (Matthew 16:26).
The life meant here was both physical and spiritual: work should not
grind the worker down into illness, and it should not obscure the more
important matter of the worker's standing before God. So the activities
that required leisure—art, worship, science, family sharing, play, and
others—traditionally helped Christians to limit the claims of work and
of chasing after a material living.

Social Justice

One of the most powerful social convictions in the Christian repertoire
of ethical ideals has been the sense that the goods of the earth exist for
all the earth's people. Christians certainly have not always honored this
conviction, but they have all caught at least glimmers of it whenever
they attended to their tradition. The biblical pictures of creation and **redemption** supported this notion, and the early fathers of the church
honed it to a sharp edge. For example, they found the gratuity of creation
and the solidarity of all human beings, as children of one God, to imply
that no one had the right to luxuries as long as anyone lacked necessities. In many periods of Christian history, as in many periods of Jewish
history, the rich were thought to have a strong obligation to give alms.
The story of the rich man who languished in hell because he did not
help the poor man Lazarus (Luke 16) was a powerfully cautionary tale,
while the judgment scene of Matthew 25 told Christians that when they
neglected the suffering they neglected Christ himself. Christians remembered that Jesus had preached the beatitudes and healed the sick.
The many hospitals, schools, clinics, and other charitable institutions
that the Christian churches have sponsored testify to the power of these
images.[8]

Nonetheless, Christians are liable to the charge of having achieved
much less than a full **distributive justice.** Concerning material goods,
there certainly have been yawning divisions between rich and poor, and
the idyllic picture of early Christian communism given in Acts 2 seldom
obtained in later centuries. The monasteries dedicated to poverty often
accumulated great wealth, the riches of the papacy were a ready target
for the sixteenth-century reformers, and the Protestant ethic often came
to identify material prosperity with good standing before God. Women

have not been first-class citizens in most Christian churches, if one defines such citizenship in terms of full access to leadership roles. Racism has corroded most of the churches, as has been especially evident in modern colonialism, in American Christians' treatment of blacks and Indians, and in present-day apartheid in South Africa. These and other discriminatory regimes regularly have appealed to Christian Scripture and theology for their justification, as has an ugly and long-playing Christian anti-Semitism. So according to the ideal of distributive justice and fair treatment of all of God's creation, many Christians have been hypocritical or culpably blind.

On the question of war, the ideal and the reality once again diverge considerably. The tradition that Christians should be pacifists, according to the example of Jesus, had most influence in the early church and then in the so-called left wing of the Protestant Reformation. The theory that, under very stringent conditions, there could be a **just war** was highly influential, but regularly leaders who wanted to go to war skirted the theory's provisions. For example, this theory required that war be a last resort, that it seek the redress of truly grievous injustices, that it distinguish between combatants and civilians, that it not hold out the prospect of doing more harm than good, and that there be a solid chance of victory. The greatest Christian scandals, in this context, were the religious wars that various Christian princes waged against one another, often on sectarian grounds, and the Crusades against the Muslims. They show that Christians often granted themselves an exemption from ordinary morality when they could call the enemy a heretic or a threat to the faith. Legitimate self-defense has remained part of the mainstream Christian ethics of war, but few of the actual wars that Christians have waged win the approval of mainstream ethicists. (Opposition to Nazism in World War II is probably the outstanding exception.)

Today the specter of nuclear war dominates the ethics of war and peace, and indeed questions of social justice generally. Christians divide on the possibility of waging a nuclear war morally, but most of the mainstream is strongly negative. Pacifist Christians recoil from the violence that nuclear war would wreak on the biosphere, as well as from the massive toll it would take in human life. Theorists of the just-war tradition find it hard to imagine that any goods that nuclear war might bring could outweigh the colossal evils that it would bring, especially now that scientists are speaking of **nuclear winter.** Moreover, many Christian ethicists judge that the present preparations for nuclear war are immoral not just because they make such war possible but also because they divert resources from more fundamental needs. For example, the money that nations spend on arms would go a long way toward averting the millions of impending deaths by starvation, to say nothing of the malnutrition, illiteracy, sickness, and cultural poverty that much of the world suffers.

The sense that the goods of the earth are for all the earth's people has stimulated the school of Christian moral reflection known as "liberation theology" to call for a wholesale reworking of the global economy and to attack capitalism as a particularly noxious foe. Such statistics as that Americans comprise 6 percent of the world's population but are responsible for 40 percent of the world consumption of natural resources are a natural stimulus in this context, but the misery of the masses in Latin America, Asia, and Africa is even more compelling. Because world suffering has shown the links among economics, politics, sex, race, and industrialization, many Christian ethicists are calling for a brand-new vision, one equal to the new global context in which the great ethical issues now occur. Such a new vision would, of course, apply to non-Christians who now share the technological prowess developed in the traditionally Christian West.

We shall deal with the ecological dimension of these issues in the next section, but here we must note that Christian tradition furnishes valuable but definitely limited guidance. Through most of their history Christians, like Jews, have thought of themselves as a chosen people. Today that conviction has to be squared with the brute fact that the vast majority of the world's population is not Christian, and that Christians are prominent among the group that seems most responsible for both the misery of the majority and the pollution of the ecosphere. That the Communist countries, which usually are explicit in their atheistic opposition to Christianity, can be accounted strong, if not worse, oppressors in economic, political, and military terms, and worse oppressors in terms of individual human rights, somewhat tempers Christian ethicists' judgments about the churches' culpability. But the fact remains that today's awareness of global and systemic injustice is a strong pressure for a new ethical vision. Thus one finds collaborative ventures in which representatives of the different world religions discuss human rights, economic justice, and political cooperation,[9] and the increasing realization that both the arms race and environmental pollution are symptoms of a runaway pathology.

At the fringes of this current chapter in the history of Christian reflection on social justice stand the internationalists who call for a global government, but since nationalism and ethnicity have only grown in recent years, this internationalist point of view can seem hopelessly idealistic. Jews and Christians could read the biblical prophets and conclude that for justice to roll down like a mighty stream, most of their predominant social concepts would have to shift, but relatively few are doing that. Indeed, a Christian fundamentalism strongly contributes to American nationalism, while a Jewish fundamentalism strongly contributes to Israeli nationalism. Muslim fundamentalism—a topic for the next chapter—further calls into question the viability of religious prophecy.

Nature

Like Jews, Christians have taken their basic attitudes toward nature from the account of creation given in Genesis 1–3. Especially important has been 1:28, in which human beings are given a dominion over the rest of creation. Nowadays Christian ecologists are interpreting this dominion as a stewardship, but most historians of Christian attitudes toward nature, like most historians of other traditions' attitudes toward nature, find that human beings have usually achieved something less than a responsible stewardship.

In looking back on their tradition with an eye to retrieving its better intuitions concerning nature, Christians can explore several sources. The Old Testament, as noted, links the fate of the land with the fate of the people and uses the promised land as a key figure of religious prosperity. The New Testament depicts Jesus fashioning metaphors that draw on the close contact with nature that he would have had growing up as a rural Jew. Perhaps the most famous of these occurs in Luke 12:27–28: "Consider the lilies, how they grow; they neither toil nor spin; yet I tell you, even Solomon in all his glory was not arrayed like one of these. But if God so clothes the grass which is alive in the field today and tomorrow is thrown into the oven, how much more will he clothe you, O men of little faith!"

The lives of the Christian saints furnish numerous stories, many of them no doubt legendary, about the intimacy with animals and with nature generally that the holy men and women achieved. In the writings of medieval mystics such as Hildegard of Bingen, Mechtild of Magdeburg, Meister Eckhart, and Julian of Norwich one finds a great love of creation and a strong sense that the divinity is present in all things. Francis of Assisi is famous for his canticles that praise the sun his brother and the moon his sister. John Calvin stands out among the early Protestant theologians for his deep appreciation of God's creative power, while later Protestant groups such as the Shakers, the Quakers, and the Amish evidence a nonconsumerist, pacifist, and ecologically sensitive religious ideal. In Eastern Orthodoxy many of the Russian **starsy** or holy monks developed a great love of the solitary wastes and snows, while the notion that Jesus is the Lord of all creation and that the Spirit fills all creation often inclined Eastern Orthodoxy to consider nature a second revelation alongside Scripture.

H. Paul Santmire, who has provided the first full study of the ambiguous Christian heritage concerning the theology of nature, offers examples of positive metaphors that flourished in the past and that might serve today's theologians as models to help in renewing the Christian theology of nature. So, for example, Santmire says of the second-century Greek father Irenaeus's naturalistic metaphors: "Such are the fruits of one theologian's energetic and consistent envisioning of reality in terms of the metaphor of migration to a good land, and then, in the context of that vision, also in terms of the metaphor of fecundity. Since God is the God who pours out blessings in the 'landedness' of the end times, flooding his whole creation with new life, Irenaeus's mind as a matter of course finds it congenial to think of God also in terms of fecundity, not only then but now. In Irenaeus's vision the whole creation is full of goodness, harmony, beauty, and life at all times, all continually pouring forth from the hands of God. God is not some distant ruler, far removed in the heavens, sending out his commands through intermediaries. Rather God is one who contains all things, works richly in them, gives them their individual places within the whole, and thus bestows harmony on all things. The human creature likewise is at home in the creation, not a stranger and pilgrim in an alien world. Humanity is constantly blessed by the fruits of the earth in general, and by the sacraments in particular."[10]

To cite just one more of Santmire's historical sources, we may listen to the praise heaped on creation by the church father Saint Augustine, who lived during the fourth and fifth centuries: "Shall I speak of the manifold and various loveliness of the sky, and earth, and sea; of the plentiful supply and wonderful qualities of the light; of sun, moon, and stars; of the shade of trees; of the colors and perfume of flowers; of the multitude of the birds, all differing in plumage and song; of the variety of animals, of which the smallest in size are often the most wonderful; of the works of ants and bees astonishing us more than the huge bodies of whales? Shall I speak of the sea, which itself is so grand a spectacle, when it arrays itself as it were in vestures of various colors, now running through every shade of green, and again becoming purple or blue?"[11]

Modern science and technology arose from a Western Christian substratum, though historians of science debate whether a Christian sense of dominion or an Enlightenment sense of autonomy and confidence in human reason was the fatal misstep that led to ecological abuses. The roots of the current ecological crisis certainly lie in the Industrial Revolution, but only in the present century has industrialization clearly outstripped nature's capacity to cope with the wastes that humanity produces.

What seems beyond dispute, however, is that when we take a hard look at the present state of the major ecological systems—the air, the water, the land—we find a trend whose continuance can only spell disaster. From soil erosion to acid rain and the greenhouse effect, descriptions and statistics that are now common knowledge paint a very grim future. Nuclear wastes have toxic potential and longevity that stagger the imagination. Chemical dump sites now dot the landscape of the developed countries, seeping destructive agents into the soil and the water. Love Canal symbolizes the danger that is already with us, while the growing body of statistics on people exposed to radiation from atomic testing makes it plain that nuclear energy is carcinogenic. All such factors make environmental ethics a new and pressing area of Christian moral reflection.

Some Christian ethicists move beyond the human costs of environmental pollution to consider the injuries wrought to nonhuman creation, but they are not yet numerous enough to warrant our speaking of a creation-centered Christian ethics. Still, the figures on famine, income, and the use of raw materials are powerful enough to provide Christian ethicists, and the ethicists of other developed nations, much of their present agenda. Consider, for example, the following passage from a book on Christian environmentalism: "This year [ca. 1983], world-wide, twenty to fifty million people will starve or will die as a direct result of inadequate nourishment. More than one-third of all people alive today suffer chronic protein and caloric malnutrition. The World Bank has documented the fact that infant mortality in the Third World (Asia, Africa, Latin America) is now more than eight times higher than that in the developed world. Life expectancy is one-third lower. The nutritional level of one hundred million children is not sufficient to permit optimum brain development. Seven hundred and fifty million people have a per capita income of less than $100 per year and another billion earn less than $500 per year. What is clear is that, tragic as it is, famine is only the spotlight on the stage of the world's food problem. Of more basic concern to the two billion have-nots are chronic hunger, the diseases induced by malnutrition, and the continuing competition for food supplies with the rich nations. Unbelievably, the Third World is a net exporter of protein to the overdeveloped world, a trade imbalance further complicating the already harsh conditions of suffering people."[12]

It is among ecologists that one finds the greatest awareness of the connections among our current environmental problems and the greatest objection to past ideals and practice. Similarly, it is among the Christian ethicists who have pondered the statistics on pollution, famine, industrialization, international trade, per capita income, and the rest that one finds the best inklings of the changes necessary to turn things around. One such change is to move from models of continued economic expansion to models of a steady-state economic order predicated on the carrying capacity of nature. Another such change is effective worldwide population control and greatly simplified life-styles for the presently affluent people of the Northern nations. The path to ecological health seems to lead in the direction of conservation of both energy and resources. The way to avoid locking poorer people into poverty forever—as opponents of steady-state economic models often charge that these models will do—seems to lie in a redistribution of the international wealth. Christians thinking along this line often probe their past ethical tradition, try to reject its anthropocentrism and its assumption that Christians are chosen people, and retrieve the notion that the

right to private ownership of land and resources has classically been subordinated to the common good of the people at large. In reading about
the church fathers or the visions of the mystics and reformers, one finds
that they often had a love of simplicity, charity, and poverty, and a reverence for creation that suggest a conservationist spirituality. The non-
Christian socialist thinkers usually make considerable sense to Christian egalitarians and environmentalists, though few Christian ethicists
approve of the disregard of human rights that the socialist regimes often
manifest. What virtually never escapes unscathed in Christian environ-
mentalist ethics is the consumerist life-style of the contemporary affluent nations.

Neither the Christian ethicists nor the Christian masses at large
seem to appreciate fully the damage that current consumerism is doing.
Only a fraction of either group pays much attention to the different rates
of consumption of raw materials in the United States and India, for example, and such neglect makes a discussion of population control one-
sided. Only a few Christians take seriously the statistics on the consumption of nonrenewable natural resources, and so only a few make
fully cogent analyses of current policies on energy production and use.
Those Christians who hold power in the Northern nations regard conservation of animal species as an affair for bleeding hearts. The links
among the industries that produce machines of war, industrial pollution, racism, sexism, and Christian or secular anthropocentrism are
clear to only a few.

Models

Without doubt Jesus has been the primary model of the Christian ethical life, so much so that in many periods Christian spirituality as a
whole reduced to an imitation of Christ. For ethics proper the first implication of such an imitation was that love replaced justice as the motivational center. The idea was not that justice was unimportant, but that
the fullest justice came only when love brought warmth, mercy, and
fuller understanding. In addition, Christians remembered that Jesus himself suffered injustice to the extreme of having to forfeit his life, and that
despite his pains he did not retaliate or try to inflict hurt for hurt. The
cross of Christ therefore figured significantly in the (unreflective) ethical
ideals of pious Christians through the ages, inclining them to be more
patient and long-suffering than they likely would have been apart from
faith. This is not to say that the example of Jesus made pacifism, nonviolence, or the return of love for hatred the dominant tendency of the
average Christian. Clearly it did not. Yet as long as Christ hung on the
cross in the local church, Christians were forced to think twice about
the ultimate significance of their sufferings. Similarly, as long as Easter

and the story of Christ's resurrection remained the axis of the **liturgical year,** the paradox of the divine ways of justice cautioned all Christians not to lose heart or decide too quickly what was possible.

Jesus also was remembered as a person who had devoted himself to others, and so Christian ethics promoted the giving of one's time, money, talents, and concern to others—especially to the poor, the sickly, and the bereaved. The **corporal works of mercy,** such as visiting the sick and those in prison, spelled out an important part of the Christian ideal, while offering others the spiritual succor of listening, encouragement, and good counsel formed much of the Christian pastor's goal.

During the centuries when Christianity dominated Western culture saints such as Catherine of Siena used the prophetic example of Jesus to summon Christian leaders, including the Pope, to a more ethical life, while the church regularly housed social critics and reformers who pointed to Jesus cleansing the Temple or opposing the Pharisees as the grounds for their criticism. Implicit in many of these critiques was Jesus' apparent concern for the spirit of genuine religion and his equally apparent judgment that the fine points of any law, religious or secular, were of secondary importance to its spirit. True enough, Christian officials could cite Jesus' statement that he had not come to abolish the law but to fulfill it (Matthew 5 : 17–18), but Jesus' example—for instance his healing on the Sabbath—was much bolder than such words. Indeed, because of Jesus, Christian ethicists have always worked in a somewhat anomalous situation. The model of Jesus did not promote the production of rigid principles or laws to direct Christian behavior. Many ethicists did attempt to produce such principles, of course, but never without puzzling their fellow Christians who had heard the New Testament sayings about the primacy of charity or the freedom of the Spirit to breathe where it will, or who knew of Jesus' summary of religion in terms of a twofold commandment of love.

Nonetheless, there were peculiar problems with proposing Jesus as Christians' ethical model, since Christians believed that Jesus was divine as well as human. As the Epistle to the Hebrews put it (4 : 15), Jesus was like us other human beings in all things save sin. This exception, naturally, proved to be monumental, so in the periods of Christian history when the divinity of Jesus was especially stressed (for example, after the rise of the Arian heresy, which denied the divinity of Jesus, in the third century), Christians instinctively looked for more approachable models. Medieval Christianity developed considerable devotion to the infant Jesus, and Eastern Orthodoxy regularly pictured Jesus as a rather regal child in the arms of his mother Mary. Mary herself drew much attention and functioned as an ethical model for Christian women. She was considered perhaps more approachable than the adult Jesus, and people in suffering could imagine themselves standing next to her beside Jesus' cross. That Mary was believed to have been both virgin and mother somewhat complicated her status as a model for Christian women. But just as many Christians generally found Jesus counseling them to mildness and compassion, so many Christians—especially women but also men—found Mary's religious attitude good guidance for their own efforts to accept God's will for them. This attitude was expressed in her response "Behold, I am the handmaid of the Lord; let it be to me according to your word" (Luke 2 : 38) to the angel who told her of her mission.

Christians remembered that Jesus and Mary had been simple and poor folk, and this kept them from feeling comfortable with worldly images of success that accented wealth and power. The holy family of Jesus, Mary, and Joseph served Christian spouses and children as an ideal, the keynote of the holy family being its humble status in worldly terms. Similarly, the saints who gained greatest popularity in Christian history tended to be those who had been humble and approachable. Thus Francis of Assisi was greatly beloved for his joyous freedom, which many ordinary Christians realized was intimately related to his romance with his Lady Poverty. Francis Xavier, the sixteenth-century Jesuit missionary, was beloved for his selfless work on behalf of **"infidels,"** and many were drawn by his reputation for helping people gain physical cures. The medieval saint Thomas à Becket, archbishop of Canterbury, and Thomas More, the saint of the English Reformation era, suggested by their martyrdom that standing up to secular powers that wanted to dilute the faith or turn it to their own purposes could cost one one's life. In Eastern Christianity the masters of prayer-forms such as the **Jesus Prayer** furnished much of the ideal, and the common people looked to the monks for inspiration. The monks were supposed to be poor, chaste, selfless, and helpful, and their removal from society at large suggested to Byzantine and Russian Christianity that ethical perfection demanded a considerable separation from general society. Most of the Catholic and Orthodox saints were not ordinary lay people who had married and worked in the world. Some of them belonged to the laity, but not enough to make the average Christian expect to gain sanctity (full ethical success) in the world.

The Protestant Reformation worked against this notion, upgrading the status of the laity and urging a holy secularity. In its wake marriage gained a higher esteem (even though, perhaps paradoxically, the Protestants did not consider marriage a sacrament), and so did the world of secular work. The Protestants generally disapproved of the cult of the saints, and of such entailments as pilgrimages to the saints' shrines. Indeed, they even disapproved of the veneration of Mary, whom the Catholics greatly loved as the Virgin Mother of God and the Orthodox called the **theotokos** or God-bearer. Protestants feared that this veneration was idolatrous, and as their model they chose either Jesus himself or the person who was steeped in biblical piety. As they studied the Old Testament, many Protestants drew close to the biblical prophets, loving both their poetry and their call to social justice, concern for the widow and orphan, and mercy rather than sacrifice. Protestants who were the minority of a country remembered that prophets such as Elijah and Jeremiah had stood up to irreligious kings. They also remembered Peter and the other members of the tiny Christian band who, after the Resurrection, had preached in the Temple in Jerusalem. When told to desist, they had proclaimed, "We must obey God rather than men" (Acts 5 : 29). Martin Luther and John Calvin, of course, became influential models, especially in their devotion to the Bible as the sole norm of Christian life, and from these and other reformers Protestants took to heart the idea that the church itself was always in need of reform.

Summary

We sketched the historical context of Christian ethics by first noting the message of Jesus and the **eschatological** expectation that he shared with Paul. By the end of the New Testament era a this-worldly emphasis balanced such concern for the end of history, but Christian ethics has always been pressured to look beyond any purely temporal success. We noted the influence of the church fathers and Saint Augustine, the humanism developed in the Middle Ages, the positive view of creation developed in Eastern Christianity, and the Protestant return to scriptural origins. Finally, we suggested how a secularist modernity challenged Christian ethical assumptions but is now itself on the defensive.

Philosophically, we discussed Christians' use of the two key Jewish notions of creation and covenant and then sketched the changes that the Christian doctrine of the Incarnation has brought about. This led us to Catholic and Orthodox sacramentalism, and then to the Protestant emphasis on the divine Word. We discussed the distinctively Christian view that God is a trinity of divine persons, noting the mysteriousness of this doctrine. We also noted the Christian sense that sin or aversion from God is finally a mysterious irrationality. Our final reflection dealt with the possibility of a Christian humanism that would balance concern with this world and concern with heaven, and undue optimism and sickly pessimism.

In regard to Christian family life, Scripture is ambiguous. Some texts suggest the radical equality of men and women, while others suggest a male dominance or patriarchy. We noted the liabilities that Christian otherworldliness and celibacy worked on the Christian view of marriage, and then we listed the string of prohibitions, from adultery to birth control, that shaped traditional Christian sexual morality. Balancing this were positive views of marriage, such as the ceremonial view of Eastern Orthodox Christians and the covenantal view of Protestants. The most important scriptural text, however, was probably Ephesians 5, which set a parallel between Christ's headship of the church and the husband's headship of the wife, both of which could involve either tender love or complete control.

Christians have viewed work in terms of the fall of Adam and Eve depicted in Genesis 3. They learned from Romans 8 that all of creation is in labor, and in the ages when a theory of natural law reigned, their sense of human possibilities was rather constrained. The main virtue relevant to work probably has been justice, and in modern times Christian ethicists have come to champion the rights of workers. In other periods Christianity tolerated slavery and often did not take fully seriously the spiritual dangers that Scripture found in riches. Believers were supposed to realize that they could not serve both God and mammon, while traditional Christian views of the Sabbath and holy days were meant to prevent people from becoming obsessed with their work.

Perhaps the key to the Christian sense of social justice has been the realization that God has given the goods of the earth to all the earth's people. Although Christians themselves often have disregarded this conviction, the Christian tradition has used it as a basis for criticizing unjust economic or political regimes. The doctrine of a just war shaped much traditional reflection about human conflict, though pacifism was a strong inclination, and today discussions of nuclear warfare and arms building place a great burden of proof on the militarists. More broadly, liberation theologians and others are pointing out the systemic qualities of most injustices, arguing that the divisions between Northerners and Southerners, men and women, and whites and other races are not accidental. Whether today's increasingly global culture will bring a new internationalism to heal such divisions is debatable, but increasingly Christian ethicists see the interconnectedness of the major problems of social justice.

The word *ecology* certainly summons the idea of such interconnectedness, though the views of creation given in Genesis 1–3 historically have not brought the majority of Christians to realize their obligations to subhuman creation. Nonetheless, both Scripture and the model of the Christian saints show the positive religious role that the land (including the water and the air) can play. One finds at least the seeds of an ecological theology in medieval mystics such as Julian of Norwich and the classical Reformer John Calvin, while many of the Russian *starsy* manifest a great love of the northern wilderness. The pollution now racking the earth shows modern industrialization, nuclear radiation, and chemical toxicity to be assuming the aspects of great sins. The mounting disparity between the wealthy and the poor, which is most painfully clear in the figures of those dying of malnutrition, links land use with distributive justice. Thus some Christian ethicists are calling for steady-state models of economic development, and virtually all are criticizing Western consumerism.

Jesus has clearly been the dominant ethical model for Christians in all parts of the world; his love, simplicity, poverty, and concern for other people have been relevant in all ages. Jesus' acceptance of suffering has greatly influenced many Christians brought low, while his resurrection has offered an enormously powerful basis for hope. Christian social critics have looked to Jesus the prophet, and Jesus' freedom from legal punctiliousness has kept the church lawyers from predominating. Mary and the saints have also been significant models, their humility and willingness to suffer for principle being especially important. Because the monastic or otherworldly status of most of the saints has made imitating them difficult, Protestant theology has emphasized the lay state and this-worldly responsibilities. In all ethical matters, however, the Christian bottom line has been the love that Jesus manifested, which has meant an ethics hardly separable from prayer and social service.

STUDY QUESTIONS

1. Explain the importance of eschatology (the view of the end of history) in the ethics of Jesus and Paul.

2. What place does the doctrine of the Incarnation have in the Christian sense of reality and the good life?

3. Explain the traditional Christian prohibition of adultery and the negative attitude toward divorce.

4. What does Leviticus 25 suggest about the biblical view of work?

5. Explain why the church fathers taught that no one had the right to luxuries as long as any one lacked necessities.

6. How does ecological devastation exemplify the Christian notion that sin is a vicious irrationality?

7. Analyze the ethical model suggested by the life of Saint Francis of Assisi.

NOTES

[1] For an overview of Christian history, see Williston Walker et al., *A History of the Christian Church*, 4th ed. (New York: Charles Scribner's Sons, 1985).

[2] We have offered a concise interpretation of the Christian world view in our text *Christianity: An Introduction* (Belmont, Calif.: Wadsworth, 1983).

[3] See Elisabeth Schüssler-Fiorenza, *In Memory of Her* (New York: Crossroad, 1983).

[4] Demetrios J. Constantelos, "Marriage in the Greek Orthodox Church," *Journal of Ecumenical Studies* 22 (Winter 1985), 21.

[5] Wilson Yates, "The Protestant View of Marriage," ibid., 53–54.

[6] See, for example, Anthony Kosnik et al., *Human Sexuality* (Garden City, N.Y.: Doubleday, 1979).

[7] "Pastoral Constitution on the Church in the Modern World" *(Gaudium et Spes)*, no. 67, in *Dictionary of the Council*, ed. J. Deretz and A. Nocent (Washington: Corpus, 1968), p. 484.

[8] For a good overview of Christian social teachings, see George W. Forell, *Christian Social Teachings* (Minneapolis: Augsburg, 1971).

[9] See Arlene Swidler, ed., *Human Rights in Religious Traditions* (New York: Pilgrim Press, 1982).

[10] See H. Paul Santmire, *The Travail of Nature* (Philadelphia: Fortress, 1985), p. 430.

[11] Augustine, *City of God* 22.24; quoted in Santmire, *The Travail of Nature*, p. 66.

[12] Alan S. Miller, "The Environmental and other Bioethical Challenges for Christian Creation Consciousness," in *Cry of the Environment*, ed. P. Joranson and K. Butigan (Santa Fe: Bear & Co., 1984), p. 384.

3

Muslim Ethics

Historical Orientation

Muhammad lived from 570 to 632 C.E. in Arabia. Prior to his rise to religious power, the religion of the Arab tribes was mainly polytheistic. Muhammad grew up as an orphan, married a wealthy widow, and when he was about forty began taking himself off into solitude to think about his life. He began to receive revelations, and after he had convinced himself that these were not a sign of madness, he accepted the command of a strictly monotheistic deity, mediated to him by the angel Gabriel, that he recite the divine Word to his countrymen. These recitals comprise the Qur'an, which is the sole scripture of orthodox Islam.

Initially Muhammad was rejected by his fellow Meccans, and in 622 he withdrew to the nearby town of Medina. There he assumed a politico-religious control, and in 630 he returned to Mecca as a conqueror. Before his death in 632, he applied the social theory that he had worked out in Medina, so his followers had a sketch, if not a full blueprint, of the new regime that they wanted to spread throughout the world.

Islam spread with such stunning speed that in less than a century Muslims had gained control not only of the Middle East but of the Mediterranean from east to west. They had entered the Indus Valley, conquered North Africa, occupied Afghanistan, and stormed southern Europe. Although different parts of this Islamic realm had different rulers, and the Muslim community experienced considerable internal strife (including assassinations), the vacuum of political, military, and cultural power in the areas adjacent to Arabia virtually determined that the Muslims would seize control.

This control was by no means merely military. Muslims looked upon Jews and Christians as "people of the book" who shared their derivation from Abraham, so they tended to offer Jews and Christians a decent, if second-class, status in their realms. Many Muslim rulers supported science, both Hellenistic and Persian; and architecture, poetry, and legal scholarship all flourished. These first centuries, in fact, comprised a golden age of Islamic culture. At capitals such as Baghdad, which was founded in 762, and Cairo, which was founded in 966, Muslims developed great universities, while the conversion of the Persians and the Turks began a rich diversification of Muslim ideals into languages other than Arabic. Until the Christian crusaders conquered Jerusalem in 1099, Islam had many more victories than defeats. The Mongols sacked Baghdad in 1258, but in 1453 the Ottoman Turks conquered Constantinople and so gained hegemony over Eastern Christianity. Islam did lose Spain in 1492, but it continued to dominate northern India until the first half of the eighteenth century.

Around 1800 a generally weakened Islam encountered modern Europe in the form of French and British armies against whom it could offer little resistance, and in the nineteenth and twentieth centuries Islam had to come to terms with modernity. Some Muslims have urged that Islam develop its tradition of intellectual inquiry and its confidence that Allah undergirds all of creation, in an effort to open itself to Western science and political theory. Others, who probably have predominated, have fiercely resisted Western secularism and used the challenge of the West to reinvigorate Muslim faith. At present, Islam numbers perhaps 750 million adherents (some observers would say nearly one billion), and it is growing rapidly in Africa. Indian Muslims have secured the separation of the two areas now called Pakistan and Bangladesh from Hindu control, while Indonesia and Malaysia number well over 100 million Muslims. The central and eastern republics of the Soviet Union are heavily Muslim, something that complicates the official state policy of atheism and also the state's control by Russians. Muslims form a significant portion of the population of China, and increasingly one finds Muslim groups in many Western cities.

The major schism in Muslim history, which is somewhat parallel to the split of Western Christians into Protestants and Catholics, came in the wake of the assassination of the fourth caliph or ruler of the Muslim community in 661. This fourth caliph, named Ali, was a relative of Muhammad (though the first successors of Muhammad had not been relatives). His supporters, known as the **Shia** or "party," were deeply alienated by his assassination, as they were by the murder of Ali's son Husain in 680 C.E. The **Sunni** or "traditionalists," who did not think that leadership in Islam had to pass on according to Muhammad's bloodline, became the predominant force, but the Shia have remained a significant opposition. In fact the Shiites have dominated certain areas, most notably Persia or Iran, and developed their own variants in Muslim doctrine, devotion, and "sensibility." Comparisons of the two Muslim groups usually portray the Shiites as the more emotional and fervent of the two, and as dominated by religious festivals at which they relive the indignities or sorrows of their martyrs. The Sunnis, who have been dominated by teachers centered in Cairo and Baghdad, appear sober by contrast, and have furnished the leading Muslim philosophers and legal scholars.

Another historical development that has greatly shaped Islam, especially in Sunni areas, is **Sufism**. Sufism first appeared as a marked movement in the ninth century C.E., bearing a banner of reformation. In the eyes of the early Sufis, the tremendous success of Islam had brought the danger, if not the reality, of compromise and corruption. So the Sufis proposed a simpler life-style and stressed spiritual values as a counter to materialistic prosperity. From the ninth to the thirteenth centuries they were a fresh stream of Muslim creativity, so impressive that al Ghazali (1058–1111), who had been a prestigious university scholar, left his worldly success to travel the Sufi path. Only through Sufi mystical techniques did he gain the deep peace of soul that he was seeking, and his testimonial to the Sufi way has become a historical benchmark: "I learnt with certainty that it is above all the [Sufi] mystics who walk on the road of God; their life is the best, their method the soundest method, their character the purest character; indeed, were the intellect of the intellectuals and the learning of the learned and the scholarship of the scholars, who are versed in the profundities of revealed truth, brought together in the attempt to improve the life and character of the mystics, they would find no way of doing so."[1]

Sufism declined after the thirteenth century, but its many different brotherhoods continued to influence Muslim life across the Islamic world. The dominant cultural force, which sometimes seemed opposed to Sufi mysticism, was the Islamic **Shariah** ("Law" or "Guidance"), which strikes the comparativist as quite parallel to Jewish Torah. As we shall see in the next section, the Muslim world view allows little separation between the secular and the sacred realms, so the same law was supposed to direct Muslims in both business and devotion. From time to time a philosophical school tried to assert its independence from Shariah, but on the whole the lawyers have dominated Islamic teaching. Like the Jewish rabbis, they have tried to make the will of God known and observed in all areas of life, from the greatest of concerns to the smallest.

World View

The foundation of the Muslim creed is the reality of God (Allah), who is the sole divinity. Muhammad is the prophet who has made Allah known, the one in whose recital or proclamation (collected in the Qur'an) one can meet Allah and learn the divine will. That there is no God but this God has swept the Muslim psyche clear of all idolatry. Muslims believe that only the sovereign creative mystery is worthy of worship. Thus Islam has accounted idolatry (**shirk**) the greatest sin, and Muslim reformers have not hesitated to castigate materialism, secularism, nationalism, or anything else they have deemed a threat to the Islamic tradition or purity of faith, as idolatry.

On occasion one reads interpretations of Muslim theology that link its almost fierce monotheism with the desert backdrop of traditional Arab culture. It is as though the desert emptiness, silence, and lack of nourishment for the eye prepared the ear or psyche of Muhammad and his followers for an especially powerful revelation of the divine Word. Muhammad had apparently had contact with Christians and Jews, so he linked his revelations with the Jewish and Christian traditions, but there was not the slightest doubt in his mind that what Allah was giving him was the fulfillment, perfecting, and supersession of what God had given to prior prophets such as Moses and Jesus. Thus Muslims have considered Muhammad the "seal" of the prophets: the one in whom the divine self-disclosure came to consummation.

This belief in the complete sovereignty of Allah, the Lord of the Worlds, explains the exalted status that Islam has accorded to the Qur'an. Perhaps even more than the Bible, the Qur'an has functioned as *the* Word of God, and orthodox Islam has generally considered it to be eternal, coexistent with Allah. According to the predominant theory of inspiration in Islam, Allah dictated the Qur'an to Muhammad. Strictly speaking, one cannot translate the Qur'an, since the divine revelation is intimately tied to the Arabic in which Muhammad expressed it. In principle the Qur'an contains all one needs to know in order to live a perfect Islamic life and gain the approval of Allah on judgment day.

The main principles of Islamic religion derive from the foregoing convictions about Allah, Muhammad, and the Qur'an. Basically, Muslims conceive of human beings as created by Allah to follow the divine will, praise the divine splendor, and thereby both order life on earth and merit a paradise after death. Human beings are not, as in Christianity and Judaism, sinful so much as weak and forgetful. By remembering the Qur'anic revelation, they can offer Allah the submission that a creature owes its all-powerful Lord, and they can develop the attitudes necessary for the proper ordering of the human community, the proper treatment of nature, and the happiness of the individual personality.

Specifically, the so-called **five pillars** of Islam are the obligations to

(1) accept the summary of the creed ("There is no God but Allah and Muhammad is his prophet"), (2) pray five times a day, (3) give alms to the poor, (4) fast during the month of Ramadan, and (5) make the pilgrimage to Mecca at least once, if possible. All Muslims are held to these five obligations, which have been interpreted both narrowly and broadly. Islam has generally been considered a lay religion, with no clerical caste destined for special authority, but in fact teachers, lawyers, and religious gurus or sheiks have exerted considerable influence. Still, each Muslim has had the right and the obligation to study the Qur'an and fulfill the five primary obligations, and each Muslim could think that by doing this he or she (we shall deal with women's status in Islam in the next section) could achieve salvation.

The Islamic conception of God as the absolutely sovereign creator of the universe, when combined with the generally lay character of Muslim doctrine and ritual, has made Islam a religion that resists any significant distinction between the sacred and the secular. And while it is true that all the other great world religions have similarly resisted such a distinction (only in modernity has the distinction come to have great force), Islam still strikes the comparativist as a tradition in which the holism or integrity of culture has been almost imperative. For Muslims have felt that all aspects of life reflect the power of Allah, and so Islam has sensed that all aspects of life fall into their proper place or gain their proper perspective only when one fits them into Allah's revelation.

So powerful a hold has this revelation had in Islam that Muslim conquerors have not troubled themselves much to interact with other traditions, let alone to work out a pluralistic culture that would grant other religious traditions a civic equality with Islam. It is not accurate, historically, to depict Muslims as having forced those whom they conquered to convert to Islam or lose their heads, but it is true that the Islamic rulers of the golden age seldom suffered any failures of nerve or had second thoughts about the utter supremacy of their prophet's revelations. The very starkness of the summary of faith, no doubt, helped to keep doubts or second thoughts at bay. One God and one prophet make for a simple and very powerful vision.[2]

Part of Muhammad's proclamation centered on the coming divine judgment, and in the Qur'an one frequently finds the prophet warning infidels—polytheists or adherents of a divinity other than Allah—that if they do not accept the one true God they will suffer in hellfire. A certain dualism obtains, such that Allah becomes a refuge from the darkness and evil that corrode human culture. Thus surah (chapter) 113, one of the last and shortest in the Qur'an, says: "In the name of God, the Merciful, the Compassionate. Say: I take refuge with the Lord of the Daybreak from the evil of what He has created, from the evil of darkness when it gathers, from the evil of women who blow on knots, from the evil of an envier when he envies."[3] The translation at least hints at the poetic grandeur that Muslims find in the Arabic original, and when one realizes that traditionally Muslims have experienced the Qur'an as recited by a skillful proclaimer, one can imagine how the words have riveted believers' souls and moved their emotions, functioning much like **mantras.**

The Qur'anic philosophy or basic outlook, then, pivots on the supremacy of Allah and the divine revelation. In light of this revelation, human beings are but bits of dust or clots of blood. God is all-sovereign, and the prime task and glory of any creature's life is to submit to God in both obedience and reverence. Nature, it follows, is not a numinous or divine reality. God completely transcends nature and human affairs alike, so any worship of a creature is hateful to God. On the other hand, God is **immanent** in all of creation, for without God creation would cease to exist. So the Qur'an says that Allah is nearer than the pulse at one's throat, and the Sufis have joined mystics of other traditions in practicing the awareness of the all-pervasive presence of God.

For Islam the individual human being is not so much the image of God as the representative of God in creation. Human beings, collectively, have the right and responsibility to supervise creation and make the subhuman world bear fruit for their satisfaction. All created things are good in themselves, so Islam in principle approves food and sex, business and family life. Yet traditionally Islam has proscribed alcohol and such foods as pork, and it has secluded women from the public arena in the name of chastity and sexual control. Muslim society is theocratic, deriving its cohesion and laws from Qur'anic legislation. Traditionally the mosque has been the center of village life, and religious ethics have coincided with the group's general mores. From architecture to literature and law, traditional Muslim culture has been a seamless whole.[4]

Family Life

The shape of Muslim family life has been determined by the Qur'an and the traditions (Hadith) that report what Muhammad said or did on various occasions. Both the Qur'an and the example of Muhammad allowed polygamy, up to four wives, but with the firm stipulation that a husband be able to provide for all of his wives financially and emotionally (give them equal affection). Marriage in pre-Muslim Arabia originally may have depended on the woman's free assent, but there was also a practice of capturing a bride and hauling her off. The main intent of marriage was procreation, and sexual satisfaction was considered normal and healthy. Both men and women were circumcised, the example of Abraham justifying the practice for men and sexual control influencing the practice for women.

Geoffrey Parrinder's chapter on Islam in his *Sex in the World Religions* describes current practices: "Boys are circumcised with great pomp,

but girls without festivities. Clitoridectomy was Sunna [rightly tradi-
tional] as far as it involved removal of the tip of the clitoris, and further
practices were excision of the clitoris and labia minora, and infibulation
which included excision and then sewing up the vagina. Modern western sexologists hold that all orgasms in women are caused by clitoral
stimulation, and therefore clitoridectomy not only causes pain but deprivation, hence some modern Muslim doctors and educated women in
the eastern Mediterranean countries have urged the abolition of clitoridectomy in all its forms, but there is often great social pressure on parents to maintain the operation on their daughters."[5]

Muslim tradition strongly disapproved of fornication, and adultery
could bring death by stoning. On the other hand, the tradition stipulated
that a judgment of adultery required that four people had actually witnessed the adulterous intercourse, a requirement initiated because of the
experience of Muhammad's wife Aisha, who had been falsely accused of
illicit relations. Divorce was more readily available to men than to
women, but originally the prescription that a husband could obtain a divorce simply by saying three times, "I divorce you," stipulated that a
month elapse between each of the sayings. The divorced woman was to
receive support for at least three months, until it was clear that she was
not pregnant by the man divorcing her. Islam generally considered divorce repugnant and believed Muhammad had opposed it.

Women could obtain a divorce, under conditions more restricted
than those for men, and the marital contract upon which Islam insisted
(usually this was worked out by the families of the two prospective
spouses) could provide safeguards for the wife in matters of property, retention of the dowry (gift given by the groom at the time of the marriage), inheritance rights of her children, and so forth. The Qur'anic
ideals for marriage and provision for women's security were actually a
considerable improvement over pre-Muslim practices, and even though
these ideals were often flouted in later Islam, the basic Muslim conception of marital life accorded it great dignity.

Islam did not approve of celibacy or a solitary religious life; it considered marriage the normal human estate. The prophet was remembered as a contented, faithful spouse of the widow Khadija, his first wife,
and his taking several other wives after Khadija's death was largely a
matter of political alliance. Still, it contributed to making sexual vigor
part of what later Islam reverenced as the Muslim ideal.

Islam has reserved sexual activity for marriage, and current-day
Muslims such as Lois al Faruqi argue that this practice, along with a
consequent separation of the sexes from before puberty, is much healthier
than Western laxity.[6] Virginity has been more stringently required of
brides than of grooms, and a perhaps somewhat artificial homosexuality
or pederasty often developed. The practice of secluding women from
public life (**purdah**) and requiring them to be veiled no doubt could have

had the positive aim of sparing women vexations, but along with the institution of the harem (mainly for the wealthy), it contributed to women's
exclusion from education, travel, and religious culture. Indeed, through
most periods of Muslim history women have not been free to attend the
mosque, which has been the heart of the community's cultural life.

In terms of freedom to marry outside of Islam, women have not had
the same rights as men. Where Muslim men might marry non-Muslims,
especially Christians or Jews, Muslim women have been obliged to marry
only Muslim men. Recent studies of women in Muslim countries regularly turn up the women's perception that their first function is to produce male offspring, while the popular imagery of the Garden that will
be the reward of faithful Muslims after death has featured buxom maidens (hur) available for the male's complete gratification. Some of the traditions attribute misogynistic sayings to the prophet, and Muslim women
have been accounted less reliable witnesses than men in Islamic courts.
Where men were to have their religious lives evaluated in terms of their
obedience to God, women often have been given the yardstick of obedience to their husbands. The traditional depictions of Judgment Day
placed more women than men in the Fire, and the main reason that such
women were condemned was disobedience to their husbands. Another
popular figure was that women would be dragged into the Garden by the
umbilical cords of their children—that is, that their salvation would
come from child-rearing.

The traditions have included the notion that intercourse is not permitted during menstruation, that contraception through coitus inter-
ruptus is permissible, and that sexual activity should be preceded by
prayer. One of the key passages of the Qur'an on these matters is 2 : 222–
23, which includes the image that a wife is like a field to be tilled: "They
will question thee concerning the monthly course. Say: 'It is hurt; so go
apart from women during the monthly course, and do not approach
them till they are clean. When they have cleansed themselves, then
come into them as God has commanded you.' Truly God loves those who
repent, and He loves those who cleanse themselves. Your women are a
tillage for you; so come unto your tillage as you wish, and forward for
your souls; and fear God, and know that you shall meet him."[7]

The basic pattern of Muslim family life, then, has been patriarchal
and focused on procreation. The priority of men over women has been
taken as part of the divine order, though strictly speaking women have
been deemed as capable of salvation or sanctity as men. Concern for fertility and respect for God's part in procreation have greatly restricted any
approval of abortion, and Muslims have remembered as a pagan horror
the pre-Islamic custom of burying unwanted children (usually females)
alive. The predominant sense has been that submission to Allah would
help wives and children to follow male rule, while it would help husbands and fathers to rule kindly and considerately.

In such Muslim areas as North Africa anthropologists have observed that language, religion, and women have been the issues over which Islam has most fiercely resisted Western incursions. In other words, trade and political contact have been tolerated much more willingly than penetration into the heart of the traditional Islamic culture through intermarriage, or involvement in the piety of the local Sufi brotherhood, or taking a Western language such as French into the family circle.[8] Relatedly, the education that most traditional families have prized for their children has been structured by study of the Qur'an, and even when middle-class families have sent their children (their sons more than their daughters) for a Western education, they have wanted this education to deal with only the technological or external aspects of culture. Muslims have felt, understandably enough, that Westerners could never understand their native cultures without accepting Allah and the seal of the prophets.

Work

Both family life and work have been shaped by the extended family, which has been the rule in traditional Muslim culture, and also by the deep Islamic sense that all things lie in God's hands. Taking the latter first, we note that Muslims have seen birth and death, as well as riches and poverty, as God's to distribute as God wishes. **Predestination** and **providence,** then, have been powerful forces in both sophisticated Muslim theology and the faith of the common people. Islam usually has avoided any **fatalism,** proposing instead that human beings are responsible for their final destiny and so must be free, but certainly it has drawn from its profound appreciation of the divine sovereignty the logical conclusion that history could not unfold contrary to God's will. Thus traditionally one began any activity by referring it to God's will, and one would plan for the future or make appointments only with the provision "if Allah be willing."

The extended family has not only influenced relations between the spouses and child-rearing but has colored Muslims' work. Generally the clan has done the trading or carried out the agricultural work, and the roles individuals played could shift within this clan framework. In rural areas women often worked in the fields as well as in the home, something that frequently gave rural and poor women more freedom than middle-class and wealthy women, whose roles were quite circumscribed. Muslim men of means wanted their wives to be leisured, because this reflected well on the men's financial standing. In recent decades women have gained more opportunities for higher education and professional careers as doctors or teachers, but these freedoms were only won through considerable struggle. The upper-class women who spearheaded the modest Islamic movement for greater women's freedom often suffered derision in their own families, and when rigorous Muslim regimes have come into power, as in Iran, the regular pattern has been for women to return to veiling and to seclusion from public life.

The obligation to give alms has influenced not only Muslim notions of social justice but also the Islamic tradition regarding work, functioning as another reminder, both symbolic and practical, of the social solidarity of all Muslims. The amount of the alms has varied somewhat, 2 to 3 percent of one's income being a rough estimate. From the outset Muhammad wanted to impress upon his followers that their new identity as submitters to Allah was to be more basic than even their blood-clans. The tradition of fasting during the days of the lunar month of Ramadan taught Muslims to curb their appetites, while the celebrations that were permitted during the nights of Ramadan kept this asceticism from becoming gloomy. Islam therefore has had a basis for thinking of work as a useful discipline that, like fasting, could keep the body subordinate to the needs of the spirit.

The theological prohibition against representing God influenced Islamic art, while the tendency of Islam to minimize the distinction between religious matters as such and ordinary daily matters meant that art, architecture, and many of the crafts came to favor **arabesque** adornment, calligraphic skills (to adorn texts of the Qur'an), and poetry. The majority of Muslims have been very poor, at least by modern standards, and their work has been artistic only in the sense that it has tended to follow the rhythms of nature rather closely. Special holy days and freedom to travel to shrines, above all to Mecca, suggested to all Muslims that work was far from an all-absorbing occupation. Scholarship has involved principally legal study, but one does not sense in Islam the sacralization of such study that one senses in Talmudic Judaism.

Indeed, in many periods the Sufis appear to have sponsored a view of human wisdom that tried to turn worldly values upside down, and like many of the Christian saints the Sufi exemplars frequently were poor and itinerant. Islam certainly was not as suspicious of wealth as some of the writers of the Christian New Testament were, but on the other hand no pious Muslim could think that God regarded worldly success as significant. Al Ghazali expressed this conviction as follows: "Regard no one with an eye that sees his worldly estate as great, for this lower world is insignificant in the eye of God, and all that it holds is little. No matter how much people of this world may exalt you, they have exalted worldly matters, while you dwindled in the eyes of God."[9]

Traditional Islam urged tradespeople to be honest in their dealings, citing the tradition that the prophet, passing by a pile of grain, put his finger into the middle of it and found it wet. He asked why this was so, and on hearing that some of the grain had been damaged by rain, he directed that this damaged grain be put on top, where people could realize what they were buying. His punch line in this story was a sober call to honesty in business dealings: "Whoever practices fraud is not one of us."[10] The Qur'an disapproves of gaining interest from a debt, agreeing with traditional Judaism and Christianity that usury is irreligious. Thus 2:275–76 expressly distinguishes between "trafficking," or ordinary business dealings, and usury, seeing the former as permitted by God but the latter as a pathway to Satan. God will forgive usurers who repent of this practice and desist from it, but those who relapse will head for the Fire.

Complementing this is the notion that God himself gives interest to the believer for the alms that the believer offers. In the eyes of heaven, usury displays a restriction of faith and a lack of gratitude for all of God's gifts, while almsgiving shows a generosity pleasing to God. According to the Hadith Muhammad forbade begging, urging a man instead to go to the woods, collect firewood, and bring it back and sell it. Because of this official rejection of begging, the solicitations that one receives outside many urban mosques are considered opportunities for almsgiving.

Nowadays the Muslim attitude toward work and commerce frequently is examined in the context of the debate between capitalism and socialism. Muslims have tended to be put off by Communism because of its atheism, and some of them have approved the capitalist stress on industry and business; others have disapproved of the individualism that capitalism frequently seems to foster. Thus Ali Masuri, a contemporary African Muslim political scientist, has written: "Commercial activity is . . . part of the origins of Islam. . . . Muhammad might well be the only founder of a major religion who was once a man of commerce. He attended to some of the trading interests of his wealthy wife. Mecca itself was at that time, and before Muhammad's time, almost as much a center of commerce as a religious focus for Arabs from distant parts of the peninsula. A verse from the Qur'an assures Muslims that it is not wrong to seek a livelihood in trade and exchange in the course of the pilgrimage [surah 2:198]. Moreover, the Prophet himself is credited with the saying, 'Nine portions of God's bounty are in commercial activity.' In Africa, too, the spread of Islam came to be associated with trade."[11]

Masuri goes on, however, to distinguish Muslim commerce from extreme capitalism, and to speak of the social responsibilities that Islam has kept prominent. His overall verdict is that Islam is neither a fully ascetical religion, turning away from the secular world of business and profane work, nor a tradition that approves of worldly activities uncritically. One might say, indeed, that the work Muhammad himself and his train of followers have most favored has been work that one could be proud of before God in prayer. Muhammad clearly was a man of action, willing to lead troops in war and rule the political life of the Islamic community, but he saw everything as belonging to a single realm of creation that owed its complete being to God. If one forgot the origin and destiny of creation or the self, one missed the path that was straight and truly religious.

Social Justice

As the obligation to give alms perhaps suggests, Islam has drawn a strong sense of social solidarity from Arab society, which was originally composed of clans. In some modern Muslim thinkers' eyes, this has meant translating the tradition as a form of socialism. Thus Mustafa Sibai, a leading Syrian thinker of the past generation, has described five fundamental rights that Islam should guarantee to all citizens: (1) the right to life, and therefore to health and protection from illness; (2) the right to liberty, especially to political liberty; (3) the right to knowledge, both material and spiritual; (4) the right to dignity; and (5) the right to property (a right that has notable limitations). Concerning property itself, Sibai has elaborated five further principles that should govern an Islamic polity and economy: (1) Work should be the most important way of acquiring property, and the possessions that just, honest work acquires should be considered legal. (2) The state should defend the right to private property. (3) The state should forbid using private property as a means of oppression or exploitation. (4) Wealth brings with it such social responsibilities as giving charity, providing pensions for relatives, and entering into mutual-aid pacts with other citizens. And (5) the state should safeguard the right to inherit.[12]

Sayyid Qutb, another influential thinker of the past generation, who spent years in prison under the Egyptian leader Nasser because of his views, related his social thought to the holism of Islamic culture that we have stressed. For him Islam equally embraces both worship and work. Thus Qutb finds it appropriate for Muslims to be as interested in this-worldly justice as in questions of heavenly reward, and he places genuine Muslim social theory alongside secular socialism in granting the poor a claim on the wealth of the rich. Indeed, he thinks that Islam condemns as "self-oppressors" those poor who do not fight for their rightful share in the overall wealth of their society. For this reason, Qutb prefers Islam to both Christianity and Communism. In his interpretation, "Christianity looks at man only from the stand-point of his spiritual desires and seeks to crush down the human instincts in order to encourage those desires. On the other hand Communism looks at man only from the standpoint of his material needs; it looks not only at human nature, but also at the world and at life from a purely material point of view. But Islam looks at man as forming a unity whose spiritual desires cannot be separated from his bodily appetites, and whose moral needs cannot be divorced from his material needs."[13]

Riffat Hassan, a Pakistani Muslim now teaching in the United States, has written about the traditional Muslim teaching on human rights. She notes the wide gap that often separates Islamic ideals from the actual practices of Muslim political regimes, and she dismisses the Muslim tendency to distinguish facilely between the theocentric basis of Islamic social ideals and the supposedly anthropocentric basis of Western social ideals, noting that Christians and Jews would claim to be as theocentric as Muslims. Then, just as honest Jews, Christians, and adherents of other traditions have to do, she holds the ideals of her own tradition up to the current practices of many regimes, using the ideals as a mirror for honest self-criticism: "For hundreds of years now, Muslims have been taught that they were created to serve God by obeying those in authority over them and by enduring with patience whatever God willed for them. For hundreds of years, Muslim masses have patiently endured the grinding poverty and oppression imposed on them by those in authority. Not to be enslaved by foreign invaders whose every attempt to subjugate them was met with resistance, Muslim masses were enslaved by Muslims in the name of God and the Prophet, made to believe that they had no rights, only responsibilities; that God was the God of Retribution, not of Love; that Islam was an ethic of suffering, not of joyous living; that they were determined by "*Qismat*" [fate], not masters of their own fate."[14]

Positively, Hassan's list of the rights that the Muslim sense of social justice ought to promote includes the rights to life, to respect, to freedom, to privacy, to a good reputation, and to a good living. In this enumeration of general rights, she goes out of her way to cite the Qur'an (2:256) as forbidding compulsion in matters of religion. The Qur'an also enumerates as human rights a secure place of residence, a means to make a living, protection of one's possessions, the pursuit of knowledge, the enjoyment of God's bounty, the protection of one's contracts, free movement, asylum from oppression, autonomy for minorities, and the protection of one's holy places. Hassan writes eloquently of the ways in which women and children have been shortchanged, and her overall presentation of the Islamic ideals shows the passion for social justice that faith in Allah and acceptance of Muhammad often have generated.

The two features of traditional Islam that have drawn most criticism from Western observers are polygamy and **jihad** or holy war. Even after noting the allowance of polygamy to the patriarchs of the Hebrew Bible, and both the restrictions on polygamy that Islam has required and the move of Muslims toward monogamy, Western critics have tended to fault the followers of Muhammad for having an ideal of family life and marriage that falls below their own standards. Today, discussions among African Christian churches have again raised the question of polygamy, since in parts of Africa polygamy has been part of the traditional mores, while the condition of marriage and family life in the West has hardly left Westerners with a basis for preaching. Similarly, the question of holy war has turned out to be rather complicated. The Bible seems to sanction forms of holy war for Israel (indeed, to the extreme of slaughtering all the enemy), while the almost constant warfare of Christians through the ages has vitiated their claims to be outstanding lovers of peace. Nonetheless, both the traditional and the contemporary Muslim doctrines of holy war raise serious questions about militancy in religion. Even after considerable qualification, Islam does seem to permit, or even to advocate, taking to the battlefield as a means of protecting or even of advancing one's faith.

In the Qur'an, many surahs (2, 3, 8, 9, 22, 29, 47, 61) speak of Allah's desire that believers fight for their faith, of Allah's presence with the fighters, or of slaying idolators who have defaulted on their covenants with Muslims. Muslims who find fighting hateful are to do it nonetheless, when it is a matter of protecting the faith. Even in the holy month of Ramadan, when fighting normally would be forbidden, any rejection of God, interfering with mosques, or persecution of Muslims overrides the prohibition and calls Muslims to take up the sword. Muhammad himself was a great warrior, gaining control in Medina and Mecca only through arms. The spread of Islam after Muhammad's death took place through military conquests, even though, as we have mentioned, the historical matter is more complicated than any simple compulsion to convert people to Islam under pain of death.

What seems clear is the imperative to preach Islam that Muhammad received, and its persistence among his followers, who have been so convinced that Allah commissioned Islam that any force opposing the proclamation of Islam has assumed the aspect of an enemy. This has not produced the modern notion of a free-market approach to religion, in which all of the traditions would be allowed to compete or sell their wares unhindered. Generally, the only legitimate conversion has been to Islam, as the view of marriage that we elaborated suggests (Muslim males may marry non-Muslims, who would come under their control, but Muslim females may not marry non-Muslims). There have been periods in Western history when Christians, Jews, and Muslims debated their beliefs relatively amicably, and we may hope to be on the verge of another such period today. But on the whole the cities such as Toledo, Spain, where one can encounter vestiges of a past culture that was significantly pluralistic, are depressingly few.

Nature

When we deal with the place that nature has held in a religion such as Islam, ideally we would portray not just the estimations or evaluations that the theologians have made, but also the way that nature has functioned in the daily lives of the ordinary believers. This obviously varies considerably, depending for instance on whether one is speaking of rural or urban adherents. It also depends on a close acquaintance with the texture of daily life, which only personal visiting or first-rate reporting can produce. Our personal visits to Muslim countries have concentrated more on the cities than the rural areas, and we have found cities such as Tehran and Cairo to be as polluted as Western cities, primarily because of automobile emissions.

A skilled journalist such as V. S. Naipaul can convey the integration with nature that traditional Muslim peoples such as the Afghanis have enjoyed for centuries. Naipaul's book *Among the Believers* beautifully renders many scenes of contemporary Muslim life (its overall cultural analysis, however, is very critical of current Islam, especially the more fundamentalist varieties): "All afternoon we passed them [the older women of the tribe]; noted their tenderness to their animals, greater than their tenderness to themselves; those faces so lined and burnt, so old though young. Not many had the complexions and health of the girls in that encampment. Once I saw a man carrying a goat; once I saw a goat wrapped in a blanket and carried on a donkey's back. . . . High up, at Shogran, it was overcast and cool, cold when it began to drizzle. The pines were immensely tall, and in places the land fell away so sharply from the road that it wasn't easy to look down to the roots of the pines. On the safer side of the twisting road there was peasant destruction: the barks of the great pines had been hacked away, for kindling. Kindling was scarce here, where there was so little flat land and so little vegetation, only pines growing in the thin drift of soil around rocks."[15]

One sees from this description that a religion originally conceived in the desert and rooted in the commercial life of desert towns has become the spiritual sustenance of mountainous people, just as it has become the sustenance of people in steamy parts of Indonesia. Naipaul visits Iran, Pakistan, Indonesia, and Malaysia, each of which offers a different physical and cultural setting. The constant in these different Muslim countries is the message of the prophet Muhammad and the sovereignty of the God Allah. In each locale Muhammad is the main guide to social life and Allah is the Lord of creation.

The Qur'an eloquently proclaims this Lordship, making it impossible for a Muslim to conceive of the world as necessary or eternal. The world obviously need not exist. It completely depends on the decision of God to make it. And since the highest of the ninety-nine names of God is that he is merciful, one suspects that the creation of the world is a mercy of God rather than a boast, a trial, or a sport. God places human beings in the world as the caliphs or rulers of nature. Just as the caliph in the community is the one who should guide it in its holistic life, so human beings should help nature to achieve the bounty that God has made possible for it. Islam therefore easily conceives of a system of economics and technology in which human enterprise develops the resources of nature to fulfill the needs of both society at large and individuals. There is no sacredness to nature such that one need hesitate before plowing it or building with its raw materials. The divine is not immanent in nature in a fashion that makes animal life untouchable. God is beyond the world, though also present to the world as its ongoing creator, and his creative plan is quite hierarchical. Human beings stand at the top of the scale of creatures, commissioned to take charge. If they should bow low to acknowledge their complete submission to Allah, they may hold their heads high when among their fellow creatures.

Concerning ecology proper, the problem of misusing natural resources and injuring the natural environment has begun to impinge on Muslim consciousness, as on the consciousness of other religions, only in recent years. Like members of other religions (for example, Shinto), Muslims have had their images of perfection in which gardens and pools symbolized an ideal integrity of nature and humanity. But they have not hesitated to denude the hills when they needed kindling, and even when their modern thinkers turned to the problems of economic development and social justice that the Western agenda set, they seldom linked these problems with questions of scarcity of natural resources, pollution, or aesthetic harmony with the surrounding environment. In more recent writings, however, concern for nature has begun to intrude, and one finds an adaptation of such traditional notions as "divine arrangement" (rububiyyia), human governance (khilafa), and dynamic purification (tazkiyah) to the task of sketching how human beings ought to approach development.[16] One finds a Muslim contributor to an interfaith symposium on the requirements of a new world order citing pollution as a good example of the problems that now transcend national boundaries. Indeed, he sees with admirable clarity the connection between assaults on the biosphere and poverty: "Reducing pollution, due respect for the natural environment and improvement of urban life in manageable agglomerations go hand in hand with eradication of poverty, slum clearing and rural development. It is now an established fact that pollution spreads across national boundaries and extreme poverty is as damaging to the environment as over-industrialization, over-urbanization and over-consumption. Once more we face a one-world problem."[17]

Islam approaches questions of nature from a scripture whose awe at the divine **creative fiat** stands second to none in the inventory of the world religions. The "Lordship" of Allah, according to the Arabic etymology, can connote a nurturing of creation, and some modern Muslim thinkers have used this connotation to justify an evolutionary understanding of the way in which God deals with nature. Certainly the Muslim God, like the God of the Christian apostle Paul (Romans 1), can be discerned in the creation that he has fashioned. In fact, nature functions as a series of "signs" that Allah has given, and the rational investigation of nature that goes forward in modern science is completely congenial to

Muslim natural theology. Islam does reject the notion of **animistic** or naturalistic gods (personifications of the forces of nature), mainly because this detracts from the sovereignty of Allah, but also because it detracts from the rulership of human beings over nature. Muslim piety on occasion speaks of the whole of creation as summoned to Islam, picturing the stars and the animals as called to bow low in obedience and reverence toward their creator. Thus surah 3 : 83 associates material creation with the human worship of God, but while one is necessary the other is free. In other words, what human beings are called to do freely, as a knowing and grateful response to their God, the mute creatures of the universe do spontaneously and necessarily, in that they must obey the laws that God has encoded within them.[18]

Islam does not appear to have drawn from this perception the sense that nature is more perfect than human beings, as Japanese Buddhist thinkers sometimes have done. Perhaps the Muslim appreciation of human freedom is so strong that the unthinking perfection of nature has little appeal for it. Correlatively, where Buddhism seems uncomfortable with the emotional complexity that accompanies reflection, wanting to get human beings away from desire and self-concern, Islam tries to attain objectivity and maturity by focusing outward on the sovereign divinity. In this process it calls upon the signs that God has strewn throughout nature, but it seldom proposes natural objects, even the sun and the stars, as models that human beings should admire as their superiors.

Models

The ethical model that Muslims should study is Muhammad, whose place in Muslim piety approaches the place that Jesus has had in Christian piety. To be sure, the Qur'an is adamant in insisting that God has had no Son. Thus the Christian doctrine of the divinity of Jesus Christ is abhorrent to Muslim monotheism. Yet Muhammad's role as the seal of the prophets has brought Muslims to venerate him as the perfect exemplar of Islam. According to all orthodox Islamic thought, he remains fully human, yet in popular piety he has acquired a string of attributes that exalts him above all other human beings.

For example, many uneducated Muslims have thought that Muhammad lived many thousands of years ago, because they equated antiquity with holiness. Muslims have admired the roundedness of Muhammad's life, seeing in his ability both to commune with God in the highest flights of mysticism and to handle the this-worldly affairs of the community a perfection that other holy personages, such as Jesus, could not achieve. The Qur'an (96 : 2/2 : 31) makes a parallel between the names that God gave Adam at creation and the Qur'an that God gave to Muhammad. Indeed, some Muslim thinkers have taught that Muhammad was illiterate, so as to emphasize the purity of his direct reception of truth from God (in contrast to the dilutions and distortions that had slipped into the prophetic line between Adam and Muhammad). At other times Muhammad's reception of the Qur'an has been likened to Mary's immaculate conception of the divine Word. With time, speculation on the birth of Muhammad led Muslims to exalt it over the Night of Power in which he first received Qur'anic revelations. The Qur'an portrays Muhammad as sent as a mercy for the worlds of creation (21:107), and poets have depicted him as a raincloud of the divine mercy. (Buddhists have used the same image for the Buddha.)

Annemarie Schimmel, from whose study of the prophet as a center of life and thought in Islam we have been drawing these characterizations, stresses the Qur'anic notion (33:21) that Muhammad is a "beautiful model" for the pious Muslim to imitate. Muhammad's way of life (Sunnah) in fact became the first determinant of Muslim **orthopraxy** or behavioral fidelity. The hadith were collected mainly to afford Muslims examples of how the prophet had acted in various circumstances, on the assumption that such action would have perfectly expressed the Islamic spirit. The finality of the revelation given to Muhammad was probably the logical basis for his exemplary exaltation—that is, if he was the seal of the messengers of God, his whole life must have expressed the fullness of the divine revelation.

Although Muhammad himself seems to have denied that he ever worked miracles, later piety soon attributed many marvels to him. Some circles expected that on the Day of Judgment Muhammad would function as an intercessor on human beings' behalf, while such Qur'anic imagery as Muhammad's "splitting the moon" (54:1) was often taken literally. The devout have embellished the prophet's birth with legendary feats, and the mystics have situated their experiences in "the light of Muhammad"—the heavenly radiance that issued from him from the time of his birth. Five hundred years or so after the death of Muhammad, followers began to celebrate his birthday on the twelfth day of the third lunar month. This holiday has served to unite Muslims in many lands and has stimulated much Muslim poetry and song. The devotional practice known as **dhikr** ("remembrance"), in which Muslims have tried to retain a sense of the presence of God by reciting pious formulas, often has used the "blessing of Muhammad" that the Qur'an (33:56) suggests.

Some circles considered Muhammad to have been sinless, and some schools of mysticism fused this concept with the notion that spiritual light emanated from and through the prophet: "It is told that the Prophet did not cast any shadow, for he was filled with light: 'Your body is all light, and your cheek is the *Surat an-Nur* (the sura 'Light')' sings an eighteenth-century Indian mystic, following his predecessors in Islamic mysticism who had applied the sura *Wa'dduuha*, 'By the Morning Light' or the sura 'By the Sun' to the radiant face and body of the prophet. The concept of light made manifest through his body is theoretically an external projection of his *isma*, his complete freedom from moral defects. Otherwise, how could he have been the moral authority for the faithful, if he had not been without sin? 'He had to be without sin, for otherwise God would have made sin a duty for the believer!'—that is how Bajuri, the great Egyptian theologian of the nineteenth century, expresses this view."[19] Schimmel notes that the idea of Muhammad's sinlessness ran into the difficulty of the Qur'an (93:7) seeming to speak of his "erring," but another text (94:1) was taken to indicate God's opening of Muhammad's breast and purifying him for the divine revelation.

Scholars of Islam frequently claim that Westerners commit some of their most grievous mistakes by underestimating the great esteem in which Muslims have held Muhammad. To imply any disrespect for the prophet is a great insult. Similarly, many Westerners have not appreciated the place that saints have held in Muslim piety, often in connection with the Sufi lodges or brotherhoods that have functioned as semisecret societies. A holy man or sheik has usually directed such organizations, his authority emanating from the spiritual power (*baraka*) he manifests. The dervishes of Turkey, who dance themselves into ecstasy, have received special attention; but in many communities less dramatic dancing, along with rituals for healing, punctuate the religious life.

The Sufi theory includes the notion of a path along which one can progress to union with God. Adepts in such prayer or mysticism have commanded great respect, and frequently their techniques have been like those of the Jewish Cabalists in giving numerical values to letters of key Qur'anic texts, or like those of Indian yogins in utilizing a rhythmic recitation of litanies (for example, of the names of God). The result of these practices has been to point the Muslim ethical ideal toward an action that would stem from a deep sense of the presence of God. Ideally, one would move through the world with the freedom and insight that only union with Allah could grant. This could mean an action expressing much love and power, but it could also mean an action perfectly conforming to or expressing the Shariah (Guidance) that the community considered its religious constitution.

The esteemed cultural anthropologist Clifford Geertz has written a fascinating comparative study of Moroccan and Indonesian Islam, showing how the different cultural substrates of the two countries have molded the cultures' different senses of spiritual perfection.[20] In Morocco, the prototypical saint is almost fiercely masculine, a prophetic figure who can clash with kings and whose regime is spartan. In Indonesia, Hindu influences appear to have sketched a more stereotypically feminine ideal, according to which the saint is subtle, graceful, wise, and full of mysterious meditative powers. He can work wonders by the power of his mental absorption in God. Symbolically, he is apt to attract a powerful disciple by causing a banyan tree to become laden with money. In Morocco, the keynote miracle of a parallel saint might be drinking without harm water polluted by washing the leprous sores of an ailing saintly elder.

The saints and the embellished Muhammad have served as models between ordinary Muslims and the transcendent Allah, easing the typical Muslim's way. Women have frequently focused their piety at the tombs or sanctuaries of famous local saints (some of them female), where they have gathered to pray or give vent to their sufferings. Reformist Muslim movements, such as the **Wahabism** that has prevailed in Saudi Arabia in recent generations, often have thought darkly of saints, Sufism, miracles, and sanctuaries. Yet across the Islamic world and throughout history, such elements of popular religion have exerted great influence. The ethical model they have built has correlated piety and morality, taking the Qur'an as both a guide to right action and a book of prayers.

Summary

To orient our study of Muslim ethics historically, we sketched the career of Muhammad, stressing his reception of the Qur'an, and described the rapid spread of Islam after the prophet's death. We noted some features of medieval Islam, described the encounter between Islam and the modern West, and explained the division of Shiites and Sunnis. Finally, we described the influence of Sufism and the central importance of Shariah.

Philosophically, we began with Muslim monotheism, noted the gravity of idolatry, explained how Muhammad has been considered the seal of the prophets, and detailed the Islamic conception of the Qur'an. These then led us to a consideration of the Muslim understanding of creation, judgment, and the five pillars that summarize the believer's main obligations. We noted the holism of Islam, as expressed in its refusal to separate the sacred and the secular, and we reflected on the Muslim sense of revelation.

Muslim family life has been structured by the Qur'an and the hadith. We considered the place of procreation and circumcision, and we discussed Muslim attitudes toward fornication, adultery, divorce, and polygamy. We also described purdah, women's perception of their status, strains of misogyny, and the basically patriarchal view of family life that Islam has shared with Judaism and Christianity.

In considering Muslim views of work, we noted the context of an extended family circle, the role of predestination and providence, patterns of women's work, the obligation to give alms, some features of Muslim art, and religious defenses against obsession with work. We considered al Ghazali's disregard of worldly status and wealth, noted the tradition that the prophet had proscribed any fraud in business dealings, and dealt with both the Qur'anic prohibition of usury and recent Muslim views of economics and commerce.

Concerning social justice, we began by stressing the Islamic sense of social solidarity, then referred to recent Muslim social theorists' views on human rights. We reflected on the Muslim traditions concerning polygamy and holy war, and we tried to explain the force of the commission from Allah to spread Islam.

In describing Muslim attitudes toward nature we stressed the variety of ecological contexts in which Islam has taken root, the Lordship of Allah over all of creation, the supervisory role that human beings have, and recent Muslim efforts to rethink human beings' relations with the environment. We then noted the Islamic conviction that Allah may be discerned in the patterns of nature, and the notion that all of creation is Muslim in being called to obey the divine will.

Our study of Muslim ethical models gave primacy to Muhammad, noting the many accolades that Muslims have heaped on the prophet through the centuries. We stressed the completeness or holism of this model, which has depicted a man both rapt with God and fully competent in the world. We showed some of the ways in which Islam has separated Muhammad from ordinary humanity—for example, by speaking of his sinlessness. And finally, we sketched the place that the Muslim saints have had in the piety of the faithful, discussing their spiritual power and their adeptness at mystical prayer.

STUDY QUESTIONS

1. What is the main difference between Shiites and Sunnis?
2. How does Qur'anic revelation shape the Islamic world view?
3. Why have Muslim women not been allowed to marry non-Muslims?
4. Why does the Qur'an forbid usury?
5. Explain why Islam considers some wars holy.
6. What can nature tell the pious Muslim about God?
7. How has the model of Muhammad called Islamic ethics to combine mysticism and this-worldliness?

NOTES

[1] W. Montgomery Watt, *The Faith and Practice of Al Ghazali* (London: Allen & Unwin, 1953), p. 60.

[2] See Frederick Mathewson Denny, *An Introduction to Islam* (New York: Macmillan, 1985).

[3] A. J. Arberry, *The Koran Interpreted* (New York: Macmillan, 1955), Book 2, p. 354.

[4] See John Alden Williams, ed., *Themes of Islamic Civilization* (Berkeley: University of California Press, 1982).

[5] Geoffrey Parrinder, *Sex in the World Religions* (New York: Oxford University Press, 1980), p. 161.

[6] See Lois Lamya' Ibsen al Faruqi, "Marriage in Islam," *Journal of Ecumenical Studies* 22 (Winter 1985): 66–68.

[7] Arberry, *The Koran Interpreted*, Book 1, p. 59.

[8] See Paul Rabinow, *Reflections on Fieldwork in Morocco* (Berkeley: University of California Press, 1977), p. 27.

[9] Al Ghazali, *Revivification of the Sciences of Religion*, as quoted in Williams, ed., *Themes of Islamic Civilization*, p. 27.

[10] See Kenneth Cragg and Marston Speight, eds., *Islam from Within* (Belmont, Calif.: Wadsworth, 1980), p. 89.

[11] *Ibid.*, p. 232.

[12] See John J. Donohue and John L. Esposito, eds., *Islam in Transition* (New York: Oxford University Press, 1982), p. 120.

[13] *Ibid.*, pp. 125–26.

[14] Riffat Hassan, "On Human Rights and the Qur'anic Perspective," in *Human Rights in Religious Traditions*, ed. Arlene Swidler (New York: Pilgrim Press, 1982), p. 54.

[15] V. S. Naipaul, *Among the Believers* (New York: Vintage, 1982), pp. 187–88.

[16] See Donohue and Esposito, eds., *Islam in Transition*, p. 221.

[17] Isma'il Abdalla, "World Chaos or a New Order: A Third World View," in *World Faiths and the New World Order*, ed. Joseph Gremillion and William Ryan (Washington: The Interreligious Peace Colloquium, 1978), p. 66.

[18] See Kenneth Cragg, *The House of Islam*, 2d ed. (Belmont, Calif.: Wadsworth, 1975), pp. 10–11.

[19] Annemarie Schimmel, "The Prophet Muhammad as a Centre of Muslim Life and Thought," in *We Believe in One God*, ed. Annemarie Schimmel and Abdoldjavad Falaturi (New York: Seabury, 1979), p. 46.

[20] Clifford Geertz, *Islam Observed* (Chicago: University of Chicago Press, 1971).

PART
TWO

Eastern
Religious
Ethics

The traditions that we are calling Western agree in deriving their sense of proper (moral) action from the will of a personal God. Judaism, Christianity, and Islam all are scriptural religions, and the desire to know what God wants their people to do has played a large part in their veneration of a written revelation. So Torah, the Gospel, or Shariah traditionally has lain close to the Western religious ethicist's hand. Ethics has been the effort to prescribe how the life idealized in such holy codes might be lived in the present. Jews, Christians, and Muslims have all felt singled out by the one God for special intimacy. The price or consequence of this chosenness has been the command to live a holy, worthy life.

The Eastern traditions to which we now turn have not had so personal or willful a deity. Certainly their ethicists have all assumed or argued that the mores honored by the community are grounded in ultimate reality, but "revelation" has not been so prominent a motif as it has been in the West. Thus the **dharma** (teaching) that Hinduism and Buddhism emphasize is not so prophetic as is the Word of God stressed by the biblical spokesmen for God. The law codes of the Indian and East Asian thinkers seem more human, and in interesting ways more sophisticated, than the codes of the Westerners who take the Bible or the Qur'an literally. In the East, history has been viewed as more cyclic than it has been in the West, and Ultimacy has used seers or sages more provisionally. This has not diminished the importance of tribal or societal codes, but it has blurred the face of the divinity thought to be their ultimate sanction.

To be sure, there are patches in the Eastern quilt where the imprint of a personified deity is clear. The Hindus who have gone out of themselves in love of **Lord Krishna** certainly have had a different sense of caste than the **Brahmins** who tried to ritualize the Vedas. The Buddhists who followed **Shinran** in throwing themselves on the mercy of the Ultimate have perceived the moral task differently than the **Theravadin Buddhists** who stressed self-salvation. But in both cases rules handed down from past Hindu or Buddhist societies have kept these divergent parties within the same family circle.

For example, the followers of Krishna did accept the general **caste** structure of Indian society, even though their religious assemblies sometimes suspended the distinction between priest and worker. The Buddhists who stressed the mercy of the Ultimate still were marked by the **sila** (moral code) that preoccupied the Theravadin self-savers. So even though we must provide for personalism and theism in the Eastern traditions, we have to keep these in perspective. On the whole both the impersonalism of the ultimate reality and the weight of traditional societal ways have been stronger than the revolutionary revelations of a personal God.

One place where East and West appear to converge, though not to coincide, is in their reverence for the sage. The sage arguably is the most important person in Eastern religious cultures, both those developed in India and those developed in East Asia. In the West the sage is contested, and probably bested, by the prophet. Yet the West also has honored the sage, and like the East the West has always given the notion of wisdom an ethical connotation. The insight that has been the ideal in both hemispheres has been one that could transform and perfect human action. One sees this in the wisdom literature of the Hebrew Bible, which scholars note owes a great deal to the prudential maxims of Egypt. In the wisdom literature the wise person is the one who keeps to the middle way, knowing the fragility of human motivation and looking only to God for full security. Certainly the Western mystics, Jewish and Muslim as well as Christian, occasionally show that wisdom has deeper roots in a perception of the presence of the divine, but the rabbis, priests, and mullahs on the whole have been lawyers more than **mystics.**

In the East the connection between mystics and ethicists probably has been a bit closer. The **rishis** (seers) who stand behind the **Hindu Vedas,** for instance, were thought to have seen aspects of the world of the gods. The writers of the **Upanishads,** whom Indian tradition has regarded as the successors of the Vedic seers, simplified this world and sought a perception of the underlying unity of all creation. It was from this perception that dharma ideally would flow, and dharma in turn was supposed to be conducive not merely to social harmony but also to mystical union with the **Brahman** or **Atman** that Hinduism considered the final basis of all reality.

The situation in traditional China was somewhat different, since the idealized Chinese sage typically was less speculative than the idealized Hindu or Buddhist holy man. Confucius, certainly, described himself as merely concerned to pass on the wisdom of the ancients who had flourished in a (mythical) golden age at the dawn of Chinese history. He had little patience with talk about God, since there was so much work to be done at the humbler, more accessible level of human problems such as social justice, peace, and political order. The Buddha also had little patience with speculation about **nirvana** or ultimate reality, saying that if one had been shot by an arrow the first task was to get the arrow out, not to determine who had shot the arrow or what the character of his family had been. On the other hand, Indian Buddhists quickly made the Buddha's dharma matter for intense speculation, so much so that wisdom, in the sense of directly perceiving the structure of ultimate reality, came to predominate over morality and meditation. It did not remove the necessity for these two other pillars of Buddhist religion, of course, but in many circles it did win the greatest prestige.

The analogue in China might be the development of a Neo-Confucian speculation some centuries after the Master's death, or perhaps the forays of Taoists into the foundations of reality. The Taoists did supply China with a meditative or mystical alternative to the soberness of Confucian moralism; they were more poetic and visionary. But in ethical matters the Confucians certainly carried the day, and just as Indian society clung to the hierarchical relationships epitomized in caste, so Chinese society clung tenaciously to the hierarchical relationships according to which Confucius had organized social life.

We shall examine some of the particulars of these generalized descriptions in the chapters that follow. Throughout, however, it would be wise to remember that Eastern religionists have been as fully human as the adherents of the Western traditions. By this we mean that certain elements—birth, death, injustice, creativity, love, hate—have played in Asian lives just as they have played in European lives. The Eastern traditions therefore have dealt with many of the same problems that the Western traditions have pondered. We also mean, however, that Easterners, in terms both of their religious traditions and their individual lives, are unique, just as Westerners are. Thus Buddhists probably have differed from Hindus as much as Christians have differed from Jews, and Mahayana Buddhists probably have differed from Theravadins as much as Catholic Christians have differed from Protestants.

Moreover, a traditional Hindu or Chinese man or woman could be as quirky—as eccentric in regard to the expectations of his or her tradition—as a traditional Muslim or Christian man or woman could be. Despite the great influence that tradition exerted in all premodern societies—both Eastern and Western—individual talent, temperament, experience, and genes always led many people to break free of the prescribed profile, usually in merely slight ways but sometimes in ways quite major.

4

Hindu Ethics

Historical Orientation
World View
Family Life
Work
Social Justice
Nature
Models
Summary, Study Questions, Notes

Historical Orientation

The religious culture of India that the word *Hinduism* brings to mind is perhaps 4500 years old. Archeological evidence from two sites in northwestern India suggests that from 2500 B.C.E. an urban culture thrived. The two sites, Harappa and Mohenjo-Daro, were the spearheads of a region known as the Indus Valley. This region depended on agriculture, had a form of writing, and appears to have had a highly structured social life. Artifacts suggest that fertility was a prime religious concern, while remains of houses and public buildings allow scholars to argue that the people were quite sophisticated builders.

Around 1500 B.C.E. invaders known as Aryans or Indo-Aryans migrated into the Indus Valley and eventually provided the foundations for what we now consider classical or formative Hinduism. These people were nomadic, warlike, and given to expressing themselves in oral poetry. The Vedas, which are the nearest Hindu equivalent to a sacred scripture, are largely collections of songs, spells, rituals, speculations, and other sorts of Aryan self-expression or lore. The gods one finds in the Vedas are mainly personifications of natural forces such as the wind, the sun, and the storm. Some of this literature deals with sacrifices that apparently were conducted in the hope of harmonizing the people with such forces. The Aryan tradition has it that the Vedas represent the visions of holy figures called rishis. One likely explanation for such visions was the ritual use of a psychotropic or hallucinogenic drink called **soma.** A great god of the seers was **Agni,** the divinity manifested in fire. Agni could also stand for divinity in general, so the performance of **sacrifices** to Agni could bring the worshiper into harmony with the entirety of a sacral universe.

We have been drawing on the historical schematization employed in David R. Kinsley's little book, *Hinduism.*[1] For Kinsley, the next major period of Hindu history is the period from about 800 to 400 B.C.E., during which the distinctive activity was the effort to go beyond sacrifice (which seems to have become routinized) and penetrate to the underlying unity of all cosmic phenomena. The most important literature in which we find this activity is the Upanishads, which regularly take the form of a dialogue between a teacher and a student. The main teaching that emerges in these dialogues is that all of reality ultimately is one, since all is enlivened or kept in being by a single source called Brahman. The Upanishads, we therefore might say, are metaphysical: concerned with the ultimate causes of things. They differ from an academic philosophy, however, in that the reason they seek ultimate causes is freedom from life's sufferings. The Upanishads further suggest, rather obliquely, that people interested in perceiving Brahman regularly resorted to yogic techniques. **Yoga** generically means "discipline," but the sort of discipline the Upanishads usually mean is one that quiets the person's consciousness and enables him or her to appreciate the simple, unrepresentable being and unity of all realities.

The millennium from about 400 B.C.E. to 600 C.E. sponsored a wealth of literature that Hindus have come to consider classical. Such epics as the **Mahabharata** and the **Ramayana** collected stories, images, and traditional lore that all later Indian generations have considered a great treasure trove. This literature spelled out many of Indian culture's social ideals, depicting, for example, how a king or a wife ought to behave. Like Greek tragedy, it often expressed the main cultural conflicts that people could experience, such as that between the written law and the unwritten code that a child ought always to obey its father.

This is also the period in which dharma, in the sense of the teaching that told all Indians what their caste responsibilities were, fully developed; so ever afterwards priests and warriors, farmers and workers, and even outcaste people could know what was expected of them. The Bhagavad Gita, which most scholars consider the most influential Indian religious writing, is part of the Mahabharata. In the Gita we see the catholicity that Hinduism had achieved by the end of its epic or classical period. There were many different yogas or paths to salvation. Depending on one's predispositions or circumstances, one could withdraw from action to study or meditate, or one could act purely, trying not to become attached to the fruits of one's actions. Perhaps the most popular discipline, however, was the way of love. Known as **bhakti,** it allowed millions of ordinary people, a majority of them women, to fashion a religion of devotion to a personal god such as Krishna or **Shiva** who was thought to represent ultimate, sacred reality.

If we called the period from 600 C.E. to 1800 C.E. India's medieval epoch, then we would have to say that bhakti was the most important feature of medieval Hinduism. Through much of this period the northern half of India was dominated by Muslim rulers, who presided over a significant Indian Islam, and a certain mutual influence of Hindus and Muslims made each group quite different than no doubt it otherwise would have been. The Hindu **bhaktas,** for example, often found Sufi themes quite congenial to their own stress on devotional love of God. Indian religion grew into a lush collection of devotions, as balladeers carried the message of the god Krishna or Shiva to the people. In the process of clarifying their own philosophical schools, Hindus disputed with Muslims and Buddhists, and the regional differences that had always characterized India (the name India was but a convenient label for a collection of remnants of many different kingdoms and linguistic areas) continued to develop. The caste distinctions derived from the Vedic period continued to obtain, while the world view that we shall sketch in the next section inclined most Hindus to relativize the significance of worldly activities.

From 1800 on the British were clearly in control of India's economic and political fortunes, though from the latter part of the nineteenth century a movement for Indian independence from British rule kept gathering strength. The British introduced many Western notions into the subcontinent, but Christianity never took hold as the new Indian religion. British legal and educational forms have shaped modern Indian culture, and a group of intellectuals impressed by Western ideals of justice and progress were at the front of a Hindu renaissance. Hinduism slowly became known in the West, often gaining the reputation of being the most spiritual religion in the world; and the philosophy of the sage **Shankara,** which put the Upanishadic ideas about the unity of all reality into a brilliantly coherent, systematic form, was the inspiration for numerous Vedanta societies in Western cities.

Since independence after the Second World War, India has struggled with great problems of poverty, increased population, and accommodation to modern technology. It has carried on a love-hate relation with the West, usually admiring the Western talent for getting things done but criticizing Western materialism. Politically, recent Indian leaders have tried to keep their country free of both Western and Communist alignments. The sheer size of the Indian population, which now is nearly three times that of the United States, has made for huge problems at the basic level of food and housing, while the volatile relations between

Muslims (and now **Sikhs**) and Hindus has led to both the partition of the country (the creation of Pakistan and Bangladesh as Indian Muslim realms) and many continuing conflicts.

World View

The central religious problem in Indian tradition is human imperfection and suffering. From the time of the Vedas one finds hints of dissatisfaction with hedonism and other forms of this-worldliness. The Upanishads represent a revolt against the religion of the Vedic priests, who tried through their sacrifices to keep people in harmony with the processes of nature. As they struggle to imagine the ultimate constituent of all things, the Upanishadic thinkers cross the border between a common-sensical philosophy (a search after ultimate causes) and a mystical desire to escape from the whole network of causes. The yogins whom later Hindu tradition made the prototypical sages (men, primarily, who could instruct others in wisdom) tended to be ascetic, and to teach that the way to escape suffering or to defeat human imperfection was to drop desire.

The principal notion that Hinduism has developed to project its intuitions of what a successful escape would be like is **moksha.** We sometimes translate *moksha* as "salvation," but perhaps "deliverance" or even "release" is a better term. For where *salvation* connotes healing, *moksha* more connotes quitting the human condition itself. Thus the classical yogin tries to achieve a state of enstasis or self-containment that would render him impervious to life's various assaults. (Where the shaman, who is the prototypical religious figure in nonliterate cultures, goes "out" of the ordinary self and so is ecstatic, the yogin goes in—or down or under—the ordinary self to rest on the bedrock of being: Brahman). When a religious philosopher such as Shankara worked out the implications of this experience, he found that it implied denying the reality of change, sense experience, and the emotions.

The state that the yogin is trying to achieve, then, is like the constant reality of Brahman. Hindus did describe moksha in positive terms (*being, bliss,* and *awareness* are the most famous nouns), yet nearly always it carried the connotation of existing so far beyond body-bound human existence that it was inconceivable. The yogin therefore did not mind having to sacrifice sense impressions, thoughts, and feelings as he descended toward the depths of his spirit-being. The journey he was taking called into question the reality of all three, since none explained itself or seemed stable in being. It was illusory to credit any of the three with lasting significance, and so it was natural to think that most people wandered in illusion (**maya**). As long as they clung to the supposition that what they sensed or thought or felt was lastingly significant, they would be trapped in a realm of affliction.

The name that Hinduism gave to this realm of affliction was **samsara.** By contrast with moksha, samsara is not fully real, not blissful, and is shot through with ignorance. Indeed, where biblical religion speaks of sin, Hinduism speaks of ignorance. People are mysteriously unaware or beclouded about the most important truths of their lives. Samsara could be portrayed as a wheel or a circuit from birth to death. Moreover, Hindus believed birth and death occurred many times, and they thought the universe itself moved through an enormous span of day and night or expansion and contraction that was quite like human birth and death. This condemnation to dying and being reborn, in fact, put the sharpest edge on the Hindu notion of suffering. Only when one completely escaped from samsara, so that there would be no more births and deaths, could one be considered either successful or blessed.

The Upanishads and the Bhagavad Gita both testify, however, that something immortal persists through all our dying and being reborn. This spiritual core of our identity, often called our **Atman,** is the basis of the Hindu notion of transmigration. After death the Atman takes up residence in a new material container—another human being, an animal, or a god. Many of the Hindu gods themselves need salvation, since they too exist in realms within the samsaric order.

The force that determines the character of one's transmigrations is called **karma.** This is a sort of moral causality, such that what one has done in the past shapes what one is in the present. Sometimes Hindus have spoken as though karma takes away free will, but usually they insist that one does have real choices and is somewhat responsible for whether one makes progress toward moksha or regresses. Still, the doctrine of karma could carry the consoling overtones of at least semi-inevitability. Since the temporal perspective of the process of attaining moksha was immense—hundreds of millions of years—one could be patient with the self and situation that karma had produced. For people in difficult circumstances, such a point of view was both a blessing and a curse. Certainly many poor or sickly people found comfort in resigning themselves to forces beyond their control. On the other hand, belief in karma could keep people from mustering the initiative to change the human or technological factors that were responsible for many of their miseries.

Karma related to important social assumptions about caste and dharma, in that whether one was a priest or an outcaste—was at the top or at the bottom of the social scale—had nothing to do with one's deeds in this present life. It did have a connection with one's deeds in past lives, however, so Brahmins had a basis for pride and outcastes had a basis for shame. The best psychological explanation for such a stratification of social life probably is the clarity that comes when people use slots or boxes to make all of their social interactions tidy. In the beginning the Aryans may have used color as a basis for assigning social status, but after hundreds of generations the complexities of the Hindu social system came virtually to defy analysis. They have not been harm-less, however, for prohibitions about touching outcaste people or having any decent dealings with them certainly have greatly increased the pov-erty and pain of the untouchables' lives. The Mahatma Gandhi, who was the leader of the Indian fight for liberation from British rule, called the outcastes or untouchables "the children of God," seeing in their misery the place where a worthy God would most energetically be at work to give help.[2]

Dharma, as we have explained, is both teaching in its generality (and so something like Torah) and the class responsibilities that come with one's particular status as a priest or a merchant. The Hindu theologians of course tried to ground dharma in the divine foundation of the world, but humanistic scholars can point to many historical factors that helped to shape how Hindus actually came to think about home life or social justice. The great codes or law books that arose prior to the medieval pe-riod fixed the ethical duties of each estate with considerable precision. Thus Manu, the foremost of such codes, punctiliously spells out the du-ties of the priest, both what he must do and what he must avoid.

Women fell somewhat outside the dharmic scheme, since the fore-most judgment about women was that they could gain moksha only after they had been reborn as men. Nonetheless, the Hindu theology consistently represented divinity as androgynous or male-female, and some of the most powerful deities in popular religion were ambivalent mother-goddesses such as **Kali.** They were ambivalent because, on the one hand, they symbolized an ultimate source of life, nourishment, and protection, while on the other hand they could turn destructive and death-dealing. Kali, for instance, frequently was depicted with blood dripping from her mouth and bedecked with garlands of skulls. Hindu theology perhaps was trying to say that only by making opposites coin-cide or clash can we catapult the mind out of the limitations of ordinary human thought and so open it to the transcendent reality of true di-vinity. Insofar as Hinduism has wanted true divinity to balance a cere-bral passivity with a carnal or creative energy, it has pictured the God-head as male-female. That the creative energy, called **shakti,** has been considered female may suggest why Hinduism has considered female-ness always to need male control.

Family Life

Classical Hindus have considered family life in the context of their in-triguing notion of the ideal life cycle. At least for males of the upper three castes, who received the sacred thread at an initiation ceremony comparable to the Jewish bar mitzvah or the Christian confirmation, physical development was considered subordinate to a progressive en-

lightenment. The four stages punctuating this progressive enlightenment were studenthood, householdership, forest dwelling, and sagehood.

In youth, one's task was learning from a religious teacher (guru) the
elements of the Hindu tradition. One would study the Vedas and the
great commentaries, learning by heart many passages of the classical
Sanskrit texts. One would live simply and chastely, obedient to all of
one's teacher's commands. Thus traditional India in effect gave its elite a
monastic education, trying to assure that both their minds and their
wills were thoroughly formed by the long-venerated ideals.

Householdership or marriage, which will take up the rest of this section, usually came in one's early twenties and was looked upon as a return to the world to take up familial and social responsibilities. When
one's hair had turned gray and one saw one's grandchildren, it was time to
begin withdrawing from these responsibilities and preparing one's soul
for death. Through simplification of one's material life and increased
meditation, one could imitate the holymen of old who had dwelt in the
forest, apart from the seductions and burdens of the world. The fourth
stage, sagehood, came as the consummation of a fully successful forest
dwelling. Having gained enlightenment (the grasp of ultimate reality
that could bring moksha), the sage or **sannyasin** was pictured as wandering the world, partly as an expression of his freedom from attachments,
and partly to instruct others.

The religious goals of marriage and family life derived from this
sense of personal time. The needs of the individual spouses, as well as
the needs of society, of course played a strong part in these goals, but
family life always was somewhat provisional: a stage on life's way. The
main purpose of marriage was procreation, so the main function of wives
was motherhood. Men were to profit from the experience of fatherhood,
but they also were to assume responsibilities in business and in the overall, extended family that Indian life sponsored. It was important to have
children to perform one's funerary rites, and also to provide for one's material needs in old age. Women were under the control of their fathers
until they married, and then they passed to the control of their husbands. In moving into their husband's family, they usually came under
the direction of their mother-in-law. Until they had produced children,
especially sons, they had little status in the family circle. On the death
of their husband they passed to the control of their eldest son, and perhaps the sorriest figure in Hindu society was the childless widow, who
was forced to live on the charity of people outside her family circle. Wid-
ows suffered the further burden of being thought to have figured in their
husband's death. In many periods of Indian history this notion of karmic
responsibility undergirded the practice of **sati,** according to which a
widow was supposed to join her deceased husband on his funeral pyre
and be consumed in his flames.

Hinduism considered marriage the normal human estate, and so it pressed upon young adults the responsibility to marry and procreate. Women had virtually no alternative to marriage, but men could renounce marriage to follow an ascetical religious life. The arrangement of marriage was complicated by the tradition of the dowry, many families going into debt to arrange the marriage of a daughter to a desirable (upper-caste) young man. Generally people were expected to marry within their own caste, but marriage of a woman to a man of higher caste was allowed. Marriage to a man of lower caste was frowned upon, since it was expected to lead to the whole family's devolution. (Progress toward moksha often was pictured as movement up the scale of caste, and sometimes the assumption was that only from the highest caste—as a Brahmin—could one actually achieve moksha.)

The parents of the prospective bride and groom generally arranged Hindu weddings, and fixing the wedding date involved consulting an astrologer to determine an auspicious time. The marital rite itself unfolded in six stages. First, there was reception of the groom at the house of the bride, and a ceremonial pouring of honey or exchange of garlands of flowers to start things on a note of sweetness and mutual acceptance. Second, there was a ceremony (perhaps separated in time from the initial reception) at which, in the presence of a holy fire, the father of the bride would hand her over to the groom, admonishing him to be true to her in matters of social responsibility (dharma), finances, and physical satisfaction.

Third, the core of the actual marriage transaction occurred when the groom clasped the hand of the bride, symbolically taking her to himself. Fourth, the bride would step on a stone situated near the holy fire, to express the hope that she and the marriage would put down all threats to familial prosperity. Fifth, the bride would offer fried rice to the fire, symbolically feeding the divine forces of light and warmth. And finally, the bride and groom would walk around the fire seven times with the ends of their garments joined. The words said at each circumambulation show that this ceremony was a petition for manifold marital blessings: sap, vigor, wealth, comfort, offspring, seasons (many years), and friendship between the two to old age.

Traditionally Hinduism put many obstacles in the way of divorce, but in recent legislation India has removed most of them, and divorce by mutual consent became possible in 1976. Wives have been counseled to be submissive to their husbands. Indeed, they have even been counseled to regard their husbands as gods. The many centuries in which Hindus lived under Muslim rule have left their mark on Indian attitudes toward intermarriage. Since Hinduism usually has not been a missionary or proselytizing religion, the trend has been for marriage between Hindus and non-Hindus to suppress the Hindu partner's faith.[3]

The Hindu ideal of **ahimsa** or noninjury encouraged all people to reverence both infants and fetuses, though the Upanishads could speak of the person united to divinity as beyond the reach of such crimes as murder or abortion.[4] Sexual pleasure apart from procreative intent was accounted legitimate, though the profile of a happy family life sketched the wife as highly fertile. An extensive erotic literature testifies to India's approval of sexual pleasure, and in the form of religious discipline known as **Tantra** sexual intercourse was used as a way to overcome desire and progress toward moksha. Intercourse also was assimilated to a religious sacrifice, and something of the magical power of the words and elements of the Vedic sacrifices was retained in efforts to secure contraception by the man's chanting during intercourse, "With power, with semen, I reclaim the semen from you."[5]

Although Hinduism tolerated polygamy in royalty, monogamy has been the general rule. The law code in Manu prescribes death for adultery (the wife who commits adultery with a lower-caste man should be torn apart by dogs), but other authorities were more lenient. Because children had the obligation to support their parents in old age, they sometimes encouraged their parents in the asceticism of forest dwelling in order to free up the parents' property. Death was considered **polluting,** and there were elaborate funerary rites whose execution was a solemn obligation incumbent on good children. In oldest times corpses apparently were simply abandoned to the wild beasts, but later cremation became the standard practice. Children were indulged until they started their schooling, and several rituals sanctified their birth and early life. However, the birth of a male was more joyous than that of a female, and having many daughters (all of whom would require dowries to marry) was a sign of bad karma.

Work

The yogic sages were very concerned with the place of work or, more generally, of action. Since their ideal was the self-containment that we have called enstasis, activity, with its tendency to disperse the personality, seemed a problem. By the time of the Bhagavad Gita a solution had arisen, and with it the discipline called **karma-yoga.** For those whose situation forced them to work—for example, parents, laborers, soldiers, and even ritualistic priests—purification and so progress toward moksha could come by acting with detachment. If one's intentions in working were pure, so that one neither desired success nor feared failure, the work would not be enslaving or samsaric. Figuratively, a pure intention would keep the karmic possibilities in work from touching one's Atman. Mahatma Gandhi used this notion of karma-yoga when he elaborated a spiritual rationale for his activities intent on gaining India's independence. He used the spinning wheel to symbolize the purity of intention that could make any work, political or mercantile, nonsamsaric, urging his followers to spin their own cloth not just as a way of boycotting English yard goods but also as a religious discipline: by emulating the patient, endless revolution of the wheel, they could fit themselves to a more godly sense of time and destiny.

Nonetheless, Indian society on the whole was not ascetic. The holy men who went off to the forest made it clear that moksha was the highest social value, but Hindu society considered three other goods legitimate. Under moksha came dharma, in the sense of caste-duty. Under dharma came **artha,** which was wealth or material prosperity. The final good, but one still fully legitimate, was **kama,** which embraced sensual pleasure and emotional satisfaction. The fact that wealth was deemed a blessing no doubt contributed to Indian economic life a solid religious sanction, if not a religious incentive.

In his marvelous study of Indian life before the coming of the Muslims, A. L. Basham has written of Indian economics: "In most early Indian literature the world is viewed from the angle of the well-to-do. Poverty, it is more than once said, is living death; to serve another for one's keep is a dog's life, and not worthy of an Aryan. From the time of the **Rg Veda,** which contains many prayers for riches, worldly wealth was looked upon as morally desirable for the ordinary man, and indeed essential to a full and civilized life. The ascetic, whether Buddhist or Jaina, who voluntarily abandoned his wealth, performed an act of renunciation which entitled him to the utmost respect. Though by this renunciation he assured himself of spiritual advancement, and was well on the way to salvation *(moksha),* the fourth and ultimate aim of existence, the ascetic's life was not that of the ordinary man, and the theoretical classification of the four stages of life . . . gave ample scope in the second stage to the householder, who was indeed encouraged to build up the family fortunes, and to spend part of them at least on the pleasures of the senses. Thus the ideals of ancient India, while not perhaps the same as those of the acquisitive West, by no means excluded money-making. India had not only a class of luxury-loving and pleasure-seeking dilettanti, but also one of wealth-seeking merchants and prosperous craftsmen, who, though less respected than the brahmans and warriors, were honored in society."[6]

The center of the Indian economy tended to be the individual craftsman, aided by members of his own family circle, but larger manufacturing concerns, cooperatives, and guilds also developed. Indian crafts attained sufficient quality in such areas as stonework, metallurgy, and weaving to qualify them as artistic. Merchants were supposed to be honest in their dealings, but Indian moralists allowed usury, except for Brahmins. One gets a good impression of how Indians regarded different sorts of work by studying the occupations closed to Brahmins as unsuitable for those closest to moksha. Agriculture presented problems, because inevitably it involved some violations of the ideal of ahimsa (for example, injuries to animals or insects). Trading in cattle, slaves, weapons, or liquor was also frowned upon. To retain the full prestige of his upper-caste status, a Brahmin had to function as a ritual priest or a religious teacher. Otherwise his engagement in economic activities detracted from his Brahminical dignity.

Indian tradition did allow slavery, but probably Indian slavery on the whole was less extensive and virulent than it was in many Western countries. Slaves were not strictly a caste (the lowest caste, the **Sudras** or workers, were freemen); originally most slaves were enemies conquered in warfare. Slaves could be ransomed, but their children became the property of their masters. Free men could sell themselves or their families into slavery to avert great distress. They could also be forced into slavery as a punishment for crime or debt, but only temporarily. The law codes provided protection for slaves, such as requirements that elderly slaves not be abandoned and female slaves not be subjected to sexual abuse. This does not mean, of course, that many slaves did not in fact suffer these injustices; and even the fact that the historical annals report slaves functioning in important roles little suggests that the average Indian would have regarded slavery as a desirable situation.

The work of the first portion of the life cycle, when one studied the tradition, included gaining a good sense of the ethical life that family responsibilities and business would require. The Taittiriya Upanishad (1.11.1−4) contains a sort of graduation address that sketches the virtues incumbent upon adults. Among them are truthfulness, fulfilling the responsibilities of one's caste, continuing to study the Vedas, procreating, attaining prosperity, reverencing the gods and one's ancestors, treating one's parents as gods, treating one's teacher as a god, honoring Brahmins, giving alms out of faith, and in general supporting all decency and irreproachableness. The wealthy were thought to have a responsibility to be liberal in helping the poor, while part of the profile of a good king was that he serve as a treasury of material benefits.[7]

In recent times, Hindu sages have looked upon work that helped alleviate the plight of suffering people as the equivalent of worship. Thus Swami **Vivekananda,** the foremost disciple of the saint Ramakrishna, learned and taught that needy people ought to be regarded as presences of the divine. Such work as teaching the illiterate, feeding the hungry, and bringing medicine to the sick was a fine expression of the love the disciple ought to have for God. Vivekananda developed this notion to the point where he urged Indian social workers to feel the sufferings of other people, learn the remedy for such sufferings, and comport themselves unselfishly in trying to bring that remedy to fruition. He considered India's neglect of the masses a national sin and accounted it a major cause of India's low situation in the international world.

In Vivekananda's view, Indian culture lived off the work and suffering of the lower classes, but instead of appreciating this essential contribution, the upper classes abused and disdained the suffering masses. Until

Indians stopped regarding the lower classes as virtual slaves, they would deserve no great prosperity. A **mahatma** or great soul, to Vivekananda's mind, could only be one whose heart bled for the poor. Such a saint (Gandhi comes to mind as fulfilling this prescription and so deserving his title *Mahatma*) would join together the traditional ideals of renunciation and service. The monks of the Ramakrishna mission that Vivekananda developed have tried to live out this belief that social service is worship of God. In so doing, they have joined with India's achievements in science, art, and politics to dispute the stereotype that Hinduism has made India hopelessly otherworldly.[8]

Social Justice

If one asks traditional Hindus about the rights to which all human beings are entitled simply because they are human, the question of caste quickly presents itself as a huge problem. The Hindu justification of caste was mythological, in that accounts of the creation of humanity described the division of the primal man into the four main groupings that stratified historical India. Kana Mitra, writing about her Hindu tradition for a book on human rights in the world traditions, refers to Manu for an authoritative presentation of the dharma concerning caste. As we follow her exposition, it will become clear that "human rights" are a modern concept that traditional Hinduism, like many other religious traditions, is ill-equipped to handle.[9]

First, the caste system assumes that people belonging to different castes have neither the same duties nor the same privileges. As things actually work out, there are many more than the four principal castes, since different trades serve to segregate people, but the main significance of caste still comes through if we contrast the functions of the four main groups. The priests, for example, have the duty of acquiring and spreading knowledge. To them is entrusted the heritage of the Vedic revelations, a heritage so highly esteemed that the priests are theoretically exempt from all secular labor (in practice many have had to earn their living in nonritualistic or nonintellectual occupations). The warrior caste serves society by protecting it from criminals and political dangers. In return, the warriors have the privilege of sharing in the benefits of both the Brahmins (knowledge) and the merchants (wealth). It is considered fitting, as well, that they receive the service of the workers who comprise the fourth and lowest caste. The third caste, which includes farmers, merchants, and other producers, is the part of Indian society entrusted with generating wealth and material exchange. Its members can expect to be taught by the Brahmins and protected by the warriors. As well, they can expect to be served by the workers, who are also obliged to serve the other two castes. The benefits due the workers for this service include the protection of the warriors and a share in the wealth of the merchants. (Significantly, the workers are not entitled to share in the knowledge of the Brahmins. Only the upper three castes have been candidate for initiation into the path of enlightenment and liberation.) Completely outside the caste system have been the untouchables, who have had to fend for themselves and usually have been the most wretched members of society.

One finds a suggestion that Hinduism realized the limitations in the stratifications of caste in the fact that the person in the fourth stage of the life cycle, having come to enlightenment and set out to wander the world as an example of detachment and the primacy of moksha, was outcaste in the sense of being bound by none of the dharmic responsibilities that he would previously have had as a Brahmin, warrior, or merchant. Another such suggestion comes from the groups of bhaktas and Tantrists who formed countercultural assemblies on the margins of official Hinduism. Frequently they neither discriminated between males and females nor retained the distinctions of caste. An anthropologist such as Victor Turner might describe both of these states as "liminal," meaning that ordinary conventions fall away and a culture allows itself to express the fundamental equality of all human beings before the mystery of existence. In so doing, the culture also suggests, of course, that the majority of our social classifications and discriminations are arbitrary, if not in fact ignorant or sinful.

At any rate, Hindu reformers such as Gandhi have tried to appreciate the benefits in such traditions as caste or the veneration of the cow without letting them sanction what by today's standards are considered cruelties, indignities, or superstitions. Thus Gandhi, as we mentioned, championed the plight of the untouchables. A sign of the changes that this championing has effected is the legislation in the mid-1950s that removed the barriers to intercaste marriage.

In the Bhagavad Gita the warrior Arjuna is repulsed by the obligation to do battle and likely kill, which his caste dharma has foisted on him. The Lord Krishna explains to him that the Atman can never be killed (which in effect removes the final seriousness of war), but then Krishna goes on to counsel Arjuna to fulfill his caste responsibilities. According to the Gita, it is better to carry out one's own caste responsibilities badly than to carry out the responsibilities of another caste well. Thus Arjuna should prefer fighting to standing up for ahimsa, as a Brahmin might be called upon to do. Behind this principle we can sense the horror of disorder that ancient India felt. It was so important to observe the order the gods were thought to have encoded in creation that one should kill or be killed rather than challenge that order. Similarly, whatever injustices or indignities the female half of the race suffered were excused on the basis of the relations between the sexes that had been ordained in the creation of human nature. Hindu notions of social justice therefore sometimes run directly counter to modern intuitions, since much of our modern way of life is predicated on the freedom of the individual to create his or her own destiny.

Despite the ideal of ahimsa, the story of the Indian kingdoms down the ages reveals an amazing amount of warfare and aggression. The period when the Buddhist Asoka ruled, about 269 to 232 B.C.E., stands out as an exception because Asoka tried to mute military violence and put into practice the Buddhist extension of Hindu notions of nonviolence. It may be that the Aryan beginnings of Hinduism, at which we find a lusty people used to raiding and warfare, always played subconsciously in the interpretations of dharma that justified the nearly constant subjugating and being subjugated. It is also worth noting that Hindu divinity has never been the complete positivity or goodness that the Western God has been. Rather, the Hindu Ultimate has embraced both creativity and destruction. The god Shiva, for example, is called "the Destroyer," in apparent recognition of the fact that the cosmos moves along as much by dying and sundering as by birth and constructive activities. At any rate, the Indian kings regularly considered conquest and expansion of their realm a primary ambition. Although some treatises on statecraft and military matters argue for what we might call codes of honor, on the whole this realm seems remarkably amoral or Machiavellian. Soldiers were bolstered by the prospect of improving their lot in the afterlife by being slain at their posts, while kings and their entire families could look forward to annihilation if the royal army lost the key battle.[10]

India's military destructiveness and apparent unconcern for its outcastes make one wonder whether an analyst such as V. S. Naipaul, who has called India a "wounded civilization,"[11] unfortunately isn't on to something. No doubt Naipaul is prejudiced against his ancestral homeland. No doubt one could find equal or perhaps even greater wounds in other civilizations, those of the West certainly included. But the apparent unconcern for human suffering that the doctrines of karma and caste seem to have created in many Indians (though certainly not all) makes those doctrines difficult for modern students to accept. If social justice should top the list of a religion's concerns, as the liberation theologians of several continents now claim, then Hinduism has some radical rethinking ahead of it.

Naipaul's book *India: A Wounded Civilization* is based on the mid-1970s, when Indira Gandhi declared a state of emergency and suspended many constitutional rights. Naipaul would locate the flaws that recent pressures in India have revealed in its failure to link self-realization—culminating in moksha—with a mundane, workable justice or contractual sense between ordinary human beings: "In the high Hindu ideal of self-realization—which could take so many forms, even that of worldly corruption—there was no idea of a contract between man and man. It was Hinduism's great flaw, after a thousand years of defeat [by Muslims and the British] and withdrawal."[12]

Nature

Hinduism's great virtue or genius, in the opinion of a comparative ethicist such as S. Cromwell Crawford, has been its reverence for all of creation. Where Western anthropocentrism has often led to neglecting or even outrightly abusing nature, Hinduism has conceived of reality, moksha, and the loving compassion that should develop with religious maturity as applying to everything that moves or exists.

Crawford understands Hinduism to locate the highest good (moksha) not in something reserved exclusively for human beings but in the entire cosmos. The self that religious discipline tries to liberate is related to all other creatures. Thus the Upanishads can describe the Atman as occurring in both a human being and a gnat. Whatever has being and life depends on the Atman or Brahman, so whatever has being or life is more like than unlike all other existents. Because of their common reference to Brahman, all creatures are kin. Crawford concludes his exposition of these traditional Hindu convictions with a firm deduction of their relevance to a present-day naturalistic ethics: "This belief in *Brahman* provides the philosophic basis for the Hindu's veneration of the natural world. The natural world is not a commodity which man possesses but a community to which he belongs. The universe appears to be material, but it is the universal consciousness of *Brahman*. Since all is one, the conquest of nature cannot be true to reality, and our sense of separateness, isolation, and egotism is the product of ignorance. Man cannot act ethically toward nature as long as he is ignorant of himself. Lacking his own sense of identity, he cannot identify with the trees and the mountains, nor can he feel empathy for the beasts of the fields. Nature is empty because he is empty. He manipulates nature because he manipulates himself."[13] One wishes that Crawford would sense the unity of men with women sufficiently to avoid the sexist language defacing his thought, but the main thrust of his appropriation of Hinduism is powerful and provocative.

The intuition that one Brahman pervades all of reality undergirded the ideal of ahimsa that we have already sketched. One ought not to harm other creatures because each is a presence of the holy Ultimate. Moreover, harming other creatures, even gnats and trees, would corrode the actor with bad karma. Thus occupations that seemed inevitably to entail harming (himsa), such as farming, butchering, or warfare, were either proscribed or devalued. To be sure, Hinduism has been a sufficiently complicated or sophisticated tradition to have embraced other lines of thought that justified doing violence to enemies or sources of food. If the Atman or Brahman that all beings possess is itself immortal, then any injury done to another creature is less than final.

When Krishna made this argument to Arjuna in the Gita, he let loose an ambiguous line of thought. A person intent on justifying murder or suicide could use this line, or similar lines of thought available in the Upanishads, to relativize the seriousness of such harmful action. On the other hand, of course, this line of thought held out considerable consolation. What any creature, human or nonhuman, suffers may not be final or fully radical, since all being derives from a source that none of our puny efforts can destroy. In the Gita, Krishna finally reveals himself to Arjuna, showing the magnificent divine splendor that even the humblest creature houses. J. Robert Oppenheimer, the leader of the scientific team that detonated the first atomic bomb, was perceptive in linking this revelation of Krishna with the power unleashed in the division of primary matter. Reality does cohere because of extraordinary energies, and no modern theology or religious system worthy of its name can fail either to correlate these energies with "God" or to provide for their proper reverence (not worship) through a truly ecological ethics.

Still in the context of the patterns of violence and counterviolence through which the biosphere seems actually to have evolved, we must also note that the doctrines of karma and Atman could sanction a view that what happens to any creature, human or subhuman, finally is bound up with the mystery of that creature's karmic destiny. Thus a general could survey a field littered with the corpses of his enemy and think that such defeat must have been their karmic fate. More recently, public officials working to clear an area of poisonous snakes or noxious pests could grant themselves an exemption from the apparent implications of their professed commitment to ahimsa by saying that it must have been the poor animals' karmic fate to have run up against this human necessity to exterminate them.

The Hindu practice therefore has been considerably more complicated than the simple appreciation of Brahman might suggest. Because the universe that Brahman undergirded was unimaginably vast in both time and space, there was plenty of room for such forces as karma, moksha, and ahimsa to operate. Indeed, the majority of Hindu cosmologists have believed the universe to be eternal. It may pulse between a **Brahma Day** and a **Brahma Night,** expanding and contracting, but at no time has it ever not existed and at no time will it cease to be. This raised a question concerning moksha, of course, for a moksha not escaping the physical universe would seem to be no true escape from the realm of samsara or ceaseless becoming. This question finally defeated Hindu theologians, as it did Western theologians, because of course they could not imagine a realm completely free of creaturely limitations. They could say, however, that the ultimate was "neti, neti": not this limitation and not that restriction. In other words, their theology or view of the ultimate framework in which the ecosphere resides was like the "negative theology" of the Western traditions: convinced that the Absolute or God is of a completely different order.

Hindus have expressed their veneration of natural objects in their worship, so much so that many scholars of religion describe Hindu ritu-

als as sacramental. Like Catholic and Orthodox Christians, Hindus have
felt that smells, sounds, sights, tastes, and touches all help the worshiper
to experience divinity, and thus that all are legitimate. The Hindu rituals
that paced the individual through the life cycle, from birth to death, associated human fate with representatives of the rest of the earth. The
traditional marriage ceremony, as we have indicated, employed honey,
flowers, fire, rice, and stone. Hindu erotico-religious art carried this sacramental instinct to the extreme of portraying the divine creative powers
through huge figures of human genitals, both female and male. Alternatively, it regularly depicted a great god and his consort in copulation,
to signify the divinity of the powers sustaining material life.

As is true with most other religious traditions, one often stands
amazed that such positive intuitions should not have produced a better
cultural praxis. Thus Hindu sexual life has suffered the repression and
misogyny one finds in most other religious cultures, while Hindu treatment of nature—forests, water, air—is now no better an ecological model
than what one finds in the West. Indeed, the smog of New Delhi probably
is worse than the smog of Los Angeles, and India has had no regulations
constraining automobile pollution comparable to those enacted in California. One moving from India to Japan notes a perceptible shift from
dust and carelessness to an almost compulsive neatness and love of
tended landscapes. A trip along the Ganges can be a moving religious
spectacle, as one watches the many pilgrims who come to bathe, but
it sends shivers of distress along the spine when one thinks of the mi-
crobes that the animals and the diseased bodies are setting loose in the
water. So venerating nature or all of life as an expression of Brahman
turns out to be a complicated matter. Simply proclaiming that nature is
an expression of the Absolute or a creation of God is no guarantee that
one will treat nature lovingly or wisely.

Models

When the average Hindu asked how he or she ought to act, several sources
of models lay ready at hand. Most influential, perhaps, were the stories
of the gods and the legendary heroes of primal times. These stories provided entertainment, the transmission of the Indian cultural heritage,
motivation or explanation for the rituals that sanctified daily life, and at
least tacit paradigms of how the good ruler, the good warrior, or the good
wife would tend to act.

The classical Hindu epics, such as the Mahabharata and the Ramayana, were probably the main source of the stories and images that filled
the average Indian's mind. Even when such a person was illiterate, story-
tellers, village plays, and enactments of the annual religious rituals com-
municated the substance of this tradition. The bhaktas, for instance, de-

pended on many stories about Krishna, who probably has been the most influential **avatar** (incarnation) of the deity.

One glimpses how the legends about Krishna and Radha, his favorite lover, could paint the fantasies and so the religious world of even mature modern Indian women in the following excerpt from an anthropologist's study of the **habisha,** a ritual that middle-aged Indian women perform to try to secure the long life of their husbands (and so avoid a premature widowhood): "Then the women reenacted the familiar legend of Krishna and the milkmaids. One woman in the role of a milkmaid churned milk in a small clay bowl. Tila [the anthropologist's informant], playing the role of Radha, the chief milkmaid and divine lover of Krishna, placed the pot of churned milk on her head. The women, holding hands, formed a circle, danced, sang loudly, and clapped their hands, imitating the devotional worship of the milkmaids for Krishna. One of the women, in the role of Krishna, reenacted the practical jokes he played on the milkmaids—hiding their clothes while they were bathing in the river, moving the boat that would ferry them across the river, and delaying its return. Pretending not to know who he was, the milkmaids loudly criticized the boatman until he revealed himself as Krishna, beloved to all of them. One of the women, in the role of Krishna's mother, played with her son and tried to prevent his mischievous pranks, while the other milkmaids danced, sang, and laughed noisily."[14]

The religion that these devotees of Krishna tend to develop is understandably quite joyous. They have reasons to think that the divinity is not just the ultimate guarantor of the meaning of their existence but also a lover with whom they can play. Adherents of the fiercer god Shiva might be more ascetic or given to lamenting their sins, but they too could draw on a wealth of mythology that portrayed how Shiva's power of fasting, sexuality, and destructiveness gave human lives direction and depth. The majority of ordinary Hindus, especially those in the rural villages, probably have cast their hopes on a local version of a nearly pan-Indian Mother Goddess. Certainly women in childbirth or afflicted with family problems have used such a goddess, along with the exemplary mothers and wives of the epic literature and the **Puranas** or cycles of devotional tales, to bolster their courage and hope.

Other significant models throughout Indian history have been the flesh-and-blood teachers, saints, and religious masters that Hinduism has always liberally produced. Ramakrishna and Gandhi, to whom we have already referred, are only two of the most recent in this long-standing Indian tradition. It is significant that both focused on service to their fellow human beings as a primary way of loving and serving God. However, it is unlikely that either holy man would have commanded great respect and so become a model unless it had been manifest that his social sensitivity derived from a profound interior life of meditation or devotional prayer.

Gandhi took on the spare dress, the diet, and the celibacy of the archetypal Hindu guru, when it became clear to him that the political tool he needed to fashion (**satyagraha:** the force of truth) was religious. He formed an **ashram** (religious community), again in the tradition of many prior gurus, giving people interested in his movement a place to which they could retire and absorb his teaching. The fact that recently several self-styled gurus have set up ashrams in the West, seduced confused youths, and then been revealed as charlatans does not vitiate the notion of guruship or ashram-life itself. In Tantrism, Hinduism has developed a subtradition in which apparently licentious sex and self-indulgence play a role (in authentic Tantra, discipline and self-denial are supposed to make sexual activity or drinking alcohol but another way of realizing the binding character, and so relative worthlessness, of samsaric activities). The mainstream of Hinduism, however, has demanded that its gurus be pure, honest, and beyond material gain.

When one reads accounts of other present-day gurus such as Ma Jnanananda of Madras, one senses that religious maturity ought to lead to an outgoing concern to teach others and to hand on the fruits of one's spiritual attainments. Ma Jnanananda is a woman gifted with powers of deepest meditation or trance (**samadhi**), and thus is venerable as one who has completed the classical yogic journey. She has moved from marriage and parenthood to the renunciation of worldly things typical of the sannyasin, and the basis of her responses to people who ask her about their personal problems is the love of God she has experienced.

Thus when people caught in the throes of sexual desire or family conflicts express their sense of slavery or depression, Ma regularly promises that if they free themselves from their attachments and come to experience the divine presence, these conflicts will largely solve themselves. For a person such as Ma, it seems, the ethical life has merged with the mystical life, so that this person who has found union with God experiences few moral dilemmas. In all situations such a person (a saint, really) feels the presence of the divinity, senses the core of the issue being presented, and is able to respond appropriately. Ma Jnanananda is rather traditional in her demands upon her followers. She offers them no suspension of the restraints in business, sex, or politics that basic Hindu morality would impose, but she does point to the experiential center that makes such restraints both easy to understand and easy to practice.[15]

From the composite that the epic heroes and the modern saints fashion, we might stress that the ordinary Hindu has been given an ideal of finding the divine in all things that could make the exact performance of dharmic or caste duties quite meaningful. The priest who labored to perform the sacrificial rituals perfectly, the warrior who spent himself in defense of the realm, the tradesman who rendered honest value, or the worker who hammered or swept diligently all had a basis for thinking that their fidelity advanced them along the path to moksha. So did the wife who bowed low to her husband or the mother who devoted herself to her children. The traits that human beings have praised across all the different cultures—kindness, helpfulness, honesty, love, wisdom, integrity, self-sacrifice—had many exemplars in Indian theology and mythology.

These were more than simply human virtues, however, because any such power was considered an expression of the divine source of being and light. One who honored parents, was faithful to friends, enjoyed the goods of the earth, avoided injuring other creatures, generously sacrificed to the god or goddess one found most appealing, and used the stimulus of old age to think deeply about the transiency of material life would be considered both good and blessed. One who used wealth generously, put up with poverty bravely, worked hard to master the traditional religious lore, or treated his wife and children kindly would be praised as both religious and ethical. Religion and ethics could not be separated. For Hinduism, doing what was good or correct meant being close to the holy source of life.

Summary

We sketched the history of Hinduism in five stages. First, the formative period was in full swing when there were cities in the Indus Valley about 4500 years ago. The Aryan invaders who conquered this area about 3500 years ago produced the Vedic literature, which portrays many natural divinities. Second, from about 800 to 400 B.C.E. religious philosophers and yogins tried to penetrate beneath the many phenomena and deities of the Vedic age and find a single underlying reality (Brahman). Third, from about 400 B.C.E. to 600 C.E. the epic literature developed, and with it the main models for Hindu ethical life and the main law codes that spelled out caste responsibilities. The fourth period, from 600 to 1800 C.E., which has been called India's medieval age, was dominated by bhaktas who reverenced personalized deities such as Krishna. During much of the medieval period northern India was under Muslim rule. The fifth and final period was the modern era, when India was under British rule and Western influences became strong. For Hinduism the interaction between Western and traditional ideas sparked a considerable reform, much of it expressed in the social concern of saints such as Ramakrishna and Mahatma Gandhi.

When sketching the Hindu philosophical outlook we stressed the problem of human suffering and the solution of the pathway to moksha. The hallmark of this pathway was the dropping of desire, which one could accomplish through one of the several Hindu yogas. The world opposed to moksha was the samsaric realm of death and rebirth. People passed through this realm endlessly, their Atmans transmigrating, and the moral law that pushed them along was known as karma. Finally, we discussed the dharma to which Indians have referred when generalizing their inherited and obligatory wisdom.

We situated the traditional Hindu ethics of family life in the context of the Hindu schema of the ideal life cycle, noting the prior stage of studenthood and the subsequent stage of forest dwelling. We observed the stress on procreation, the subordinate place of the wife, the social setting of the extended family, the values expressed in the usual wedding ceremony, and the prevailing attitudes toward divorce, sexual pleasure, adultery, abortion, and contraception. We concluded by considering polygamy, monogamy, and both children's early upbringing and their obligations when their parents die.

In discussing work we first explained the path of karma-yoga, in which Hinduism has seen a way to make work salvific. Next we noted the legitimacy of wealth, the central role of the craftsman, the ranking of different kinds of work that one can derive from the occupations prohibited to Brahmins, the force of Indian slavery, the virtues laid before the graduating student, and the sanctification of social work that Ramakrishna and Vivekananda proposed.

Our discussion of social justice began with a consideration of the important Hindu institution of caste, and we first noted how modern ideas of human rights may not square with the traditional mentality behind such an institution. We sketched the different rights and duties appropriate for each of the four major castes, noted liminal places where India showed itself aware of the arbitrariness of such social assignments, touched on the place of the outcastes, mused about the psychology of caste responsibility expressed in both Krishna's advice to Arjuna and the Indian assumptions about women, and observed the disjunction between the doctrine of ahimsa and the marked militarism demonstrated through the course of Indian history.

Concerning ecological ethics, we first discussed the positive benefits in the Indian sense that Brahman pervades all beings. Then we noted the potentially ambiguous consequences of the conviction that the Atman is imperishable. We connected the conflicts of evolution to the Indian beliefs about karma, and Indian sacramentality came up for review when we noted the place of the material world in Hindu ritual and worship. Finally, we remarked on the current ecological problems that Indian culture faces.

In discussing models for the ethics that Hinduism has proposed, we first focused on the gods and heroes made familiar through the epics and devotional classics. Krishna was our example here, and we showed how even modern Indian women tend to act out scenes from the stories about Krishna. The Indian tradition of guruship provided another source of models, and once again we reviewed the examples of Ramakrishna and

Mahatma Gandhi. We moved on to comment on the example and teaching of Ma Jnanananda, noting the coexistence of ethics and mysticism in her life. Our final reflections dealt with the virtues that humanity's many different religions seem to praise, and how Hinduism has tended to present them.

STUDY QUESTIONS

1. What did the Upanishads do to the religious world view enshrined in the Vedas?
2. What is the relation between moksha and samsara?
3. What was the relation between the first and the second stages of the traditional Hindu life cycle?
4. What was the traditional Hindu attitude toward money?
5. Explain how the traditional Indian world view justified caste.
6. How does the Hindu view of Brahman suggest that nature is not a commodity that human beings possess but a community to which human beings belong?
7. How have Ramakrishna and Mahatma Gandhi colored the model of the ethical Hindu?

NOTES

[1] David R. Kinsley, *Hinduism* (Englewood Cliffs, N.J.: Prentice-Hall), 1982.

[2] See R. C. Zaehner, *Hinduism* (New York: Oxford University Press), 1966.

[3] See Arvind Sharma, "Marriage in the Hindu Religious Tradition," *Journal of Ecumenical Studies* 22 (Winter 1985): 73–75.

[4] See Geoffrey Parrinder, *Sex in the World's Religions* (New York: Oxford University Press, 1980), p. 12.

[5] *Ibid.*, p. 19.

[6] A. L. Basham, *The Wonder That Was India* (New York: Grove Press, 1959), pp. 215–16.

[7] See S. Cromwell Crawford, *The Evolution of Hindu Ethical Ideals* (Honolulu: University of Hawaii Press, 1982), pp. 132–36.

[8] Swami Nikhilananda, "The Realistic Aspect of Hindu Spirituality," in *The Indian Mind*, ed. Charles A. Moore (Honolulu: University of Hawaii Press, 1978), p. 230.

[9] Kana Mitra, "Human Rights in Hinduism," in *Human Rights in Religious Traditions*, ed. Arlene Swidler (New York: Pilgrim Press, 1982), pp. 79–80.

[10] See Basham, *The Wonder That Was India*, pp. 126–27.

[11] See V. S. Naipaul, *India: A Wounded Civilization* (New York: Vintage, 1978).

[12] *Ibid.*, p. 40.

[13] Crawford, *The Evolution of Hindu Ethical Ideals*, pp. 150–51.

[14] James M. Freeman, "The Ladies of Lord Krishna: Rituals of Middle-Aged Women in Eastern India," in *Unspoken Worlds*, ed. Nancy A. Falk and Rita M. Gross (San Francisco: Harper & Row, 1980), pp. 116–17. See also David R. Kinsley, *The Sword and the Flute* (Berkeley: University of California Press, 1977).

[15] See Charles S. J. White, "Mother Guru: Jnanananda of Madras, India," in Falk and Gross, eds., *Unspoken Worlds*, pp. 22–37.

5

Buddhist Ethics

Historical Orientation

Buddhism, like Christianity and Islam, began with a distinct historical figure. Gautama, who received the name Buddha ("Enlightened One") because of the power of his insight, lived from 536 to 476 B.C.E. He was born near the foothills of the Himalayas in what is now Nepal, and grew up as a prince of the warrior caste. The legends of his birth and youth stress that he was predicted to be a Buddha who would escape samsara and bring enlightenment to many. After thirty years or so of indulgence, marriage, and pleasure, he became serious about life when he started pondering the significance of disease, old age, and death. These problems so came to possess him that he left his protected life in the palace, creeping away from his wife and child before dawn, and set out to find a solution to the bedrock imperfection of the human condition.

The reports have it that Gautama studied with various ascetics and teachers, learning much about yoga and philosophy and about discipline and fasting, but finding that none of this schooling brought him to his goal. So he sat himself down, vowed not to get up until he had gained enlightenment, and won the victory he had been seeking: After some debate with himself he resolved to teach others what he had realized, and the formulation of his insight was the famous Four Noble Truths that ever since have been the core of Buddhist philosophy.

We shall elaborate on the Four Noble Truths in the next section. Here we should note that the Buddha slowly gathered a band of disciples, both men and women, and that by the time of his death at age eighty, his movement was well under way. The group that the Buddha gathered became known as the **Sangha** or Community, and the monastic part of it has been the heart of Buddhism for nearly 2500 years. Monks, both men and women, would vow celibacy and agree to live a simple community life under the direction of an abbot or abbess. As we shall see later, the rules developed for the monastic Sangha suggest much of the Buddhist ethical ideal, as does the simple ethical code (*sila*) that is incumbent on all Buddhists but is especially directed to the laity.

After the Buddha's death his followers continued to probe his teaching and pass it on to others. Several hundred years later they had accumulated a full literature that has formed the basis of the Buddhist canon, many of the items being considered **sutras** or addresses of the Buddha himself. A split developed between those who were more conservative regarding the original legacy and those who wished to speculate about its philosophical implications. This latter group, which came to be known as the Mahayanists, also was more interested in dignifying the life of the Buddhist laity. The more conservative group, known as the **Hinayanists** or Theravadins, has preferred to focus on ethics and has kept the monastic life as the acme of the Buddhist community.

The reign of the Indian Buddhist king Asoka, which we mentioned in the last chapter, suggests the social success that Buddhism had achieved within two hundred years of the Buddha's death. Buddha must first have appeared to his contemporaries as a Hindu reformer, much as Jesus must have appeared to his contemporaries as a Jewish reformer, and only centuries of debate and competition, some of it bitter, elaborated the differences between Buddhists and Hindus. In the case of Asoka, the Buddhist stress on ahimsa and consequent repugnance for war created a rule remarkable for its humanitarianism. Asoka left stone monuments describing his conversion from violence and sketching the ideals of a Buddhist realm that would prize peacemaking and harmony.

From the third to the sixth centuries of the Common Era Buddhism engaged in highly successful missionary ventures to the east, soon becoming well established in Vietnam, China, Korea, and Burma. In 594 C.E. it was proclaimed the state religion in Japan, and in 749 C.E. the first Buddhist monastery was established in Tibet. In India, Buddhism began to decline after the seventh century C.E., because of such factors as the laxity of the Sangha (which had become quite wealthy), the invasions of the White Huns and Muslims, and a resurgence of Hinduism. Hinduism proved better able than Buddhism to adapt to the invasions and new religious movements, so eventually Buddhism was more influential outside India than in its native land. Theravada Buddhism held on in Ceylon (now Sri Lanka) but missionaries made new progress in Burma, Thailand, China, Japan, and Tibet. Generally speaking, Theravada Buddhism has dominated the areas closest to India (Sri Lanka, Burma, Thailand) while **Mahayana** Buddhism has flourished in East Asia. Tibet has developed its own distinctive tradition, sometimes called **Vajrayana,** which appears to have been more influenced by India than by China.

The gross distinctions between Indian and Chinese Buddhism include the more speculative cast of Indian thought, which loves dialectical analyses and subtle psychology or introspection, and the more aesthetic cast of East Asian thought. For the Chinese Buddhists the contemplation of natural beauty merged with religious meditation, and such Buddhist notions as "emptiness," which we shall consider momentarily, exerted a great influence on both contemplation and ethical action. Mahayana Buddhism was also shaped by the Confucian mores that dominated East Asia, one of the results being that the different Buddhist sects constituted themselves like family clans, with lineages of gurus and doctrinal traditions.

Buddhism has predominated in Sri Lanka, Burma, and Thailand, gradually subjugating the native traditions, which usually were animistic, and becoming the soul of the local culture. The situation has been more complex in China and Japan, where quite articulate native traditions have responded to the challenge of Buddhism (which they first saw as a foreign import) and have either outrightly rejected it or, more frequently, amalgamated with it. Thus Confucianism became more speculative after the development of Buddhism in China, and what is known as Neo-Confucianism—a systematic world view that included meditational techniques and metaphysical doctrines, as well as elaborations of the traditional Confucian ethics—is inconceivable without the Buddhist stimulus. That Taoism furnished the early translators the essential philosophical vocabulary for rendering Indian notions into Chinese proved very significant. Indeed, some scholars think that an East Asian Buddhist school such as Ch'an (Zen in Japan) owes as much to Taoism as to Indian Mahayana Buddhism. Essentially, the East Asian preference for concreteness over abstraction, along with the naturalistic aesthetics, pressured Buddhism to undergo a rather thorough transformation.

East Asian Buddhism has fluctuated greatly in terms of its cultural influence. In ninth-century C.E. China, for example, it suffered fierce persecutions, which testified to the enormous influence that the Sangha had accumulated by that time. Similarly, when the Tokugawa **Shogunate** consolidated power in early seventeenth-century C.E. Japan, it moved to subject the Buddhist Sangha to the control of the state bureaucracy. Buddhism became the official religion of Thailand in 1360 C.E., and in the mid-sixteenth century C.E. it won over the Mongols. In all of the lands to which it voyaged it went native, adapting itself to local customs, and in many places—especially in East Asia—it split into numerous sects. Almost always, however, the depth of the Buddhist philosophy and the richness of the Buddhist rituals made Buddhist monks the officiants at the funeral ceremonies, where people summarized their sense of life and death. Today Buddhism has embarked on a world-wide expansion, beginning to take root in the West and establish American and European traditions.[1]

World View

The Buddha expressed his liberating experience in four affirmations. These Four Noble Truths have served as the foundation of the Buddhist world view. First, all life is suffering. Second, the cause of suffering is desire. Third, stopping desire will stop suffering. Fourth, the best way to stop desire is to follow the eightfold path of right views, right intention, right speech, right action, right livelihood, right effort, right mindfulness, and right concentration.

One sees the Indian-ness of Gautama's insight and project. Like the Upanishadic seers who were his contemporaries, he wanted to find something that would undercut the radical imperfection of existence as most people experienced it. What the Hindu sages called moksha the Buddhist sages have called nirvana, but the basic affirmation has been the same. Buddhists have agreed with Hindus that the realm of ordinary experience is samsaric: a cruel wheel of births and deaths. They have also agreed that karma drives this wheel. The first two noble truths express with ruthless clarity both the problem and its cause: to live is to suffer, and the reason we suffer is that we have desires and so are vulnerable to disappointment. The third noble truth accords with the yogic point of view: if we root out desire, we shall refuse karma the handle by which it can afflict us. The fourth noble truth makes Buddhism distinctive. The programmatic eightfold path put together a practical package— a how-to-roust-desire kit—that later tradition specified quite concretely.

Frequently commentators, both traditional Buddhists and modern scholars, correlate the eight aspects of the Buddhist path to nirvana with the three major aspects of Buddhist religion: wisdom, morality, and meditation. Right views and right intention have been subsumed under wisdom: knowing the truth and orientating ourselves by it. Right speech, right action, and right livelihood have been subsumed under morality. We may consider them the aboriginal Buddhist ethical precepts. Finally, right effort, right mindfulness, and right concentration have been subsumed under meditation (there have been many different Buddhist meditational schools and methods). By sitting and concentrating one's awareness, one could appropriate the full force of the Enlightened One's dharma.

We have noted that early Buddhism accepted the traditional Indian notions of samsara and karma. We could add that it accepted the reality of reincarnation and the vast stretches of cosmic space and time that we described for Hinduism. The key difference between the way of the Buddha and classical Hinduism lay in the matter of Atman (and so also of Brahman). For the Buddhists there is no Atman. Indeed, perhaps the most pernicious illusion we have to root out (the Buddhists agreed with the Hindus that ignorance and illusion are what keep us in bondage to desire) is the illusion that we are or have a subsistent self.

Three of the key Buddhist characterizations of reality are that all things are painful, fleeting, and empty or self-less (**anatman**). The Buddhists dislike the Upanishadic notion that all things are rendered alike by their Atmans, as well as the Hindu conviction that a single Brahman serves as the ground of all reality. In the Buddhist view, there is nothing under or behind the entities of the world. Rather, the entities of the world form a moving field of interacting forces that itself comprises "reality." We shall have to qualify this characterization shortly, however, because Buddhist discussions of emptiness and nirvana call for more nuance. But the Buddhist denial of Atman and Brahman, along with the Buddhist stress on interconnected phenomena, will serve adequately as a first distinction between the Hindu and Buddhist world views.

To express their sense of reality, Buddhists have spoken of **dependent coarising.** When elaborated, this notion came to denote twelve linked stages in the arising of any entity. The first and last stages were joined, so the whole could be pictured as a wheel. (The Buddhists also used the wheel to symbolize the dharma.) As you read our summary of the twelve stages, note how physical and metaphysical forces mix together: (1) aging and dying depend on rebirth; (2) rebirth depends on becoming; (3) becoming depends on appropriating certain necessary materials; (4) appropriation depends on desire; (5) desire depends on feeling; (6) feeling depends on contact; (7) contact depends on the senses; (8) the senses depend on name and form (mind and body); (9) name and form depend on consciousness; (10) consciousness depends on (is shaped by) samsara; (11) samsara depends on ignorance (of the four noble truths); (12) ignorance therefore is the basic cause of samsaric suffering.[2]

So far, then, we have seen the Buddhists spell out quite exactly the forces constituting the painful human condition, using notions common to Indian tradition. As they speculated further, however, the Mahayana Buddhist philosophers radicalized this beginning. Since the Mahayana philosophy greatly contributed to the Buddhism of both East Asia and Tibet, what we have now to explain was very influential.

The first Mahayana emphasis was in effect a leaning on the notion of anatman, to the point that "emptiness" became the primary mark of all entities. The first thing a wise person would note or stress was the selflessness or insubstantiality of each portion of reality. Second, the Mahayanins thought hard about the significance of nirvana, the state of unconditionedness—freedom from samsara—that was their goal. This hard thought led some of the best Mahayana philosophers, such as the sage Nagarjuna (who flourished around 200 C.E.), to identify samsara and nirvana. What Nagarjuna meant by asserting such an identity was that nirvana supplies whatever in samsara should be judged, in ultimate perspective, as truly or fully real. Since samsaric beings themselves—all human beings, for example—suffer pain, are fleeting (always changing), and have no self (no fully consistent or underlying identity apart from their component elements)—they are not wholly real. The reality or existence that they do possess must therefore be an expression or presence of the unconditioned, self-sufficient mode of reality (nirvana) that the mind requires if existence is to make sense. Nirvana and samsara therefore are one or inseparable.

Not even the Buddhists pretended that this advanced Mahayana philosophy was easy to understand, so the **Prajnaparamita** literature in which it was most famously elaborated has had the aura of being the cream of Mahayana dialectics or philosophical argument. Practically, however, the notions of emptiness and the identification of nirvana and samsara had great consequences, because they allowed East Asian Buddhists to concentrate on here, now, embodiment, physical nature, and the other concrete or holistic aspects of human life that the Chinese and Japanese cultures instinctively have preferred to Indian abstractions.

Perhaps Zen Buddhism has most thoroughly exploited the Mahayana philosophy, making such famous features of Japanese life as the tea ceremony, floral arrangement, swordsmanship, archery, and gardening, as well as ordinary manual labor and recreational games such as *Go*, potentially spiritual disciplines. When Buddhism very knowingly preaches living in the present, rejecting any separation between mind and body or thought and action, "just-sitting" (*shikantaza*) in meditation, and other staples of this-worldliness, it draws on the conviction that nirvana is not a physical beyond so much as an aspect of present situations. We grow enlightened in the measure that we connect ourselves with the rest of existence under this present aspect. When we are enlightened, we sense the oneness of all beings—not by referring to an objective Brahman, but by being in the midst of the moving, interconnected field through which nirvana plays.[3]

Family Life

Insofar as the monastic dimension of the Sangha has carried more religious prestige, Buddhist family life, like Roman Catholic Christian family life, has labored under the cloud of being a second-class vocation. From time to time Mahayana saints such as Vimalakirti modeled the highest virtue as married people, but on the whole celibacy was part of the Buddhist saint's profile. Buddhist family life probably profited, however, from the fact that women had the alternative of entering monastic life. In many areas there was cultural resistance to this freedom, but enough women made use of the tradition that the Buddha had accepted women into the Sangha to create a space in which females no longer had to marry mindlessly or as the pure pawns of their families. Buddhism usually required that both parents approve of a child's entry into the monastic life, and this too upgraded the significance of a woman's will.

The basic ethical precepts incumbent on all Buddhists were the five commands of *sila*. Those who had formally committed themselves to Buddhism (by solemnly avowing that they took refuge in the Buddha, the dharma, and the Sangha) were obligated (1) to refrain from killing living beings, (2) to refrain from stealing, (3) to refrain from unchastity, (4) to refrain from lying, and (5) to refrain from alcoholic beverages. Buddhist moralists naturally elaborated the implications of these five precepts, considering, for example, the degree to which farming did or did not violate the first precept. They would specify that the third precept, which forbade unchastity, also forbade adultery, sexual relations with a nun, and sexual relations with a woman betrothed to another man. (Most of the codes are written from a male point of view.) They would also move from legal interpretation to advice by suggesting, for example, that the spirit of the third precept urged restraining one's demands on a wife who was pregnant or nursing, or who had taken a temporary vow of sexual abstinence. The Indian Buddhist moralists, especially, loved to clarify the ambiguities of lying and honesty, of stealing and making restitution.

Beyond these five precepts, the laity were urged to be generous in supporting the monastic Sangha, often under the modality that the monks would transfer to generous benefactors the merit of their meditations and good works. Many monasteries offered the laity spiritual instruction in doctrine or meditation, and the laity frequently were welcome at the monastic celebration of religious holy days, such as the New Year or the birthday of the Buddha. In other aspects of Buddhist family life local culture exerted a considerable influence. So, for instance, in East Asian Buddhist families a Confucian sort of hierarchy would situate the elderly above the young and males above females.

Rita Gross has raised this observation to the general principle that Buddhism itself furnished few specific guidelines for the married life of Buddhists, the rule being that the local Indian or Chinese (or now American) customs concerning marriage and family life would tend to be animated by Buddhist spiritual ideals.[4] Thus she finds that Buddhism has coexisted with monogamous, polygynous, polyandrous, and even homosexual commitments, judging each by the degree to which it lessened egocentricity and advanced inner liberty. This same attitude has meant that divorce, childbearing, and contraception have not been treated dogmatically but rather judged case by case. Generally, Buddhism has favored monogamy, responsible childbearing and child-rearing, and marriages in which spiritual progress was the couple's main goal and reason for union. It has disapproved of divorce, irregular sexuality (for example, oral or anal intercourse), and homosexuality—but not rigidly or without regard to intentions or special circumstances that might change the ethical evaluation. The precept against killing has meant a strong aversion to abortion and infanticide (exposure of infants, especially girls, has been widely practiced in East Asia).

In providing a spiritual rationale for the mores of traditional family life in both India and East Asia, Buddhism has urged children to respect their parents, allowed present generations to venerate their deceased ancestors, helped wives be docile to their husbands, and counseled husbands to treat their wives and children considerately. Buddhism did not agree with the Hindu notion that only men might gain moksha or nirvana. Yet traditional Buddhism was beset with misogyny, much of it due to the tendency of celibate monks to consider women dangerous to their vocation, and it did not grant women equal access to monastic authority. In principle, however, men and women were equally in need of spiritual insight and equally apt to attain it.

No doubt partly because lay life seemed to carry so many distractions, married Buddhists in areas such as Burma have shifted their focus from attaining nirvana to gaining merit and so better karma for a better next life and eventually a solid opportunity to gain nirvana. This has carried in its train a great concentration on rituals that afford opportunity to gain such merit. Melford Spiro's well-regarded study of Burmese Buddhism details the daily, weekly, monthly, annual, and life-cycle dimensions of such a ritualistic religious focus, suggesting that a pious Buddhist family would be nearly saturated with prayers and small offerings. Spiro begins his detailed description of the daily cultus as follows: "For a pious Buddhist, the first and last acts of the day consist of devotions performed in front of the small shrine found in almost every Burmese household. Always on the eastern (auspicious) side of the house, and always above head level (for to be placed below another's head is a grave insult, while to be placed above it is a sign of respect), the shrine consists, minimally, of a shelf for a vase, which usually contains fresh flowers to honor the Buddha. In some cases, a polychrome picture of the Buddha or of a Buddha image is found on the shelf. . . . In addition to the flower offerings, candles are lit and/or food offerings placed on the shelf as part of the daily devotions."[5]

This quotation, like many incursions we might have made into anthropological treatments of other religious traditions, reminds us that the typical family life has been filled with little devotions, prayers to God or the saints, and other ways of helping the people (especially the women, but also the men) to orient themselves, in both sadness and joy, in the universe. For Buddhists of East Asia the greatest object of such folk or familial religion has been Kuan-yin, a **bodhisattva** (Buddha-to-be or saint) who has functioned much like a Mother Goddess. We ourselves have visited her shrine in Tokyo and observed people pinning up pictures of their newly born children, whose arrival and health they attribute to the grace of the bodhisattva. In sects such as Shin Buddhism, the priests usually are married and the devotional life of the family has a high status. Shin Buddhism also has stressed the mercy of the Buddha, teaching that faithful reliance upon this mercy is more important than mastering doctrine, engaging in austerities, or even meditating.

Overall, then, Buddhism has accepted family life and tried to make it compatible with the goal of progressing toward nirvana more than it has created a new marital theology. Because of the significance of monastic celibacy, Buddhism has probably esteemed sexuality and procreation less than many other religious traditions have. On the other hand, a generous fulfillment of one's responsibilities in family life certainly could become a good disciplinary framework. The model of the compassionate Buddha, wonderfully peaceful and beyond the wars of desire, could refresh weary householders, reminding them that the true riches of life lay in the heart or spirit. If one purified consciousness, enlightenment could come at any moment, in any situation or vocation. The point was to do what one was doing, live where one was living, with a growing appreciation of the "Buddha-nature" or "suchness" of the things with which one was dealing. All things were pure to the pure. The closer one came to enlightenment, the more spouses, children, trees, or birds could seem vessels of light.

Work

E. F. Schumacher, the British economist and ecologist whose book *Small is Beautiful* enjoyed great vogue a decade ago, spent time in Burma as a consultant. He returned home deeply impressed by the attitude toward work and material possessions that he had observed, thinking that "Buddhist Economics," as he called it, held many of the answers to the questions being raised by the inflooding data on environmental depletion and pollution. Schumacher listened to Buddhists discussing the modern implications of the fifth aspect of the eightfold path (right livelihood), and he sympathized with their desire to develop their country's economy without betraying its Theravadin Buddhist heritage. Indeed, he found in this heritage an attractive alternative to the ordinary Western view of work.

According to this Western view, in Schumacher's opinion, work is a necessary evil. Employers tend to look upon work as simply an item of cost, which they want to keep as low as possible. Employees tend to look upon work as a sacrifice of leisure and comfort. The Western ideal, one might therefore (somewhat cynically) say, would be output without employees and income without employment. In contrast, "the Buddhist point of view takes the function of work to be at least threefold: to give a man the chance to utilise and develop his faculties; to enable him to overcome his ego-centredness by joining with other people in a common task; and to bring forth the goods and services needed for a becoming existence."[6]

Just as the Western view of work has borne such consequences as the assembly line and the modern corporation that constantly shuffles alignments to maximize profits, so the traditional Buddhist view of work has influenced how Buddhists have thought about the details of manual and cooperative labor. For example, Buddhist spirituality abhors the notion that work should become so meaningless, boring, or stultifying that it would actually harm a worker's religious life. If the production of goods or the attainment of financial profits took precedence over the welfare of the human beings party to the economic enterprise, Buddhist moralists would be obligated to cry foul: the compassion of the Buddha would be violated, and an evil attachment to material things would be perverting right order, in which detachment is the path to happiness.

Similarly, a situation in which one worked frantically to attain the means to a perhaps equally frantic self-indulgent leisure would strike traditional Buddhists as almost comically wrongheaded. For certainly human health, they would say, requires serenity, beauty, and social utility in both hours of work and hours of leisure. Certainly neither profit nor pleasure should rule over peace, self-possession, purity of intention, and compassionate help for others.

One might argue, of course, that Schumacher's comparison is unfair or imbalanced because it is setting the Buddhist ideal against the Western practice, rather than comparing ideal to ideal and practice to practice. The argument would have merit, but Schumacher could reply that the Burmese society he had studied was much more diligently trying to connect its traditional religious values with its economic reforms than Western society was. Moreover, he could suggest that the Buddhist tradition is less ambiguous about the relativity or the delimited goodness of wealth and material production than the Western traditions (especially the Protestant Christianity tied up with the rise of capitalism) have been. Buddhists, of course, could interpret material wealth as a sign of good karma, but their focus on detachment meant that work was interpreted in all the monasteries as a spiritual discipline rather than as a path to a financial prosperity that could be considered a sign of divine favor or election. Christian monasteries taught the same lessons about work, but the ideology behind the rise of modern Western labor theory and economics broke with Christian monastic values. Indeed, the contemplative context of even modern Buddhist labor theory and economics puts them in a different psychological world than that of the modern West.

In describing the implications of the call to right livelihood, Walpola Rahula, a well-known interpreter of Buddhism to the West, quickly suggests that Buddhism would have many problems with occupations that now greatly shape, or perhaps even control, Western business: "Right Livelihood means that one should abstain from making one's living through a profession that brings harm to others, such as trading in arms and lethal weapons, intoxicating drinks, poisons, killing animals, cheating, etc., and should live by a profession which is honourable, blameless, and innocent of harm to others. One can clearly see here that Buddhism is strongly opposed to any kind of war, when it lays down that trade in arms and lethal weapons is an evil and unjust means of livelihood."[7]

Interestingly, however, the Buddhist groups that have had the most success in the United States have not been the sects that have stressed meditation, philosophy, and a deep penetration of the Four Noble Truths that would reveal the painfulness, fleetingness, and selflessness of all realities. Rather, the most successful groups, such as the Nichiren Shoshu of America and the Buddhist Churches of America, have married American images of drive and success to their practices of chanting homage to the Lotus Sutra (a very important traditional devotional text) or of placing their reliance in the Buddha Amida (a savior figure). In fact they have been quite like some Christian evangelical groups in promising that hard work, combined with devotional faith, will bring financial success or progress in one's business career.

Thus Charles Prebish, in a work on American Buddhism, has commented: "To recall the basis for such practice is, in this context, less important than noting that it is these two groups [Nichiren Shoshu and the Buddhist Churches of America] with their optimistic attitude and emphasis on success, that represent the two largest groups in America. We have previously identified some of the ways in which these groups resonate with patterns in mainstream American religion, and these will not be reiterated here. Nevertheless, the two groups are highly consonant in their quest with the 'American dream.' They highlight the benefits of the traditional work ethic in America, as well as the fruits of a life of strong faith, calling to memory the myth of 'rugged individualism.'"[8]

We shall have occasion to consider some of the cultural underpinnings of this sort of Buddhism when we deal with Japanese ethics. Here our main point is simply to ensure that the picture of Buddhist views of work not be falsely clear. No doubt a good Buddhist ethicist could work out ways in which the orientation of the American Buddhist devotional sects toward success could be compatible with traditional Buddhist notions of detachment and freedom from material desires. That would entail some rather sophisticated dialectics, however, as when Christian theologians try to square the notion of an evangelical call to material success with the Sermon on the Mount or with Jesus' strictures about the difficulty with which the wealthy will enter the Kingdom of Heaven.

For Schumacher, who was interested in ecology and environmentalism, the leading Buddhist virtues were clearly simplicity, self-restraint,
and harmony with the environment. The same Japanese Buddhism that
gave rise to the Nichiren and other success-oriented sects encouraged
naturalist poets who subordinated human egocentricity to an environment considered richer in Buddha-nature because of its nonstriving, integrated character. We shall note this refrain when we come to Buddhist
views of nature. For questions of industrial work, art, science, and economics, however, the specifically Buddhist contribution to the dialogue
of the world religions would seem to lie in perceptions less familiar in
the United States: the primacy of the welfare of the worker and the community, the need to keep work from being harmful to other creatures,
the demand that work square with a spirituality focused on detachment,
and the requirement that work help free us from egocentricity.

Social Justice

One of the frustrations in the study of Buddhist social ethics is the Buddha's apparent unconcern for social questions as such. Winston King,
who has contributed a fine study of Theravada ethics entitled *In the
Hope of Nibbana*, expresses this frustration as follows: "One of the features of the study of Buddhism most frustrating to the Western mind is
the effort necessary to discover a social philosophy within it. The question suggests itself: *Is* there any? . . . Where is any theory of the state,
any systematic philosophy of political power and its proper use, any interpretation of the meaning of human history? Has anyone ever portrayed the
ideal state, the Good Society, or Nibbana [Nirvana]-on-Earth?"[9] King goes
on to find elements of a social ethic in different tiles of the Buddhist
mosaic, but his initial observation is that the Buddha himself spent little
energy on social questions, focusing instead upon the individual who
needed release from a life shot through with suffering.

Walpola Rahula does not necessarily disagree with this characterization of the Buddha's main interest, but he does note that the Buddha's
teaching dealt with the life of laity in the world. So, for example, the
dharma takes up the various relationships that a person has to juggle,
noting that children should hold their parents sacred and venerate them
almost as gods. Parents, in turn, must bring their children up well,
providing them with education, a good marriage, and finally property
(through inheritance). Pupils should reverence their teachers, while
teachers should take a holistic view of their pupils' welfare, including
such matters as helping to secure them good jobs. Spouses should treat
one another with a religious respect. Indeed, the Buddha specified many
of the obligations of each spouse: "The husband should always honour
his wife and never be wanting in respect to her; he should love her and be

faithful to her; should secure her position and comfort; and should please her by presenting her with clothing and jewelry. . . . The wife, in her turn, should supervise and look after household affairs; should entertain guests, visitors, friends, relatives, and employees; should love and be faithful to her husband; should protect his earnings; should be clever and energetic in all activities."[10] Other relations clarified in such general yet helpful terms include those between friends, between masters and servants, and between monks and laity.

In literature attributed to the Buddha, Rahula finds the view that poverty causes immorality and crimes (this is why the Buddha opposed simply punishing offenders harshly), and the view that virtually no war is just. In his treatment of the ten duties of a king or governor, the Buddha showed how moral probity underlies good government, demanding that the ruler be liberal in dispensing his wealth, keep the five precepts of sila, put the interests of the people before his own, be honest in all his dealings, be kind, be austere in his personal habits, harbor no hatred or grudges, show patience, and not oppose the will of the majority.[11] Asoka has often been cited as the ruler who best exemplified this ideal, and his efforts to establish a nonviolent reign represent a high-water mark in the history of Buddhist pacifism. An interesting modern case involved the efforts of the Burmese politician U Nu to structure his country's affairs according to Buddhist principles, efforts that developed toward a Buddhist socialism.[12]

Most Buddhist politicians, including U Nu, have found it necessary to moderate the ideal of nonviolence (for instance, in dealing with insurgents against their country), and the majority of Buddhist countries have kept some form of capital punishment. Similar accommodations have been reached regarding killing animals, though nonviolence towards animals (and so vegetarianism) has remained the ideal. In all of these cases, the presence in society of a vigorous monastic Sangha in which the ideals could be quite strictly realized was both an assumption and something greatly desired.

Trevor Ling, who has written a good general account of the Buddha's life and the historical development of his teaching, notes a certain tension between the egalitarian government proposed for the monastic order and the monarchical government tolerated, if not in fact proposed, for lay society: "The unwisdom of the multitude, the need for social and economic stability as a prerequisite of the prescription to overcome this unwisdom, the emergence of powerful monarchically ruled states— these things together provide an explanation of why the Buddha, who seems to have regarded the republican *sangha* as the ideal form of government, nevertheless gave a large place in his teaching to the important role of the righteous monarch."[13]

For all the merit in the claim that the Buddha and later teachers dealt with the concrete problems of life in the world, the sense that the average person was unwise or ignorant, when combined with the powerful conviction that the greatest good in life was the attainment of nirvana, painted all this-worldly occupations in somewhat dark hues. Despite their importance, such material activities as gaining adequate wealth and securing social harmony seemed to the Buddha not worth one-sixteenth of the spiritual happiness that a faultless life could bring.[14]

One catches this tone in the chapter of *The Dhammapada,* a greatly beloved little ethical text, that is entitled "The World." The emphases are reminiscent of the very influential Christian work by Thomas à Kempis, *The Imitation of Christ:* "Do not follow the evil law! Do not live on in thoughtlessness! Do not follow false doctrines! Be not a friend of the world. . . . Look upon the world as a bubble, look upon it as a mirage: the king of death does not see him who thus looks down upon the world. . . . This world is dark, few only can see here; a few only go to heaven, like birds escaped from the net. . . . The niggardly do not go to the world of the gods; fools only do not praise liberality; a wise man rejoices in liberality, and through it becomes blessed in the other world. Better than sovereignty over the earth, better than going to heaven, better than lordship over all worlds, is the reward of the first step in holiness."[15]

As this translation suggests, early Buddhism had to work with Hindu notions of gods and other worlds. *The Dhammapada* also suggests how the Buddha and his followers undercut Hindu caste, because it makes the Brahmin not the person whose birth has set him or her at the highest social station but the person of greatest religious development. In other words, for Buddhism Brahminism or religious preeminence became a matter of personal character rather than social caste. Buddhism disregarded caste when it came to eligibility for the monastic life (it could cite Hindu traditions about the yogic vocation for support). That the Buddha himself came from the second caste has led some Buddhist historians to dispute the traditional preeminence accorded the priests, but further reflection moved the whole notion of spiritual leadership to another plane. Indeed, Buddhism has been remarkable for stressing that the only solid basis for such leadership is actual enlightenment. No doubt this criterion sometimes has not been fully honored, but in principle Buddhism has been a meritocracy: you are the wisdom you have attained.

The so-called "atheism" of Buddhism relates to this stress on personally achieved insight. In the oldest strata of the Buddhist ethical tradition one is counseled against any spiritual reliance except upon one's own will and mind. An example of such self-reliance is the Buddha himself, who did not gain release by means of the Hindu traditions and teachers but through the direct experience of meditative seeking. At a basic level, therefore, Buddhism has considered all human beings equal. Later Mahayana philosophy would teach that all possess the enlightenment-being and need only come to realize this. When ethicists were so minded, they could unite this sense of equality or democracy with the counsel to compassion and urge people to help the sick, give alms to the poor, and teach the ignorant, as expressions of Buddhist faith well rooted in the example and teachings of Gautama.

Nature

The teachings of Gautama largely assume the view of nature that prevailed in his time. According to this view, the realm of samsara includes all living things, and even the realm of the gods is less than nirvana. We may interpret the original Buddhist world view as still shaped by the cosmological myth, in that all beings are thought to share a similar sort of stuff (Buddhist-nature); but the Buddhist intuitions of an unconditioned realm at least strain the cosmological myth (which implies that nothing in nature is experienced as unconditioned, except perhaps the cosmos as a whole) and perhaps break it.

Ecologically, then, Buddha shared much of the Hindu sense that the world is a community to which human beings belong as only one set of citizens. Buddhist nonviolence toward animals symbolized the reverence that one ought to have for all being, and at the foundation of this reverence was the pervasive reality of the Buddha-nature (inner lightsomeness or intelligibility), which somewhat approximated the Hindu Brahman.

As we have mentioned, East Asian Buddhism took to heart the love of nature that was indigenous to the region, and poetic monks frequently used naturalistic themes to illustrate the religious ideal. Thus the Japanese monk Saigyo, who loved to wander aimlessly and point out that going is as important as arriving, would praise the spontaneity of trees and animals, in contrast to the painful reflectivity of human beings.[16] Where a pine tree or a carp just is what it is, without fuss and labor, a human being has to become human through education, experience, meditation, and much suffering. Japan always loved the image of holistic, spontaneous perfection. So did Chinese Taoists, in whose view the Tao of painting or calligraphy best expressed itself when the artist seemed to work with "no mind"—directly and effortlessly. Zen Buddhism took over this notion, urging warriors to attack and defend instinctively. The entire East Asian Buddhist notion of art and work was colored by such naturalism, for nature stood before all people as proof that life and productivity can occur without endless agonizing or splits between body and mind.

Buddhism had its equivalents of the Western eschatological literature, in which devout people could find projections of heaven or final perfection. The myth of the perfect realm of Shambala suggests that at the end there will be no need for an institutional Buddhism, and that life will be "seamless," as it is in physical nature: "For in the myth of

Shambala from the *Kalacakra*, after the destruction of the armies of the fanatical egocentrics led by their planetary Dictator, there is no temple or monastery, as the Holy Dharma is fully, 'seamlessly' expressed in the lives of all peoples."[17] Similarly, when Buddhists spoke of the Pure Land where the Buddha Amitabha (the object of much devotional love) would preside, they employed many naturalistic images. Thus they thought the Pure Land would have "a great variety of flowers and fruits, [be] adorned with jewel trees, which are frequented by flocks of various birds . . . on all sides it is surrounded with golden nets, and all round covered with lotus flowers made of all the precious things. Some of the lotus flowers are half a mile in circumference, others up to ten miles."[18]

The Jataka tales, in which various feats of the Buddha are described, portray the Enlightened One assuming the guise of various animals, reminding the reader of Buddhist views of karma and reincarnation. Obviously a world in which all beings are enmeshed in the same processes of birth and death is quite ecological. That the Buddha should assume the guise of a bird to help other creatures to salvation therefore seemed quite reasonable. Relatedly, the bodhisattva vow important in Mahayana Buddhism specified that the saint or Buddha-to-be would remain in the world, delaying full entry into nirvana to labor for the release of all living creatures, not just fellow human beings.

Buddhist rituals have tended to be fairly simple, the centerpiece usually being the recitation of portions of different sutras. Yet they have regularly been adorned with incense and flowers, and Buddhist monasteries have often won fame for their gardens and peaceful ponds. The Zen monasteries of Japan are especially famous in this regard; a principal emphasis in their arrangement of natural elements has been emptiness. Thus the famous Rock Garden Monastery in Kyoto features a series of angular rocks arranged asymmetrically on a bed of plain raked sand. The impact of this rock garden is an inseparable blend of the aesthetic and the religious, for while one's senses are delighted and soothed, one's mind is being taught the sacrality of bareness, space, and simplicity. As with the naturalistic imagery of many Buddhist haiku (brief poems), the ultimate objective is enlightenment: realizing that all things are empty and flowing.

This perspective has informed the famous Buddhist saying that before enlightenment, one senses trees as trees and rocks as rocks. During the struggle to gain enlightenment, one senses the mystery of trees, rocks, and everything else—the portentous quality of any being. After one attains enlightenment, however, trees are again just trees and rocks are again just rocks. The person who is fully integrated and wise knows and accepts the simple suchness of all things. What is is, and we are perfected or realized to the extent that we can deal with what is as it is. Even when present-day Buddhist masters accommodate this teaching to contemporary technology, admitting that we now have the power to change the way that many things in either nature or society exist, they retain the basic perspective that our fulfillment lies here—is available right now—in the seamless connectedness of the beings of the universe.

It is probably impossible to understand very much of such sentiment unless one has experienced the inner world of Buddhist meditation. From the beginning, Buddhists cultivated an intense purification and elevation of consciousness. Because of this heightened and sharpened inner awareness, the masters have interacted with the natural world more intensely than ordinary folk or Western culture generally has tended to do. Many descriptions of enlightenment have unity as a motif: the person finally experiences the non-dual character of all creatures. Sometimes such people refer to the One Mind of reality, and if they are philosophically astute they know that schools such as Yogacarin Buddhism taught that all reality was finally Mind only.

Tibetan Buddhists have played their own variations on these themes, their meditations often employing naturalistic mantras, or sacred sounds, and naturalistic mandalas, or sacred shapes. The stories of the most famous Tibetan saints picture them wandering in the snowy wastes of the Himalayas and undergoing great austerities, to purge themselves of human artifacts and find their original mind or being in which all things have fallen into proper place. The Tibetan saints also display features of the pre-Buddhist Tibetan shamanism, which was greatly concerned with spells and ghosts. This reminds us that the popular Buddhist reality was alive with the lingering forms of the dead, whom the ordinary people feared and tried to placate. Buddhism came to control the funerary rites of East Asia because of its metaphysical depth, but also because its naturalistic meditators had confronted this dimension of ghosts and taken away most of its terrors. The advanced Buddhist did not fear death. Nirvana, after all, was like the reality of the fire after one has blown out the candle, or like one's face before one's parents were born. It was a realm one could reach only by transcending the dichotomies of cultural existence and coming closer to the simplicity of natural existence. The ethics that it encouraged therefore was a simple, naturalistic expression of detachment and compassion for any fellow being in need.

Models

Gautama himself certainly has been the primary model of Buddhist ethics, though the historical Buddha has been less important in Mahayana schools than the metaphysical Buddha who manifests the deepest secrets of all reality. The stories of the prince Gautama giving up an apparently perfect life of sensual gratification and political power were very influential, as were the stories of how Gautama gained enlightenment and then spent the second half of his life instructing ignorant humanity.

These stories gave flesh or imaginative power to the twin virtues of wisdom and compassion. Gautama was the founder of the "Middle Way" (between excessive austerity and self-indulgence), as Buddhism liked to call itself, because he had solved the problem of human suffering. Both conceptually and practically, he had defeated Mara, the Buddhist Satan, who wanted to keep all living things in samsaric bondage. This quality of wisdom or enlightenment stamped all later Buddhist reflection on the moral life. Only those who were enlightened could even know what a proper ethics should be, because only they could know the true end of human beings and the nature of the obstacles standing in the way. Sometimes Buddhist Tantrists and Tibetan "crazy masters" expressed enlightenment quite provocatively, using sex or liquor or forbidden foods to dramatize that no tidy moral rules ever captured the essence of enlightenment. Because enlightenment is a holistic and finally ineffable grasp of nirvanic otherness or unconditionedness, no ruler can ever render it. Usually, however, Buddhist wisdom has been calm and sober.

The second great virtue of the Buddha was his compassion. Both the historical Gautama and the metaphysical **dharmakaya** or Teaching-Body of the Enlightened One were believed to relate to all living things with a deep sympathy for their sufferings. The Buddha's great insight, expressed in the Four Noble Truths, gave his religious career a therapeutic accent. He was like a spiritual physician, more concerned to bring patients to health than to speculate about the nature of their disease, let alone to hector them with threats of punishment. True, one can find in the Buddhist sutras rather gruesome descriptions of the hells to which people of evil will and bad karma will go, but the stress in such descriptions is on how, in ignorance, criminals have chosen to follow a path that led to punishment. Buddhism has no personal God who takes sinners' offenses as a rejection of love freely offered to them. One can find the theme that sinners are unappreciative of all that the Buddha has done for human beings, but the Buddha himself stays serene, whether people accept or reject the help he offers them.

Buddhist ethics, then, has tended to remain cool and detached. The "great compassion" (*mahakaruna*) that Gautama and the major bodhisattvas have displayed certainly bears similarities to the love of the biblical God (*hesed, agape*), but it lacks the passion of the biblical deity. The bodhisattva Kuan-yin, for all her maternal gentleness and desire to help, does not come across like the maternal God of the prophet Isaiah, who could never forget her nursing child.

We have to appreciate the Buddhist sense of what is most important in life before we can adequately criticize either this ethical coolness or the apparent unconcern of many Buddhists for social justice and economic reform. Buddhists have always felt that the main injuries in life come from self-chosen or karmically predetermined ignorance. Thus the main benefactions come from leading people out of their ignorance and

compassionately showing them the way to enlightenment. Only a profound enlightenment will get people out of the samsaric realm. Anything besides nirvana is no more than a band-aid remedy. People who are
not themselves enlightened are unlikely to do much good, and to go
rushing off to improve the world before one has gained true wisdom
probably will bring more harm than good. Buddhist ethicists, in other
words, have not stressed social problems the way Western ethicists have.
Buddhist ethicists would certainly agree that poverty, ignorance, illness,
and the like make a poor breeding ground for virtue, but they are more
interested in inner constraints, thinking that fifteen-sixteenths of the
blessings possible in life are spiritual.

Apart from Gautama and the famous bodhisattvas, the major models
in Buddhist life have been the members of the monastic Sangha, local
or famous from history, who embodied the ideal of enlightened living. In
Chinese Buddhism, for instance, the sixth patriarch of the southern
Ch'an school offered a model of sudden enlightenment (which that
school taught, somewhat in opposition to the gradualism of the northern school). Similarly, the example of Bodhidharma, founder of Ch'an,
was influential, his fierce insistence on the necessity of sitting in meditation becoming a staple of religious art. In Japan the saint Shinran, who
married to bring himself closer to the laity and preached a gospel of faith
in the compassion of the Buddha, offered a model of devotional Buddhism. Shinran, like those who urged reliance on the Lotus Sutra or
the Buddha Amitabha, thought that the present age was not conducive
to harsh or profoundly demanding ways to salvation. People needed
something simple and full of hope. Much like the Hindu bhaktas, then,
Shinran taught and modeled something more emotional than what either the classical Theravadin tradition, with its stress on ethical exact-
ness and scholastic philosophy, or the meditational schools such as Zen
were advocating.

The **Vinaya** or rule for Buddhist monks sheds further light on the
model of the Buddhist saint. Monks clearly were trying full-time, in
what we might call a professional way, to gain virtue, enlightenment,
and finally nirvana. They were the main teachers of the laity, through
both verbal instruction and overall example. Thus, to the ordinary requirements of the five precepts they added regular meditation, austerity
in diet ("no stomach more than two-thirds full"), begging for their food,
and periods of wandering interspersed with periods of removal for full-
time concentration on gaining enlightenment. The four misdeeds that
have merited expulsion from the monastic Sangha are fornication, theft,
killing, and falsely claiming spiritual attainments. Lesser yet still serious misdeeds for monks have included touching a woman or speaking
suggestively to her, exceeding the designated size or modest appointments of one's cell, falsely accusing other monks of violating the rule,
and fomenting discord or causing a schism. The Vinaya goes on to detail

many other actions that are forbidden, such as sleeping in another's space, sporting in the water, or showing levity in one's demeanor. The picture of the ideal monk that emerges is a person completely self-possessed, austere, compassionate toward all beings, and balanced between engagement in and hateful rejection of the world.

Finally we should note that Buddhism, like Hinduism, has sponsored a wealth of pious tales in which the faithful could see proper doctrine and ethical action exemplified. One such story concerns the coming of the Buddha to a Hindu town where the priests did not want him. They blocked all avenues of approach but he crossed the river by levitation. A servant girl perceived the goodness of the Buddha and, violating her master's orders, gave the Enlightened One water for drinking and washing. Her master beat her so severely for this disobedience that she died, but the Buddha caused her to return as a beautiful angel. "The angel identified herself as the former servant girl and described her mansion in the heavens as a large property having many buildings with high-peaked roofs, lotus ponds, a pleasant river with pure water and white, sandy beaches, and a magic tree able to grant all her wishes. All this splendor and her own beauty was her reward for giving water to thirsty holy men, she exclaimed, and added that anyone who, with the right attitude, did likewise could expect a similar reward."[19]

Summary

To orient our study historically, we sketched the career of Gautama, noted the rise of the Sangha, described the split between Theravadins and Mahayanins, mentioned the reign of the model king Asoka, outlined the missionary ventures of the third to sixth centuries C.E., and explained the demise of Buddhism in India. We then discussed the distinctions between Indian and East Asian Buddhism and offered a few observations on the historical fortunes of each.

We began our philosophical orientation by studying the Four Noble Truths in which Gautama expressed his enlightenment. We noted the Indian background of the Buddha's teaching, then explained the correlation of the Eightfold Path with the three Buddhist pillars of wisdom, meditation, and morality. We discussed the Buddhist acceptance of karma and samsara, the Buddhist rejection of the Atman, and the three marks by which Buddhists characterize all samsaric entities. We dealt with the Buddhist convictions about the interconnectedness of all phenomena and then explained the twelve stages of dependent coarising. Finally, we described the Mahayana radicalization of this beginning in terms of emptiness and the unity of samsara and Nirvana, indicating some of the consequences of this radicalization in East Asian Buddhist life.

In treating Buddhist family life we first made it plain that Buddhism

has praised monastic existence more; then we described the five basic
ethical precepts that have been incumbent on all Buddhists. We noted
how the laity were encouraged to support the Buddhist clergy and then
took up the question of the Buddhist acceptance of local marital customs. This led to an appreciation of the Buddhist concern for intention,
as well as a sketch of what marital arrangements and sexual practices
Buddhism has tended to favor. We dealt with parent-child relations and,
using an anthropological description of Buddhist life in Burma, explained
the ritualistic focus of a typically pious Theravadin family. After describing the function of the bodhisattva Kuan-yin, we considered the basic
Buddhist counsel to seek enlightenment.

Concerning work, we examined E. F. Schumacher's observations
about Burmese values, and we saw how he linked these values to the current ecological crisis and the related Western views of work. We elaborated the contrary Buddhist notions and then noted the place of Buddhist
views of karma and Buddhist contemplation. Walpola Rahula presented
us a useful interpretation of the Buddhist counsel to right livelihood, and
then Charles Prebish reminded us that the Buddhist sects that have
thrived in America have accommodated themselves to the American
dream of prosperity. We contrasted this with more traditional stresses on
egolessness and detachment, leaving the reader to resolve the apparent
contradictions.

Our treatment of Buddhist views of social justice first noted the
difficulty of finding a systematic Buddhist social ethics. Then we described Buddhist prescriptions for such fundamental social relationships
as parent-child and teacher-pupil. We described views of poverty and war
attributed to the historical Buddha, as well as the Buddha's ten precepts
for a king. This led us to remark again on the model of Asoka and to note
the efforts of recent politicians, such as the Burmese U Nu, to establish a
Buddhist commonweal. Trevor Ling explained the tension between the
Buddha's acceptance of monarchical rule for the state and his advocating
republican rule for the monastery. *The Dhammapada* reminded us that
Buddhist thought, overall, has qualified the value of all worldly doings.
We then dealt with the Buddhist rejection of Hindu caste, linking it with
a meritocracy based on virtue. Finally, we connected this stress on indi-
vidual achievement with Buddhist "atheism."

In describing Buddhist views of nature we noted Gautama's assumption of the basic Hindu cosmology, and so the traditional Buddhist appreciation of the interconnectedness of all beings. We then described how
Buddhism accepted the East Asian reverence for nature, and we described the place of natural objects in Buddhist descriptions of paradise.
We mentioned ecological features of the Jataka tales, the bodhisattva
vow, and Buddhist ritual; and we went on to consider Zen shrines and
Zen poetry, correlating the latter with a goal of utmost realism—dealing
with what is as it is. Finally, we dealt with the meditational aspects

of the Buddhist appreciation of nature as well as with several Tibetan motifs.

For ethical models we first nominated Gautama himself, suggesting the importance of the story of his renunciation, enlightenment, and decision to teach. We stressed his wisdom and compassion, noting how the latter gave his career a therapeutic cast. We dealt with the detachment and coolness of Buddhist compassion, then tried to explain the ethical significance of the Buddhist conviction that only enlightenment and nirvana cure the radical imperfection of human existence. The next models we considered were the famous Buddhist masters, who varied considerably in the virtues or capacities they demonstrated. Third, we dealt with the monastic model of human perfection, describing the drift of the Vinaya. And finally we suggested how the popular tales about the Buddha inculcated such virtues as generosity to travelers.

STUDY QUESTIONS

1. Explain the split between the Theravadin and Mahayanin Buddhisms.

2. What is the significance of the Buddhist teaching of anatman?

3. What impact would a faithful observance of the five precepts of sila likely have on Buddhist family life?

4. Why does the Buddhist notion of right livelihood proscribe trading in arms?

5. How adequate a political philosophy is the Buddha's sketch of the ten duties of a king?

6. Explain why East Asian Buddhists have considered nature superior to human culture and made it a model for human realization.

7. What role has the enlightenment of Gautama played in the Buddhist conception of society's greatest needs?

NOTES

[1] See Donald K. Swearer, *Buddhism* (Niles, Ill.; Argus, 1977); Kenneth K. S. Ch'en, *Buddhism* (Woodbury, N.Y.: Barron's, 1968).

[2] See Walpola Rahula, *What the Buddha Taught* (New York: Grove, 1974).

[3] See Edward Conze, *Buddhism: Its Essence and Development* (New York: Harper & Row, 1959).

[4] See Rita Gross, "The Householder and the World Renunciant: Two Modes of Sexual Expression in Buddhism," *Journal of Ecumenical Studies* 22 (Winter 1985): 81.

[5] Melford E. Spiro, *Buddhism and Society*, 2d ed. (Berkeley: University of California Press, 1982), pp. 209–10.

[6] E. F. Schumacher, *Small is Beautiful* (New York: Harper & Row, 1975), p. 51.

[7] Rahula, *What the Buddha Taught*, p. 47.

[8] Charles Prebish, *American Buddhism* (North Scituate, Mass.: Duxbury, 1979), p. 185.

[9] Winston L. King, *In the Hope of Nibbana* (La Salle, Ill.: Open Court, 1964), p. 176.

[10] Rahula, *What the Buddha Taught*, p. 79.

[11] *Ibid.*, pp. 84–85.

[12] See King, *In the Hope of Nibbana*, pp. 249–69.

[13] Trevor Ling, *The Buddha* (Baltimore, Md.: Pelican, 1976), p. 174.

[14] See Rahula, *What the Buddha Taught*, p. 83.

[15] *The Dhammapada*, trans. Irving Babbitt (New York: New Directions, 1965), pp. 28–29.

[16] See William LaFleur, "Saigyo and the Buddhist Value of Nature," *History of Religions* 13 (1973–74): 93–128 and 227–48.

[17] Robert Thurman, "Beyond Buddhism and Christianity," *Buddhist-Christian Studies* 3 (1983): 35.

[18] Edward Conze, *Buddhist Texts through the Ages* (New York: Harper & Row, 1964), pp. 202–3.

[19] Roy C. Amore and Larry D. Shinn, *Lustful Maidens and Ascetic Kings* (New York: Oxford University Press, 1981), pp. 120–22.

6

Chinese Ethics

Historical Orientation
World View
Family Life
Work
Social Justice
Nature
Models
Summary, Study Questions, Notes

Historical Orientation

India and China are the two great Asian cultures, and the likelihood is that China is the older. Archeological remains suggest that China had developed cities by about 3500 B.C.E., and around 1600 B.C.E. the Shang era of Bronze Age culture was in full swing. Confucius and Lao Tzu traditionally have been placed in the sixth century B.C.E., so for more than 2500 years China has had a "higher," philosophically articulate culture.

The prehistorical substratum of Chinese culture, like the substratum of the other religious cultures that we have considered, was animistic. In the Chinese case **shamans** and mediums seem to have flourished, and their influence has never died out. Indeed, the vast majority of Chinese have been peasants, even throughout the Common Era. Even today, when China has reached the staggering population of perhaps 1.03 billion people, the peasant life, with its strong ties to the land and the village clan, continues to be an important part of Chinese culture.

Religiously and ethically, the significance of the shamanistic substratum can be seen in the role that **oracles** have played in Chinese decision making. People confronted with hard choices, as well as people beset with sickness or family troubles, would consult a **diviner** or visit a local shrine. There they would receive a "fortune"—an indication from the fates or ultimate powers of what they ought to do. Similarly, people building a house would consult a **geomancer** (a specialist in the fortune-forces of the earth), to determine the most favorable site and orientation. People planning a wedding, a journey, or a new business venture would consult an astrologer to determine the most auspicious time. This sensitivity to the spirit forces running through nature and human life shaped the vast majority of Chinese, even those educated in the Confucian classics or persuaded by Buddhist philosophy.

We shall deal with the philosophies of the classical Confucians and Taoists in the next section. Here we should note that within a century or so of Confucius' death (479 B.C.E.), this Master was well on the way to being considered the great authority on Chinese mores and political thought because of the work of such respected disciples as Mencius. With ups and downs, Confucianism generally prevailed as the "orthodoxy" that shaped higher Chinese culture, including the court protocol and the literature on which the examinations for posts in the imperial bureaucracy were based. The slogan "In office a Confucian, in retirement a Taoist" implied that the poetic and philosophical attributes of the Taoists were better suited to private life. Buddhism, which always carried the liability of having non-Chinese origins, made a considerable impact because of its metaphysical depth. But on the whole, apart from the periods when Chinese emperors themselves were Buddhists, Buddhism was like Taoism in exerting most of its influence through personal rather than civic life.

After the era of Confucius and **Lao Tzu,** China went through a time of disarray, being pacified only during the early Han Dynasty in the third century B.C.E. About this time a movement that scholars sometimes call "religious Taoism" developed, giving the ideas of Lao Tzu and Chuang Tzu (another powerful early Taoist thinker) ritualistic form. The trade in silk opened China to the West late in the second century B.C.E., and by the middle of the second century C.E. Buddhism had started to make an impact. The fourth through sixth centuries C.E. brought military incursions of the Huns, while by the early seventh century China had started to shape the culture of Japan. The seventh and eighth centuries were a time of cultural renaissance, as China dominated central Asia, Chinese poetry flourished, and (about 730 C.E.) printing was invented. In the ninth century Buddhism was severely persecuted, on the charge of being foreign. Around the year 1000 Chinese painting and ceramics were enjoying a golden age, and in the twelfth century Neo-Confucianism, a reworking of the Confucian foundations in view of later metaphysical challenges such as those of the Buddhists, found its chief spokesman in the person of Chu Hsi.

The Mongols destroyed the Chinese empire in 1234. Marco Polo was in China in 1275, and on his return to Europe he started what became a long-standing Western fascination with East Asia. The Jesuit missionary

Matteo Ricci successfully represented Christianity at the Chinese court in the late sixteenth century. The Manchu Dynasty of the seventeenth century was a time of Confucian orthodoxy. China experienced Western influence and then dominance in the modern period, but hardly without resistance, both military and cultural. The Chinese have always considered their realm the center of the earth, so that even people who conquered them militarily have remained barbarians or only semihumans in their eyes.

The great event of the twentieth century was the victory of the Communists under Mao Tse-tung after the Second World War. The Maoist programs for cultural reform took aim at Confucianism as the decadent past viewpoint that had to be overthrown. The recent decades have certainly changed the face of China considerably, but they have also shown how strong a hold the Confucian and peasant traditions have retained at the cultural foundations.

For our purposes, the self-sufficiency of the Chinese stands out even during a cursory look at their history. China has been so vast a realm geographically, and so dense a culture in terms of population, that prior to very recent developments in travel and communications it could indeed think of itself as the center of the world. The West certainly has impinged in the last four centuries, but only very recently has China felt any strong need to fit itself into the international community. The advent of Buddhism early in the Common Era brought Indian notions close to the heart of Chinese culture, but even in this case China changed the intruder as much as the intruder changed China. Thus we find that Taoist notions that translators employed in rendering the Mahayana texts tended to concretize their abstractions, while the Buddhist sects regularly took on the appearance of Chinese clans, developing lineages of masters. Confucianism continued to dominate Chinese family life and political thought, and Taoism continued to inspire Chinese art.

Because of the power of the **cosmological myth,** and the correlative lack of a transcendent deity thought to have given a revelation from a realm beyond nature and history, higher Chinese culture has both fitted itself to the rhythms of nature and spent little energy on eschatology, the study of the end of history (which usually leads to an interest in divine judgment, heaven, and hell). Thus Confucius described himself as interested in worldly ethics and Chuang Tzu counseled people to accept death as part of nature's cycles.

The peasantry, however, have been greatly interested in the afterlife, with its heavens and hells. The connections between the present generation and the prior generations of ancestors were taken very seriously, while the popular imagination was filled with images of ghosts, occult forces, and progress up or down the ladder of karma or the architecture of heaven and hell. One sees the imprint of Buddhism at this point, and a carryover from the Buddhist influence in funerary rites. In many periods of Chinese history, gaining merit or better karma was a strong ethical motivation. In the villages Taoist priests tended to be the recourse for warding off diabolical forces, and accounts of Taoist exorcisms performed upon possessed victims are colorful indeed. So the picture of a sober Confucian moralism dominating Chinese religion or ethics certainly requires qualification. In most historical periods the overall situation was much more complicated and vivid.[1]

World View

We have considered the main ideas of Buddhism. By the time of the Neo-Confucian synthesis, they had become part of the Chinese fabric. The shamanistic foundations of Chinese culture, along with the folk dimensions of religious Taoism, helped "Confucianism" (considered as a popular and synthetic view of reality, rather than as just the strict views of Confucius himself or the Confucian intellectuals) include divination and ritualistic sacrifices—in many periods to Confucius himself. One of the key notions from Chinese prehistory that got into the Confucian outlook and was expressed in these activities was that of the **yin-yang** composition of all reality. These two forces—the one represented in passivity, femaleness, and darkness, the other represented in activity, maleness, and lightness—structured the Chinese outlook as a search for balance or harmony. In diet, religious ceremony, and aesthetics one sought the ideal blend of yin and yang. Yang tended to be the favored aspect, no doubt because of Chinese patriarchalism, but yin was considered equally fundamental and necessary.

A second feature of the Chinese search for harmony was the ancient conviction that a "Way" (**Tao**) runs through all reality, giving it proportion and direction. The Confucians were especially interested in the historical and ethical aspects of the Tao, while the Taoists were more interested in the metaphysical and spiritual aspects, but both schools agreed that human society and nature alike could be harmonious, and so prosperous, only when they followed the Tao. (Nature, to be sure, had little choice in this matter, so nature became a model for the flow and harmony that human beings ought to strive to attain).

The Confucians thought that the Tao had best been realized in the rulers of a golden age at the beginnings of Chinese historical memory. Indeed, Confucius described himself as merely a transmitter of the heritage from this age, not at all an innovator. The Chinese view of history therefore was both retrospective—looking back to better times at the beginning—and cyclic (moving from periods when the *Te* or force of the Tao was better expressed, to periods when it slackened, and then moving back to better times). The basic political conviction was that if leaders were virtuous—ethically powerful—through union with the Tao and fidelity to the example of the early heroes, then the common people would take their cue and live as they ought. This conviction led the Confucians to oppose political or legal theories that stressed brute force, harsh punishment, and compulsion. Confucius spent his life looking for a docile ruler who might put his ideals into practice.

The Master exerted most of his influence through an informal academy where he was attended by young men of good birth who came to be instructed in their moral heritage. The notion was that a "gentleman," someone well educated in both the outer form of Chinese etiquette and the inner spirit of moral integrity, would serve the best interests of his family and his country. For himself, virtue would be its own reward: he would gain peace and the respect of his neighbors. In fact the sage, on the model of Confucius, was the most honored personage in Chinese culture.

The outer forms of what was a quite ritualistic and hierarchized Chinese life came under the virtue of **li.** The gentleman schooled in li knew what do to in any given social circumstance, and he could move through the interaction graciously, whether it involved giving orders to a peasant or participating in a sacrifice at the imperial court. The great inner virtue in the Confucian scheme was **jen,** which translators render variously as "love," "humaneness," and "goodness." Confucius himself thought that jen was rare, though crucial, while Mencius thought that jen was fairly abundant because human nature was basically good. Both agreed that only jen kept Chinese protocol from being stuffy or even hypocritical, and the constant charge of the Taoists against the Confucians was that legalism or formality had come to predominate over a vital inner spirit—that is, that the Confucians had too little jen.

The Confucians did love order, and they thought in terms of hierarchical relationships. To their mind, nature had set rulers over ordinary people, men over women, teachers over students, and elders over the young. This latter hierarchical relationship both gave Chinese culture considerable stability and inclined it to conservatism if not inflexibility. The elders were not simply the oldest living generation, either, for veneration of those who had died—even those who had died many generations earlier—was a powerful factor in Chinese religious life.

The Taoists complemented these predominant Confucian views, and it is important to realize that the Chinese have never felt that they had to choose between Taoism and Confucianism (and Buddhism). People have been Confucian in some aspects of their lives, Taoist in other aspects, and perhaps even Buddhist in still others. As we have noted, Confucianism tended to dominate official life—business, politics, civic affairs—while Taoism was thought richer in resources for art, personal aesthetics, and meditation. Confucianism stamped family life more than Taoism did. Buddhism attracted intellectuals, people concerned about death, and the common people—this last group insofar as they thought about gaining merit for a better afterlife.

The key Taoist idea was that the Tao is the directive force of nature and that one could connect up with this force to great profit. The classical Taoist thinkers, Lao Tzu and Chuang Tzu, spoke of the paradoxical quality of the ways of the Tao, and they tended to think that present times, when human artifice flourished, were a sorry fall from a more vigorous earlier age when people had lived better connected to their source. Lao Tzu spoke in poetic images of the empty space that was more important to the utility of a house than the definite structures that contained such space. He used the infant, the female, and water dripping on rock as symbols of the indirect, apparently passive or weak way that much natural power is wielded. The Taoist notion of **wu wei,** a sort of passive action or effective not-doing, was transferred to politics, where it was translated into the policy that the least rule is the best. Politics, Lao Tzu said, is like cooking fish; the less stirring the better. Another key image in Lao Tzu's classical work, the **Tao Te Ching,** is that of an uncarved block, which to the Taoists represented human nature before it had been shaped by culture—when its potentiality was richest. The Taoists often accused the Confucians of so ritualizing and ordering life that they had wasted much human potential. The Taoists believed that law made criminals, that technological "progress" was usually regress, and that simplicity was better than complexity.

Chuang Tzu complemented Lao Tzu's politically oriented paradoxes and archaism with parables about the natural processes that the Tao runs and the implications of appreciating the Tao in personal life. He buttressed the instinctive Chinese desire for long life by setting the human being in the cycle of an ever-turning nature, arguing that the best way to survive is to avoid public notice—to be like the gnarled, ugly tree, rather than the straight, desirable tree. The heroes of old, to Chuang Tzu's mind, lived simply. They knew how to breathe (the Chinese have often considered the breath to be the vital force) and they slept soundly. When death came they did not lament and wail but accepted what was natural, knowing that just as they had drawn the materials of their existence from the earth so it was right that they should one day return those materials to the earth. Chuang Tzu had a keen ear for the paradoxes and arbitrariness of language, and he showed that much of what we call good or bad is relative to the framework we are using. He urged people to stretch themselves to the framework of nature and the Tao, thinking that this would likely give them more peace and wisdom.[2]

Family Life

The Confucian stamp on Chinese family life was clearest in the family's reverence for parents and the elderly. To obey one's parents and bring them honor was the first rule of a child's existence. Parents arranged one's marriage, and the transition of a bride to the home of her husband led to the proverbial notion that the best of daughters wasn't worth a splayfooted son. Because a girl would leave her natal household, spending resources on her was considered weeding another's field. In the extended family, which was the norm in China, a young bride came under the direction of her mother-in-law. She had no status until she produced children, especially sons, and she could expect to be involved in an emotional tug-of-war with her mother-in-law for the affection of her husband. Some scholars refer to this emotional situation as inevitably fostering "uterine politics." The only way that women could wield influence was through their children, so they manipulated their children shamelessly.

The second hierarchical relationship that the family derived from Confucian convictions was the rule of men over women (which made uterine politics necessary). It was simply assumed that men would have the final say in politics, family decisions, and culture. As things worked out, of course, women in fact could accumulate considerable influence. For example, a man who beat his wife could become the object of destructive gossip and social pressure. When she joined the other women at the river to do the wash, the battered wife would make sure that her bruises were plain. The other women would give their husbands no peace until they forced the abusive husband to reform. Women also gained economic power in many circumstances by running the family shop or working in the family garden plot. The stereotype of the Chinese wife included a sharp tongue and a tempestuous temper—more ways of righting the imbalance of power that the official Confucian views imposed.

Perhaps the saddest index of the misogyny latent in Confucianism was the practice of female infanticide. When a Chinese family became hard-pressed it would leave "excess" female babies out to die. Once fertility had been assured (a bride could be returned to her natal home if she proved infertile) and sufficient sons produced, there was little objection to contraception or abortion. The Taoists, who saw feminine nature stereotypically (as weak, indirect, manipulative) yet associated it with the tendencies of the Tao more closely than they associated stereotypically male nature (aggressive, direct, violent), fought against female infanticide and to some extent championed women's rights. Perhaps their own position as a minority or marginal school inclined them to remind the Confucians that yin forces were as crucial to life as yang forces.

The great veneration that children were to show their parents came to sharpest focus at the parent's death. Strict Confucians (people who wanted to follow the Chinese ideal as closely as possible) would retire from public life for up to three years to grieve and to reset their own lives. In effect this provided upper-class Chinese a moratorium in middle age for considering their own mortality and what they wanted to do with the rest of their lives. Socially, a child was judged by the honor it gave its parents, so there was great pressure to grieve ostentatiously. Thus when a

Chuang Tzu made light of death, noting that it was a part of nature's pattern that none of us could escape, he poked holes in the Confucian ritualization of the critical time when the generational guard changed.

Another hierarchical characteristic of the Chinese family was the dominance of elder children over younger children. Especially important was the role of the eldest son, who succeeded to direction of the family on the death of the father. Even in later life, when siblings might be sixty and fifty years old, the eldest son would expect to have a say in the affairs of his younger siblings, and the younger siblings would be primed to seek the advice of the eldest.

In the royal household there usually was a retinue of concubines, so that historians speak of the royal harem, but in the ordinary household monogamy was the rule. Still, a husband looked upon his wife as the mother of his children rather than as his friend, lover, or confidante. She might fill those roles, of course, if the chemistry between them was right, but it was legitimate for a man to seek sexual pleasure outside of marriage, and the sexes tended to be segregated socially, so men found most of their friendship with other men. The chastity of the bride and then the wife was important, with the result that women's movement was considerably curtailed. Some feminists, in fact, see the painful practice of footbinding—wrapping women's feet so that they would not attain their normal size but would remain tiny—as a tellingly ugly symbol of men's desire to keep women from running around. Other commentators stress the aesthetic ideal that was at work here—tininess and a mincing gait were considered important features of feminine beauty—and note that footbinding actually was practiced for only a relatively short time in Chinese history (the late-medieval and premodern centuries).

When Western missionaries came to China and tried to adapt Christianity to Chinese traditions they found problems in the practice of ancestor veneration. Some missionaries thought that the Chinese were worshiping the departed members of their clans, while others (better informed) realized that the rites and obeisance enacted at family shrines were more a matter of loyalty, remembrance, and honor. The family was, to be sure, concerned to ward off the potentially baneful influence of the departed, who stayed around for a considerable period in ghostly form. The instinct was that if an ancestor had not died peacefully, or had a grievance against living members of the family, that ancestor might cause trouble or bring bad luck. When Buddhism had made its mark on Chinese thought, children had to try to gain merit to improve the karma of deceased ancestors, and popular literature of the post-Buddhist period speaks of sacrifices through which children would send money and goods to secure their parents' happiness in the afterlife.[3]

C. K. Yang, whose sociological study of religion in Chinese life is a good source of details and lore, suggests the ritualistic life of the family when he writes: "As an act of making an offering to the spirits, sacrifice in its simplest form might consist of daily burning of incense, morning and night, and reverential bowing in front of a symbol of the spirit, which was usually a wooden tablet or a portrait. The fragrant smoke spiraling from the burning incense was a means of contacting the invisible spirits of the ancestors and, in the belief of some people, constituted the daily ration for their sustenance. This means of communication with the dead, along with the visible symbol of the ancestral tablets and reverential bowing, served as a reminder of the existence of the role of the dead among the living. . . . Besides incense, there was the burning of candles and paper money as a means of communicating with and providing sustenance for the spirits. Above all, there was the offering of food and drink, always a central item on sacrificial occasions."[4]

Family life could turn harsh, of course, when one's children or spouse died. The offspring on whom one had pinned one's hopes for a secure old age could be gone in a twinkling. At such times the Chinese tended to invoke a fatalistic sense that the world moved by patterns beyond their understanding. Buddhists would seek solace in veneration of a favorite saint, perhaps Kuan-yin, or they would speak of the inscrutable influence of karma. Peasants would speak of the uncertain influence of the spiritual forces that controlled all luck, both good and bad. The main thing, however, was for the clan to continue. All peoples, no doubt, have sought fertility and continuance, but the Chinese stand out as especially fervent in their pursuit. Chinese images of the afterlife, for all their imaginative sportiveness, probably were less influential than the sort of immortality represented by many offspring and a vigorous old age. The linking of the familial generations was the dominant factor shaping the ethics of the typical Chinese household.

Work

In Chinese culture, work varied greatly with one's social station, as it did in all other religious cultures. The peasantry who formed the base of traditional Chinese society worked hard, either on their own small plot of land or on the estate of a nobleman. The mercantile class also worked hard, associating in guilds to stimulate trade (in part by sponsoring sacrifices to guild deities). The upper classes enjoyed more leisure, but the culture at large accorded them considerable respect because of the responsibilities that their position of leadership entailed.

At the top of the Chinese hierarchy, the emperor or provincial governor not only headed the civil bureaucracy but also performed priestly or ritualistic tasks. The conviction behind this fusion of secular and sacred roles was twofold. First, traditional China, like most traditional societies, made no hard-and-fast distinction between the secular and the sacred. Religion was simply the soul of the whole culture. Second, traditional China moved to the rhythms of the cosmos, thinking that human society would prosper when it best fitted itself to the patterns of the Tao. The seasonal sacrifices of the emperor therefore connected earth below with heaven above. Unless the virtue (te) of heaven above flowed through the emperor to earth below, the people could expect hard times. We shall see the political implications of this conviction in the next section, when we discuss the **mandate of heaven** that was necessary to legitimate dynastic rule in China.

Insofar as the sage was the most honored figure in Chinese society, scholarship and meditational study had considerable prestige. China associated wisdom with old age, mainly because the Chinese saw wisdom as practical or prudential and believed that one could attain it only through long experience. Also, however, much time was necessary for the potential sage to penetrate the traditional texts and learn their wisdom from within. There was a famous saying that when Confucius had reached seventy he could do as he wished, because his own will and the Tao had become fused.

The motivation to work hard in Chinese society came from the desire for material gain, certainly, but perhaps even more from the desire to honor—or not to dishonor—one's parents and ancestors. "Shame," as Western observers frequently call it, has been a powerful motive in East Asian society. It is not embarrassment at personal failure, let alone guilt about moral failure, so much as a sense of having proved an ingrate to one's lineage and brought its good name into disrepute. Students raised in this Confucian mold have felt intense pressures to do well, especially in their crucial examinations. People in the contemporary United States, pondering the remarkable academic success of Chinese, Japanese, Vietnamese, and other East Asian Americans, should indeed investigate the results of tests of raw intelligence; but in all likelihood, the sense of responsibility that centuries of Confucian family mores have ingrained is at least as powerful a factor as intelligence in this success.

Women's work also varied with their station in society, upper-class women working mainly to make themselves adornments of their husbands and champions of their children's advancement. Middle-class women regularly worked both in the house and in the family shop or trade, while peasant women worked in the fields and cared for the smaller animals. Often life was hard, food was scarce, children were numerous, and disease could sweep in suddenly. Infant mortality rates were sobering, and many women died in childbirth. Somewhat marginal women functioned as diviners or **mediums,** but the official religious work—the Taoist and Buddhist priesthoods (which entailed caring for a shrine) and the Confucian politico-ritualistic offices—was reserved for men. Women could enter the Buddhist monastic Sangha, and Chinese Buddhist nuns frequently were the objects of venomous gossip and dislike because their simple existence, outside of any counsel they might give to other Chinese women, challenged the Confucians' complete subordination of women to men.

Serving in the government bureaucracy was important work in Chinese society. For many posts, people had to pass "civil service" examinations, the basis of which was Confucian lore and classical literature. The slant of governmental policy, in other words, was ethical as much as empirical or factual. China always retained the conviction that the character of the worker was as important as the knowledge or skill. The different historical changes in the Chinese economy naturally meant fluctuations in the distribution of wealth, but through such changes Chinese social structures remained more consistent than those of the West.

Thus Jacques Gernet, writing about daily life in China in the thirteenth century c.e., on the eve of the Mongol invasions, contrasts the medieval developments of China and Europe: "The commercial development of China from the eleventh to the thirteenth centuries was contemporaneous with a similar development in Europe. But the vigorous economic expansion which took place at that time in China is on an altogether different scale from its Western counterpart. The volume of commercial growth in China was commensurate with the size of its population, the amount of its wealth, its vast area, and its advanced stage of technological development. The exaggerations of Marco Polo at the end of the thirteenth century merely express the astonishment of the traveller from the West at finding a commercial activity more intense than that of Genoa or Venice at the same epoch. And yet this sudden increase of vigour in the economy of both Europe and the Far East had very different results. In Europe, cut up as it was into a multitude of separate jurisdictions and powers, the merchant class was able to assert itself, have its rights recognized, and form an entity of its own. Towns gained their liberties and urban institutions appeared, the opposition between town and country became permanent, and the rise of a bourgeoisie which was the first step toward the formation of the Third Estate was to have important consequences for the future destiny of the West. In China, in spite of the gigantic scale of development, nothing more happened than that merchants became wealthy."[5]

The reason for this difference, in Gernet's view, was the pervasive power of the Chinese central government. For while China certainly had local or provincial traditions and differences, for hundreds of years the dominant social pattern had been one of a relatively unified empire. The mythical justification for the imperial power was the identification of the head of the ruling clan with the divinity called "Heaven." This head, somewhat like the Pharaoh of ancient Egypt, connected the realm of ultimate power with the human realm. In Europe, Christian and Greek sources had steadily elaborated a more individualistic view of human nature. The single person came to be as important as the family tribe, and a variety of different languages and customs divided up the European continent. In theory there was a single Holy Roman Empire during many eras, but in fact local kings and dukes directed most of the politics.

Chinese ethical literature certainly urged workers to uphold the standard virtues of diligence, honesty, and integrity. Indeed, the Confucian viewpoint depended more on a personal sense of integrity than it did on threats of punishment or prospects of reward by outer agencies (God, gods, saints, or demons). Laziness and corruption did exist, of course, and in some periods actually flourished. Bribery and intrigue regularly were rife at the courts, and banditry, along with dishonest trade, harassed the middle classes. Overseers could easily mistreat their peasants, whose recourse was the standard ploy of slowing down their work and playing dumb. Prostitution, drug dealing, and criminal activities kept many busy. People enjoyed watching opera and gymnastics, while art forms such as landscape painting and ceramics made China famous. Chinese technology made many notable achievements, from printing to gunpowder, while Chinese cuisine became world-famous. The overall impression, then, is of a very industrious people, not only vast in numbers but energetic in projects and deals.

Social Justice

While traditional China never had social stratifications as rigidly or as religiously sanctioned as those of Indian caste, from the formative period the Chinese did think in terms of classes that nature had established. The Confucian reforms associated with the term **rectification of names** were meant not only to tidy up the logic of official discourse but also to assist an ethical repristination based on more clearly assigning the different social tasks.

Donald Munro has explained the context and intent of these reforms as follows: "A simpler division of the basic social positions included ruler, minister, father, son, older brother, younger brother, husband, and wife. The social function of each position was spelled out, and Confucian teachers saw one solution to the political strife of the time in causing people to live up to the ideal descriptions of these positions. 'Let the prince be a prince, the minister a minister, the father a father, and the son a son,' said Confucius. One aspect of social function was the famous Confucian doctrine of the rectification of names (cheng ming), which had both ethical and logical applications in China. The original intent was ethical, based on the belief that once names have firm meanings they will almost magically serve as effective standards of conduct. For example, if the meaning of 'king' were fixed and changes in its content were impossible, no upstart adventurer would dare to call himself a king, as so many were doing; moreover, a legitimate ruler would be intimidated into acting in accordance with the ideal prescription. The same held for the other social positions. If *cheng ming* could be effectively carried out, the social order would become firmly established."[6]

These prescriptions, to be sure, arose during a period of special turmoil, and they never gained complete acceptance. Still, they suggest the Confucian desire for social stability, as well as the very conservative cast of Confucian thought. The Confucian masters, including Confucius himself and Mencius, moderated all such notions with an insistence that the ruler be virtuous and the gentleman be as filled with jen as possible. They argued that the only effective rule was by example, and that one of the keys in the example of kings and dukes was their generosity to their people. For instance, if the king or duke could persuade the people that the royal park was a public domain set aside for the enjoyment of all the people, and not just a hunting ground for the upper classes, no tract of land would seem too vast. On the other hand, if the people resented the royal park, thinking that it symbolized a rulership contemptuous of them and seeking only its own pleasure, the smallest reserved tract would draw their wrath.

When Chinese reformers or adventurers wanted to oust the present regime and start a new rule or dynasty, they could appeal to the doctrine of "the mandate of heaven." As a consequence of the Chinese sense that virtue passed down from heaven to the heads of the human realm, when things were out of joint in the human realm one could question whether the present regime still retained its legitimacy. The criteria for whether heaven was supporting the current emperor were slippery, of course, but a certain pragmatism, according to which the most legitimate rule was the one that actually brought peace and prosperity, enabled adventurers to capitalize on hard times or chaos—or even to foment hard times or chaos—and call for a revolution.

For Mencius, whose views had an impact second only to that of Confucius, the crux of whether the mandate of heaven had been lost was whether a ruler was effectively exerting himself for the people. Mencius believed that human nature essentially was good, so that when people observed their ruler laboring diligently on their behalf they were likely to be appreciative and follow his example in their own dealings. One could not say that Mencius was a forerunner of the Communists who came to power in the middle of the twentieth century, but he does seem to share with Mao Tse-tung and the Communists a conviction that political power ought to be exercised mainly on behalf of the people at large.

The history of China, like the history of India, is remarkable for the number and destructiveness of its wars. Apart from the Buddhists, whose convictions about ahimsa inclined them to pacifism, the leading Chinese ethicists seem to have accepted war as a fact of life. Their efforts went mainly toward humanizing war and lessening the sufferings it caused.

Several rather enigmatic sayings in the *Analects* of Confucius bear on this project. For example, in 13:29 the Master is quoted as saying, "When good men have instructed the people [in morals, agriculture, military tactics] for seven years, they may be allowed to bear arms."[7] The explanation set in brackets, which comes from the Neo-Confucian master Chu Hsi, implies that war is legitimate as long as the populace has sufficient knowledge to estimate what it is getting into. The quotation may also mean that a war deemed necessary after people have been brought to the point where they could support themselves and arbitrate their disputes probably is just or reasonable. That the instruction includes military tactics probably expresses the Confucian conviction that people going out to war should have a chance of avoiding being slaughtered and of attaining victory. In 13:30 Confucius is quoted as amplifying this conviction: sending people out to war without such instruction is betraying them.

Lao Tzu is much more critical of war, and Taoists generally thought that the use of force tended to bring more harm than good. Chapter 30 of the *Tao Te Ching* expresses Lao Tzu's skepticism: "He who assists the ruler with Tao does not dominate the world with force. The use of force usually brings requital. Wherever armies are stationed, briers and thorns grow. Great wars are always followed by famines. A good (general) achieves his purpose and stops. He dares not seek to dominate the world. . . . (For) after things reach their prime, they begin to grow old, which means being contrary to Tao. Whatever is contrary to Tao will soon perish."[8]

In the sixth to the tenth centuries c.e. Buddhism flourished in China, and with this flourishing came a certain modification of previous harshness in military life and criminal justice. Rulers were encouraged to grant occasional amnesties or to remit death sentences, in the name of the Buddhist compassion and veneration for life. During the first, fifth, and ninth months of the year, which were times of penance in the Buddhist calendar, the emperors forbade executions, and medieval Buddhism also stimulated many imperially supported charitable works, such as dispensaries, free hospitals, and hostels for travelers. Monks built bridges, planted shade trees, and encouraged giving alms to people outside one's clan as a way of improving one's karma.

On the other hand, medieval Chinese rulers were not beyond coopting Buddhist notions of karma and the spiritual fate of the personality for their own ends. For example, when they were having difficulty enlisting soldiers for foreign battles because burial away from home was repugnant to Confucian sensibilities (one could neither honor one's ancestors nor receive sacrifices at the family shrine oneself unless one's corpse was there), the leaders of the Sui and T'ang dynasties built shrines for the dead in the foreign lands of battle and argued that, as the Buddhists taught, the spiritual aspects of the personality were more important than the bodily aspects, and that the spiritual aspects could be as active for parents from afar as from close to home.

Finally, we could generalize about the Chinese legal system, which tried to help the Chinese actualize their ideals of social justice, by noting that it has stressed duties more than rights. John C. H. Wu sees this as leading to the fusion of law and ethics, in contrast to Western tendencies, and he does not hide his preference for the Chinese attitude: "The emphasis being on duties, the law has never been freed from its dependence on morality. This forms a contrast to the legal systems of the West in modern times, especially in the heyday of individualism, when the emphasis was decidedly on rights rather than duties, with the result that the science of law tended to be divorced from ethics, and in a number of cases the decision became shocking to the moral sense of man."[9]

Nature

The moral sense of traditional Chinese men and women was framed and restrained by their deep immersion in the cosmological myth. They thought of themselves as fellow-participants with animals, plants, and inanimate creation in a single living organism ruled by Tao. The rituals of Chinese life, which Herbert Fingarette rightly has made the cornerstone of social harmony,[10] also fitted the people to the rhythms and elements of nature. Many of the most venerated songs from ancient times celebrated seasons or beauties of nature. Nature was not only the source of human nourishment; it was also the larger context that gave human affairs their proper perspective.

Human life was short and the life of the cosmos seemed without beginning or end. Human life was troubled and one had to grope one's way along, but nature just did what it did, just was what it was. Lao Tzu consistently spoke of the ten thousand things that the Tao ruled—all creatures, great and small. The supreme folly, in his eyes, was running against the grain of nature's Way. Confucius, to be sure, was more interested in human affairs, but he too felt that those who only paid court to the "stove" (human prosperity) and neglected Heaven would have no recourse when human fragility let them down.

The religious Taoists turned to **alchemy** and various yogic regimens (breath-control and retention of the semen during intercourse, for example) to try to gain a physical longevity if not immortality. The basic world view that we may broadly call Confucian assigned different elements values of yin and yang, and it analyzed all things for their ratios of the five basic natural elements: water, fire, metal, wood, and earth. Religious Taoists employed both of these notions in rituals such as exorcism, trying to give the priest and victim allies in their fight against the demonic possessor. The divination text called *The Book of Changes* assumed that one could read or even influence the future through the patterns that different lines, representing both human and natural forces, would assume when interpreted by casting lots. The geomancy that we have mentioned expressed the Chinese conviction that how a human dwelling sat on the land—its relations to water, wind, and the directions of the compass—had a great deal to do with whether the inhabitants would prosper or suffer bad luck.

These and many other commonplace aspects of traditional Chinese life suggest the ecological cast of Chinese religion and ethics: the forces of nature were always assumed to be important actors in the drama at hand. Nonetheless, the Chinese were also quite willing to apply their current technology to nature and try to improve their share in nature's beauty or bounty. This led to numerous abuses of nature that historians of technology and ecologists have noted, often in an effort to disabuse Westerners of the notion that the East has been a paragon of respect for nature. For example, René Dubos, drawing on the classic work of Joseph Needham, *Science and Civilisation in China*, has reminded his readers that until the seventeenth century C.E., China was far ahead of Europe in science and technology, and that often it used this knowledge to massively destructive effect.[11] For example, writings of the medieval period lament the erosion and deforestation of the hills of central and northern China, which once had been beautifully treed. The likelihood, based on patterns of deforestation around the world, is that overgrazing and fires (or the cutting of trees for firewood) were the cause. In other words, human beings, not natural forces, had produced such environmental disasters. Even Buddhist monks had a share in nature's abuse, for to build their many temples they did not scruple to cut down huge numbers of trees, apparently without bothering to replant as they went. Yi-Fu Tuan, on whom Dubos also draws, estimates that in some periods Buddhist temples accounted for half the consumption of timber. Another great source of destruction was the need for charcoal, which the industrial expansion from the tenth century C.E.—an expansion involving the manufacture of metals, salt, bricks, tiles, and liquor—made a necessary commodity.

The expansion of Chinese cities, several of which housed more than a million people, also made the medieval period a time when the forest primeval was sacrificed to the needs of human development. Tuan cites as an example the city of Hangchow, capital of the southern Sung dynasty, which greatly expanded in the thirteenth century C.E.: "The demand for timber was such that some farmers gave up rice cultivation for forestry. Cities in which houses were so largely made of wood ran the constant danger of demolition by fire; and this was essentially true of the southern metropolises where the streets tended to be narrow. The necessity of rebuilding after fire put further strain on timber resources. But of even greater consequence than the accidental burning of parts of cities was the deliberate devastation of whole cities in times of upheaval, when rebels or nomadic invaders toppled a dynasty. The succeeding phase of reconstruction was normally achieved in quick time by armies of men who made ruthless inroads upon the forest."[12]

One sees from this actual ecological practice that Taoist and Buddhist lyricism about nature did not hold "developers" back from laying nature waste when urban expansion or other human needs seemed acute. Nonetheless, Marcel Granet and other scholars have shown the reverence for nature at the roots of the Chinese cultural tradition, and this reverence suggests that the Chinese who despoiled nature violated their own better roots, whether they realized it or not.

The reverence for mountains and rivers that we find in the ancient texts was part of a reliance on the prince, who interacted with these and other natural phenomena at the seasonal sacrifices, to guide the people through their socionatural existence. And it does seem that the Chinese frequently projected onto nature the order that they were trying to achieve in human affairs. (It is also true, as we have indicated, that they used the movement of the Tao through nature as a model for those human affairs.) In Granet's own analytical terms: "It has long been known that Mountains and Rivers played an important part in the official religion and in the popular beliefs of the Chinese. From the most remote antiquity, we are told, Mountains and Rivers have been objects of worship in China. This statement is liable to be misinterpreted. . . . Let us see what the texts say: 'Mountains, forests, rivers, valleys, heights, hills, have the power to produce clouds, to make rain and wind, and to cause portents to appear: of all these things it is said that they are *Shen*, sacred powers.' 'It is the sacred powers of mountains and rivers who are entreated by means of sacrifices when floods, droughts, or epidemics befall.'"[13]

The folklore that pictured mountains as the backs of dragons, upon whom the world sat, and that found spirits animating every glen and glade, fitted well the ordinary Chinese peasant's animistic sense that forces, both good and bad, ran through nature everywhere and everywhere had to be placated and won over. An intellectual such as Chuang Tzu builds on this foundation when he goes on to use familiar animals to illustrate his philosophical or even mystical teachings. For example, to make his regular point that how we evaluate what happens to us depends heavily on our perspective, he contrasts the life span of the mushroom and the cicada with longer-lived creatures: "The morning mushroom knows nothing of twilight and dawn; the summer cicada knows nothing of spring and autumn. They are short-lived. South of Ch'u there is a caterpillar which counts five hundred years as one spring and five hundred years as one autumn. Long, long ago there was a rose of Sharon that counted eight thousand years as one spring and eight thousand years as one autumn. They are long-lived. Yet P'eng-tsu alone is famous today for having lived a long time [much shorter, however, than the rose of Sharon] and everybody tries to ape him. Isn't it pitiful!"[14]

Models

As the preceding quotation implies, the ideal of traditional China was to live to a ripe old age, vigorous and surrounded by many children. For Chuang Tzu this is slightly ridiculous, since a mere glance at nature shows that the best human span is insignificant compared to the life of nonhuman creation. Yet Chuang Tzu himself urges people to follow the Taoist way (of staying hidden and accounted insignificant) as a tactic of self-preservation. He also seems to draw on a meditational regimen that vitalizes his spirit and allows him to wander imaginatively through the vastness of creation. Insofar as Chuang Tzu and other sages like him have been primary models of the Chinese ethical ideal, we can say that the actions praised in traditional China usually were those that conduced to longevity and gaining cosmic perspective (family honor was also crucial).

The most influential model that the Confucians favored was assembled from the teachings and practice of the Master himself. Confucius most revered the legendary rulers of the earliest dynasties, whom memory had gilded and mythologized. Foremost among them was Tan, Duke of Chou, whom Confucius placed first among the early rulers who had governed by their virtue, a trait that made them only slightly less noble than the *Sheng* or divine sages of the ideal beginning age. Arthur Waley's description of Shun, one of these divine sages, captures the portrait that inspired all later Confucian and Neo-Confucian disciples: "The eulogy of Shun [*Analects* 8 : 20] which follows tells us that with only five servants to help him he kept order 'everywhere under Heaven.' Elsewhere he is said to have ruled by *wu-wei* (non-activity) [a notion much beloved of the Taoists, as we have seen], through the mere fact of sitting in a majestic attitude 'with his face turned to the South.' We have here the conception, familiar to us in Africa and elsewhere, of the divine king whose magic power regulates everything in the land. It is one that is common to all early Chinese thought, particularly in the various branches of Quietism that developed in the fourth century B.C. The *Sheng*, however, only 'rules by non-activity' in the sense that his divine essence (*ling*) assures the fecundity of his people and the fertility of the soil. We find Shun assisted in his task by 'five servants,' who are clearly conceived of as performing the active functions of government."[15]

We have mentioned the traditional association of the emperor or prince with the cycles of nature. Here the added notion is that at his station in the sacro-naturalistic order of cosmic powers the ruler performs his functions by simply being. His subordinates care for the doing—the ordering, supervising, instructing, and disciplining—necessary for the functioning of the realm. In later periods, when the typical sage was not the ruler but was a private person such as Confucius or Lao Tzu trying to influence culture from the margins, the model had a more accusatory motif. Because those who were running the realm, both the heads and the bureaucratic members, were not traditional, virtuous, ordered, and selfless like Confucius, things were in disarray. The way back to peace and prosperity was to apply the teachings of the Master and follow his example in one's personal habits.

The example of the ancients and the precepts of the classical texts continued to shape Chinese culture well into the modern era. Thus the valedictory address of K'ang-hsi, the Manchu emperor who ruled from 1661 to 1722 C.E., is replete with the proverbial wisdom of the past on which he had constantly nourished himself. Written in 1717, it no doubt intends to put a final polish on his achievements, but even when taken critically it suggests the genuine moralism or desire for ethical praise-worthiness that motivated all educated Chinese: "The rulers of the past all took reverence for Heaven's laws and reverence for their ancestors as the fundamental way in ruling the country. To be sincere in reverence for Heaven and ancestors entails the following: Be kind to men from afar and keep the able ones near, nourish the people, think of the profit of all as being the real profit and the mind of the whole country as being the real mind, be considerate to officials and act as a father to the people, protect the state before danger comes and govern well before there is any disturbance, be always diligent and always careful, and maintain the balance between leniency and strictness, between principle and expediency, so that long range plans can be made for the country. That's all there is to it. . . . The 'Great Plan' section of the *Book of History* says of the five joys: The first is long life; the second is riches; the third is soundness of body and serenity of mind; the fourth is the love of virtue; the fifth is an end crowning the life. The 'end crowning the life' is placed last because it is so hard to attain."[16]

K'ang-hsi goes on to note that he is now nearing seventy, his sons, grandsons, and great-grandsons number over 150, and the country is more or less at peace. He is ending well, in other words, and he wants the respect of his people—their realization that he has exhausted his strength on their behalf. The average Chinese, throughout history, no doubt has been grateful for the rare ruler like K'ang-hsi, who at least could make a good case that the welfare of the people had been his heart's desire. Through many periods of corrupt rule, that manifestly was not the case. The average Chinese therefore took the model of the sagacious ruler with a grain of salt, thinking that ethical precepts and reverence for the ways of Heaven were all very well, but that many rulers in fact did not bother with them.

Because many rulers did not bother with the ethical ideals and many lives were rife with suffering, ordinary people—especially the women and peasants who fell outside the ranks of privilege—contented themselves with trying to gain a measure of respect in their own family circle. To be honorable within the clan was a realistic goal, and the criteria for such status included respect for one's elders, not disgracing the family lineage, and surviving the attacks of nature and one's enemies that imperiled one's own longevity. Maxine Hong Kingston has recently put many of these sentiments into artistic form, showing how they continued to form life in San Francisco's Chinatown in the mid-twentieth century.[17]

For example, one of the cautionary tales that formed Kingston's girlhood psyche was the story of her aunt's disgrace. In the old country the aunt, her father's sister, had been married to a man who left their village to seek work abroad. He had been away several years when it became noticeable that the aunt was pregnant. The villagers persecuted the family for this breach of local mores, so much so that the aunt drowned herself and her newly born infant in the family well shortly after giving birth. Prior to her mother's recitation of this tale, Kingston had not even known of the aunt's existence. Her father and the rest of the family had cut the aunt from the family tree because of the disgrace she had brought.

The sense one gets from traditional Chinese ethics is that such shaming was more important than any objective moral analysis. Had the family not been disgraced, perhaps a sympathetic reading of the aunt's lonely circumstances could have excused her misdeed. But the villagers knew everything that went on, down to the last detail, and the villagers' investment in the traditional mores (as a wall of defense against chaos, which they pictured as both nature and society running amok) was so heavy that the offending family had to be severely punished. The adulterous aunt did the honorable thing in removing herself from the family circle. Even when one has discounted the envy, perverse satisfaction in the misfortune of others, and vindictiveness that puritanism tends everywhere to generate, one has to be awed by the power of the Chinese sense of family honor. The most influential models of traditional Chinese mores were distinctly premodern in their nearly complete subjugation of the individual to the welfare of the tribe. The virtues most praised, in the final analysis, were those that guarded the family honor.

Summary

We began our historical orientation by noting the antiquity of Chinese civilization and its animistic substratum. We spoke of the "official" influence of the Confucians and of how Taoism and Buddhism shaped "retirement." We mentioned key eras in the history of China after the time of Confucius and Lao Tzu, underlining the influence of Buddhism after the second century C.E. One lesson we drew was the relative self-sufficiency that has characterized the Chinese down through the ages. Finally, we sketched the noneschatological character of higher Chinese culture, which contrasts with the great interest of the folk religion in the afterlife.

In dealing with the basic philosophy of traditional China we first explained the broader connotations of the term *Confucianism* and then the important role of yin/yang. We dealt with the concept of the Tao, explaining both its political and its naturalistic overtones. We described the leading Confucian virtues of li and jen, and then we laid out the hierarchical relationships that have structured Chinese social life. The Taoist understanding of Tao was our next concern, and finally we dealt with some of the key symbols of Lao Tzu and Chuang Tzu.

In dealing with Chinese family life, we rooted its ethics in Confucian convictions, which included the subordination of women to men and the subordination of youth to old age. We stressed the centrality of procreation, described the crucial time of a parent's death, and noted such aspects of the Chinese marital relation as its canons of feminine beauty. Finally, we dealt with the religious life of the typical household, mentioning the veneration of ancestors—something that confused Western missionaries—and the recourse of ordinary people in times of trouble.

To describe the Chinese ethical views of work we first sketched the different ranks of traditional Chinese society. We noted the impact of the cosmological myth on both the functions of rulers and the model of the sage, and then we considered the sage's ideal penetration of the tradition. We saw the likely impact of a desire to avoid shaming one's clan, and we also mused about the work of traditional Chinese women. Our next topic was the place of the Chinese civil service, which connected with the imperial organization of historical China. Finally, we dealt with miscellaneous virtues and features of the traditional Chinese working world.

To explain what ideals of social justice have prevailed in Chinese society, we first noted the stratifications that the tradition imposed and the traditional ideal of stability. Next we dealt with the notion of the mandate of heaven, and then with Chinese views of war. We discussed Buddhist mitigations of cruelties and harsh laws. We also discussed how militaristic emperors tried to utilize Buddhist notions for their own ends, and we characterized traditional Chinese law as focused on duties more than rights.

To explain Chinese attitudes toward nature, we began with the Chinese immersion in the cosmological myth. We noted Taoist and Confucian practices relying on yin/yang theory and on the notion of the five basic natural elements. We recalled the importance of geomancy, before moving to an unromantic view of how China actually has treated the environment. This showed us several patterns of abuse, most of them at odds with China's own ancient respect for mountains and rivers. We noted folkloric aspects of traditional Chinese ecological sensibilities and concluded with an example from Chuang Tzu.

The main models of the ethical life that we found came from earliest antiquity, especially as this was mediated by the teaching and example of Confucius himself. We discussed the divine sages mentioned in the *Analects*, pondered the views of the eighteenth-century C.E. ruler K'ang-hsi, contrasted his example with the likely impact of China's many corrupt rulers, and then used literary reflections of Maxine Hong Kingston to dramatize the place of clan honor in the traditional ethical model.

STUDY QUESTIONS

1. What does the practice of geomancy suggest about traditional Chinese culture?
2. What did the Confucians think about the Tao?
3. What were the main hierarchical relationships structuring Chinese familial ethics?
4. What was the work of the Chinese sage?
5. How did traditional Chinese thinkers expect the "rectification of names" to promote social justice?
6. Describe the relation between Chinese ecological ideals and Chinese environmental practice.
7. Evaluate the emperor K'ang-hsi as an ethical model.

NOTES

[1] See René Grousset, *The Rise and Splendour of the Chinese Empire* (Berkeley: University of California Press, 1953); Arthur F. Wright, *Buddhism in Chinese History* (Stanford, Calif.: Stanford University Press, 1959).

[2] See Wing-tsit Chan, *A Sourcebook in Chinese Philosophy* (Princeton, N.J.: Princeton University Press, 1963); Lawrence G. Thompson, *Chinese Religion: An Introduction*, 3d ed. (Belmont, Calif.: Wadsworth, 1979).

[3] See, for example, *Monkey: Folk Novel of China by Wu Ch'engen*, trans. Arthur Waley (New York: Grove, 1958).

[4] C. K. Yang, *Religion in Chinese Society* (Berkeley: University of California Press, 1970), pp. 39–40.

[5] Jacques Gernet, *Daily Life in China* (Stanford, Calif.: Stanford University Press, 1970), p. 61.

[6] Donald J. Munro, *The Concept of Man in Early China* (Stanford, Calif.: Stanford University Press, 1969), p. 24.

[7] Chan, *A Sourcebook in Chinese Philosophy*, p. 41.

[8] *Ibid.*, pp. 154–55.

[9] John C. H. Wu, "Chinese Legal and Political Philosophy," in *The Chinese Mind*, ed. Charles A. Moore (Honolulu: University of Hawaii Press, 1977), p. 219.

[10] Herbert Fingarette, *Confucius—The Secular as Sacred* (New York: Harper & Row, 1972).

[11] See René Dubos, "Franciscan Conservation versus Benedictine Steward-ship," in *Ecology and Religion in History*, ed. David Spring and Eileen Spring (New York: Harper & Row, 1974), pp. 114–36.

[12] Yi-Fu Tuan, "Discrepancies between Environmental Attitude and Be-haviour: Examples from Europe and China," ibid., p. 110.

[13] Marcel Granet, "The Holy Places," in *The Chinese Way in Religion*, ed. Lawrence G. Thompson (Belmont, Calif.: Dickenson, 1973), p. 29.

[14] Chuang Tzu, *Basic Writings*, trans. Burton Watson (New York: Columbia University Press, 1964), p. 24.

[15] Arthur Waley, trans., *The Analects of Confucius* (New York: Vintage, 1938), p. 18.

[16] Jonathan D. Spence, *Emperor of China* (New York: Alfred A. Knopf, 1974), pp. 143–44, 146.

[17] See Maxine Hong Kingston, *The Woman Warrior* (New York: Alfred A. Knopf, 1977).

7

Japanese Ethics

Historical Orientation

Although ethnologists still debate about the racial composition and origin of the Japanese people, it is now generally agreed that from before 4500 B.C.E. to 250 B.C.E. a hunting and gathering culture prevailed on the islands. This period is known as the Jomon era, and Japanese tradition speaks of Jimmu, the first emperor, as ruling about 660 B.C.E. The actual history of the Jomon era is sketchy, but probably the earliest emperors were simply the heads of the most powerful clans. Among the archeological remains from the Jomon period are female fertility figures, which suggest a veneration of the mysteries of life and sexuality.

From about 250 B.C.E. to 250 C.E., during the Yayoi period, the different ethnic groups that had come to the islands blended, producing the sources of the current Japanese stock. The traditional date for the original building of the great national shrine at Ise is 5 C.E., and this implies that the native Japanese religious attitudes (later articulated as **Shinto**) had by that time coalesced. The key notions of this native religion included the **kami,** which in effect were divinizations of natural powers—the sun, the storm—and clan founders. Characteristically the kami were associated with any striking natural phenomena, such as outcroppings of rock, tall trees, ponds, rivers, and winds. Another ancient notion linked the imperial family to the sun goddess Amaterasu, while the Shinto legends told (rather vaguely) of the creation of the Japanese islands and the adventures of the primal human couple Izanagi and Izanami.

The classical mythology included stories of the conflicts between Amaterasu and the wind god Susanoo; comparativists find in these stories traces of the conflict between order and creativity. Susanoo is a **trickster** figure, playing pranks and expressing the unruly aspects of the human personality (what Freudians might call the id). This mythology is poetic and helpful for understanding such later phenomena as the regalia associated with the Japanese throne and the ritual of the traditional Japanese wedding, but when compared to other cultures' mythologies it is not overly impressive.

Around 285 C.E. Confucian ideas came into Japan, and ever after Japanese social thought and family life bore their stamp. Japan has vacillated in its attitude toward Chinese culture, sometimes imitating it slavishly and sometimes revolting in bouts of nationalistic self-assertion. On the whole, however, China certainly furnished Japan the majority of the ideas by means of which it ordered its sense of reality. Buddhism arrived in the sixth century, and before long most of the Chinese Buddhist sects had established foundations in Japan. In 594 the imperial powers declared Buddhism the state religion of Japan, while the Taika Reform of 645 remodeled the Japanese government along Chinese lines. Early in the eighth century a written version of the native mythology was completed, in part because adherents of the native traditions resented the influence of foreign traditions and wanted to articulate their own lore and ritual.

Early in the ninth century the Tendai and Shingon Buddhist sects took hold, and by the end of the ninth century Japan was in a period of cultural flowering, as novels, landscape painting, poetry, and other artistic forms prospered. In the twelfth century more Buddhist schools were introduced and began the process of adapting to Japanese sensibilities and needs. Among them were Pure Land Buddhism, Nichiren Buddhism, and Zen. The first two were devotional schools that appealed especially to the laity. Zen focused on meditation and was especially appealing to the warrior class. What some scholars call Japan's medieval period (roughly from 794 to 1600) included the Heian and Kamakura eras; shrines from these eras are among Japan's great national treasures. The imperial city of Kyoto, fortunately largely spared during the Second World War, remains a stunning witness to the beauty and depth of both the Shinto and the Zen Buddhist strands of the medieval cultural synthesis.

Japan was racked by civil war throughout the period 1150–1600. By the middle of the sixteenth century it was coming under the influence of the West. The famous Jesuit missionary Francis Xavier arrived in 1549 and had good success preaching the Christian gospel. With the advent of the Tokugawa rulers in 1600, however, an era of openness ended and

Japan entered upon more than two and a half centuries of closure. The Tokugawa shoguns suspected everything Western, and under their rule Confucianism prospered. Buddhism came under the stricter control of the state, and the warrior/mercantile ethical code known as **Bushido,** which we shall examine later, was very influential. The first generations of Tokugawa leaders were flexible enough to encourage poetry, literature, and a renaissance of Shinto theology, and during the seventeenth century such luminaries as the Buddhist poet Basho flourished. Just before the end of the Tokugawa era, when both the government and the general culture were stagnating, a wave of what came to be called "new religions" began. Many of these religions were founded by **charismatic** women (who often claimed to be possessed by or in contact with certain kami), and their general intent was to give common people a livelier religious experience and devotional life.

In 1854 Admiral Oliver Perry forced Japan to reopen to the West, and from then on Japan could no longer ignore Western ideas. The Meiji emperor restrained Buddhists during the years 1868–71, as well as bringing the Shinto priests and shrines under strict state control. At the turn of the twentieth century Japan engaged successfully in wars with China and Russia, and the period from 1900 to 1945 was a time of intense Japanese nationalism, but the defeat in World War II was a great blow to national pride. Indeed, the last four decades have been a time for rebuilding the national psyche as much as rebuilding the economy and polity. Under the direction of General Douglas MacArthur, occupied Japan began the process of dedivinizing the emperor and establishing a government based on Western democratic principles. In carrying out this blueprint, the Japanese have displayed a genius for adapting foreign ideas and making them their own—often, indeed, improving them. Japan's recent economic success has caused the West to ponder deeply the Japanese work ethic, and it has afforded sociologists a fascinating entry into the Japanese sense of clan, corporation, family life, and collaboration.

Among the main motifs that emerge when one steps back to gauge the basic patterns of Japanese religious history, certainly the significance of the clan ranks high, as it does in the case of China. Perhaps equally important is the blending of aesthetics with religion and the frequent focus of this blended sensibility onto natural beauty and sacrality. The typical Japanese shrine, Buddhist or Shinto, sets the human personality in the broader and more labile context of woods, ponds, flowers, and impersonal groves. The deepest hunger expressed in journals of pilgrims visiting such shrines is to escape the confines of ego and savor the fresh, often cold or bare reality of the sacral realm of the kami. Japan also has associated sacrality with purity and cleanliness, both physical and spiritual. In its martial arts, games, and art forms such as the tea ceremony and floral arrangement, it has tried to make natural elements triggers for peace and enlightenment. The Chinese motif of shame has a strong hold in the Japanese religious psyche, and recently secularism has ridden into Japan on the back of technological prowess. But the shrines continue to suggest the religious recesses of the Japanese spirit, and most of the shrines intimate that divinity and nature are at least overlapping circles, and that perhaps they coincide.[1]

World View

From its earliest traditions Japan got a great love for its islands, with their manifold sources of beauty—water, mountains, trees, and rocks. Shamans, often female, served as connections to the kami who animated this lovely landscape, leaving the strong impression that the human spirit need only explore its capabilities to find itself traveling the world of the divinities. The oldest traditions also nourished an ethnocentrism that stands out even when one has been reminded that most peoples have considered themselves the primary instance of humanity. Thus Shinto cosmology came to consider the Japanese islands the navel of creation, and the Japanese have been slow to incorporate both the Ainu, a people who have populated northern Japan since prehistoric times, and later foreign arrivals such as Korean workers. The children of liaisons or even marriages between Japanese and Westerners have struggled outside the main channels of social acceptance, and recently the nation has pulled together remarkably to achieve its economic renaissance, business and government often being indistinguishable.

This deeply rooted sense of national identity has enabled the Japanese to appropriate huge portions of their religious mentality from other cultures, especially the Chinese. As we have mentioned, Confucian mores came to structure Japanese social life, and Buddhism at times has gained the status of being the official Japanese religion. The Japanese certainly have interacted with both of these traditions, finally creating a social thought and a meditational or devotional religion distinctively their own, but they also seem to have had the psychology necessary for appropriating whatever good ideas have come their way. Taoism, as a further example, furnished the Japanese part of their rationale for venerating nature, and even Christianity moved those who could get beyond its masculine deity and connect it with the Japanese instinct to depict divinity in maternal colors.

For one trying to sketch the traditional Japanese world view, this talent for appropriation and adaptation proves complicating. When the Japanese venerated their emperor as head of the organic national community, they appear to have expressed both Confucian convictions about the relationship between ruler and ruled and their native Shinto instinct that the emperor was directly connected to the kami (especially to the goddess Amaterasu). When they located the kami in pristine nature and created naturalistic shrines to honor them, the Japanese seem mainly to have been moved by the convictions structuring the Shinto Chronicles—but also to have been expressing a Taoist sense of how nature moves to the subtle directions of the Way, as well as expressing a Buddhist sense of emptiness or of the superiority of nature's impersonal enlightenment-being to human reflectivity.

Whatever the complexity of the lineage behind the leading Japanese ideas, however, their basic import is rather simple. First, Japanese religion has largely moved within the orbit of the cosmological myth, thinking of the cosmos as a living whole and populating it everywhere with kami (800,000 is the traditional figure). Second, Japanese social life has been structured by loyalty to the clan, with subsidiary motifs of striving mightily to avoid shaming one's clan and instinctively arranging political affairs or matters of business through a network of clannish contacts. Third, Buddhism probably has had the strongest metaphysical and meditational impact, giving the average Japanese a sense that reality is both interconnected and fleeting or processive. While social boundaries may be many and exact, the boundaries among the different elements of nature are quite fluid.

Indeed, human beings may contact the kami through trance, the dead can linger in the midst of the living, and religious peace is apt to come from losing oneself in the contemplation of natural beauty. Zen meditational techniques helped to discipline many Japanese in their approach to these matters, and Zen generally served to make Japanese religion holistic. That is, Japan has not favored the Western split between mind and body or spirit and matter. The religiocultural ideal has been the perfectly energized samurai warrior, who acts with lightning speed and is wholly unified. Alternatively, the ideal has been the refined **geisha,** who could make a preserve of grace and beauty apart from the workaday world, a preserve in which music, art, and conversation flowed pleasingly.

Both pleasure and pain had remarkable contours in this world view. Pleasure could have its crude modes, but the more telling pleasures were aesthetic. The typical Japanese home, for example, had a little garden in the foyer. There rocks, water, and an angular little tree would conspire to set a mood of serenity. The shrines where people would go in free times would express this motif on a larger scale. There, beautifully colored carp or areas of wild flowers might add further embellishments. And while developing such gardens and shrines could involve considerable work, one senses that the workers have traditionally taken pleasure in it. In other words, the work has been free—done for its own sake rather than for commercial profit. In the same way calligraphy, mastering a game such as *Go,* or coming to appreciate the Japanese theater has filled out many ordinary lives. The value pursued has not been "artistic," in any self-conscious or ostentatious way, but an attunement with something elegant or beautiful, something that could make the pieces of reality fall into a pattern the Japanese considered traditional and pleasing.

One catches a glimpse of this orientation in the novels of Yasunari Kawabata, a Nobel Prize laureate who brilliantly depicted the traumas of a recent Japanese culture caught between its traditional past and the modernity foisted on it by the West. In the following passage Shingo, a quite ordinary middle-class businessman, suggests the little rituals and aesthetic interests that have punctuated the days for many Japanese: "Shingo disliked cold drinks even in hot weather. Yasuko [his wife] did not give them to him, and the habit of not taking them had formed over the years. In the morning when he got up and in the evening when he came home he would have a brimming cup of tea. Kikuko [his daughter] always saw to supplying it. When they got home from viewing the sunflowers she hurried off for his tea. He drank about half of it, changed to a cotton kimono, and took his cup out to the veranda, sipping as he went. Kikuko came after him with a cold towel and cigarettes and poured more tea. Then she went for his glasses and the evening paper. He looked out at the garden. It seemed too much of an effort, when he had wiped his face, to put on his glasses. The grass was rough and untended. On the far side was a clump of bush clover and pampas grass, so tall that it almost looked wild. There were butterflies beyond. Shingo could see them flickering past gaps in the leaves, more than one butterfly, surely. He waited to see whether they would alight on the bush clover or come out from behind it. They went on fluttering through the leaves, however. He began to feel that there was some sort of special little world apart over behind the shrubbery. The butterfly wings beyond the leaves of bush clover seemed to him extraordinarily beautiful."[2]

Many Japanese ethical assessments of good or bad can be translated into this sense of pleasing or disliked. Equally, many experiences of pain are experiences of ugliness. If something is ill-fitting or ill-mannered it gives considerable pain, probably more than it would in a comparable Western setting. On the other hand, the Japanese have schooled themselves to endure considerable pain and privation. Sacrifice for the family, the clan, or the company is part of daily life. The instinct is to save rather than to spend, to fit in rather than to stand out. And most of these emotional/ethical assessments appear subtle, muted, refined. As such, they weave their way back and forth through the fabric of Japanese culture. Japanese ethics has not been the teaching of a church authority or of a line of religious masters who stood apart from the ordinary faithful. It has been a finely tuned evaluation of what was pleasing and displeasing, fitting and unfitting. To be sure, it was practiced exquisitely by only a few connoisseurs, but the lay majority practiced it impressively.

Family Life

The quotation from Kawabata's novel *The Sound of the Mountain* suggests not only the place that aesthetics and natural beauty have held in many Japanese lives but also the Confucian cast of Japanese family life. Shingo is constantly attended by the women of his household because he is the husband and father. To be sure, Kawabata's novels and any other literature that takes one close to the actual operation of Japanese family life show women exerting great influence and manifesting considerable independence. Within the cultural forms of their society, they have been as creative and self-expressive as women anywhere else. But the Japanese cultural forms themselves have largely followed the Confucian hierarchized relationships, meaning that in the typical Japanese family women seconded men and the young seconded the elderly. It is no mystery, for example, that Japan has been slow to develop a women's movement. Even after a generation of women who have had nearly equal opportunity in education, both business and family life remain preserves of male rule.

Actually, in current Japan business and family life overlap considerably, because when men join a business firm they commit themselves to much more than just a cluster of work relationships. The directive pattern, if not the full rule, tends to be that one will stay with one's firm throughout one's career, and that one will do much of one's socializing and recreating in its context. For Japanese executives this has meant even longer hours away from home than their American counterparts have to endure. For Japanese women it has meant, relatedly, a stronger sense that their preserve is the home.

Japanese women have followed Chinese women in being considered first of all producers of children. They might also be their husbands' friends and lovers, but that has been a secondary matter. Traditionally marriages were arranged by parents, who carefully considered not only the compatibility of the two prospective partners but also the relations between the two extended families. Apart from the Buddhist monastic life, Japanese culture made little provision for not marrying, so there was little understanding of staying single for the sake of one's career.

From the beginnings of Japanese culture, as we noted in describing the Jomon period, fertility has been a central interest. Geoffrey Parrinder connects this theme with the widespread presence of phallic and vulvar images.[3] By traditional association the peach, rice, beans, and the comb were considered female fertility symbols. Male symbols tended to be sticks, posts, and poles, some of them carved quite explicitly. Western visitors have remarked on such customs as having boys strike girls with phallic sticks at the imperial celebration of the new moon each month. Concern for children's health extended the theme of fertility, and the custom was to take children at ages three, five, and seven to the Shinto

shrines on the fifteenth day of the eleventh month to secure their continued protection. When it came to marriage, Shinto sensibilities prevailed over Buddhist sensibilities (Buddhist ways prevailed when it came
to funerals), and the traditional wedding ceremony recalled the walk of
the primal couple, Izanagi and Izanami, around the pillar of creation (either the pole connecting earth to heaven or a phallic symbol).

A certain double standard has prevailed in Japanese society, women
being held to much stricter chastity than men. As has been true in most
other cultures, prostitution has always been available, and the ministra-
tions of geishas, who usually were not prostitutes, afforded men added
feminine charm outside of marriage. Some popular literature suggests
that Buddhist monasteries and Japanese theater life encouraged homosexuality, and the so-called "floating world" or demimonde available in
most Japanese cities provided a variety of erotic pleasures.

The schooling of children hewed to the Confucian line, but traditionally only boys got advanced education. Peasant women could expect
to work in the fields, but middle- and upper-class women could take training in various domestic arts. The early depictions of women stress an
ideal of physical beauty based on easy childbearing (ample bosoms and
hips), but later the most desirable Japanese woman was fragile and pale.

Chie Nakatane, whose analysis of Japanese social structures bears
mainly on business groups, indicates the social context of all male-
female and parent-child relations when she writes of Japanese family
life: "Moral ideas such as 'the husband leads and the wife obeys' or 'man
and wife are one flesh' embody the Japanese emphasis on integration.
Among Indians, however, I have often observed husband and wife expressing quite contradictory opinions without the slightest hesitation. This
is indeed rare in front of others in Japan. The traditional authority of the
Japanese household head, once regarded as the prime characteristic of
the family system, extended over the conduct, ideas, and ways of thought
of the household's members, and on this score the household head could
be said to wield a far greater power than his Indian counterpart."[4]

Moreover, as was true in China, the "family" in question included
more than the members presently alive: "The dead are so important that
the label of ancestor worship has been applied to Japanese religion. Family unity and continuity are essential for carrying out the important rituals honoring the spirits of family ancestors. Even beyond the family, the
dead, their burial or cremation, and periodic memorials have great religious significance. The dead can rise to the status of 'gods.' A dead person is referred to euphemistically as a Buddha . . . and the tacit understanding is that after a fixed number of periodic memorials a dead person
joins the company of ancestors as a kind of *kami*."[5] Family honor follows in this Confucian pattern, the worst aspect of failure being the
shame that it will bring to one's family.

In the traditional Japanese home, religious activities included prayers and offerings made at a family shrine. Periodically the family would hold memorial services for the dead, especially on the anniversaries of their deaths. Regularly, there would be offerings of food from the family table to the Buddha or the kami. The family would celebrate the New Year by reconsecrating the house, decorating it with pine branches, and preparing special foods. Traditionally one cleaned the house at this time, extinguished the hearth flame and secured a new flame from the village shrine, and sprinkled salt and holy water throughout the house.

The extended family or clan also would gather and reaffirm itself through commemorations of the departed ancestors and other religious rites. Many of the important temples of Japan first were shrines of important clans. One can even think of the national shrines and festivals as expressing the largest grouping of Japanese: their extension as the people of their islands.

These traditions are now in transition, as Japan adapts culturally to its new technological thrust. Divorce is more frequent, and abortion is rife. Traditionally divorce was discouraged and the stress on procreation minimized abortion. (Confucian ethics, as we saw, did not scruple about female infanticide.) Today's better health care has dramatically cut infant mortality and extended the Japanese life span, so the pressures to limit family size have greatly increased. Some of the "new religions" therefore have ministries to women who undergo abortions, while other religious functionaries have developed shrines where elderly Japanese, feeling unwelcome in cramped households, can pray for a speedy death.[6]

Work

Confucian mores certainly encouraged hard work, if only as a way of honoring one's parents and superiors. Zen Buddhism enlarged the possible significance of work, seeing each task as potentially a discipline through which one could unify body and mind. What may have been more influential in the development of modern Japanese industry, however, was the fusion of devotional Buddhism with hard work that occurred during the Tokugawa era. Robert Bellah has gone so far as to credit Shin Buddhism of the Tokugawa period with preferring work to meditation, because while meditation spotlights the usually undisciplined mind and so disturbs one's peace, work tends to keep one more composed. Shin tracts, directed toward the laity, abounded in maxims such as the following: "Always think of the divine protection. Cheerfully do not neglect diligent activity morning and evening. Work hard at the family occupation. Be temperate in unprofitable luxury. Do not gamble. Rather than take a lot, take a little."[7] The impression is of a Japanese version of a puritan ethic, according to which idleness is the devil's workshop and frugality is next to godliness.

Just as stories of Horatio Alger carried this ethic home to millions of Americans, so similar stories of merchants who started poor and prospered by a combination of hard work and devout faith in the Buddha brought the ethic home to millions of Japanese. Both groups drew the implication that financial success was a blessing from God, and no doubt the complementary implication—that poverty showed the divine disfavor—afflicted not a few Japanese, just as it afflicted not a few Americans.

This Japanese ethic was not limited to business life, either. During the Tokugawa era religion was pressured to support loyalty to the national rulers and patriotism. So at one and the same time the diligent worker—peasant, merchant, or government clerk—could think himself serving the Buddha, the shogun, and his own financial prosperity. Women tended not to be the target of the overtly economic counsels, but certainly maternal and wifely hard work qualified women for analogous praise—religious, national, and familial all in one.

Many writers not only promoted diligence as a religious virtue but also tried to deepen people's desire to work hard by making such work an expression of one's proper gratitude. This gratitude was owed, in the first place, to one's parents and clan. It was also owed, however, to the nation and to the Buddha. People given much ought to return much. To be lazy or careless was therefore to show oneself an ingrate. When the prevailing consensus was that ingrates were a disgrace, laziness and carelessness became less common.

The extreme of dedication and self-sacrifice probably was the proud willingness of the samurai warrior to die rather than fail his lord. When a samurai thought he had failed, the only honorable thing was to offer to commit suicide. Honor, then, was another powerful factor in Japanese culture, and certainly it trickled down from the warrior class to the merchants and even to the peasants. Not to be a person of honor—in terms of one's word, one's loyalty, and one's diligence—was to be contemptible.

For women, perhaps predictably, much of the call to be honorable centered on chastity. Thus, parallel to the ritualistic suicide that the failed samurai warrior was to offer stood the ritualistic suicide of the violated virgin or the dishonored wife. Engaged women being dressed for their wedding would be given a small sword, so that they might commit suicide if they should be dishonored sexually on the way to the wedding. No doubt few people thought such dishonor actually was likely to occur, but the symbolism spoke volumes about the psychology of the Japanese ideal of female honor.

Japanese work was not all military or productive, however. Alongside the agricultural achievements of the peasants, the businesses of the merchants, and the adventures of the warriors stood the impressive achievements of the artists. As we noted, the Japanese have always tended to blend the aesthetic and the religious realms, so it is frequently hard to know where the religion of a given work begins and where the art leaves off. The classical pottery fashioned for the tea ceremony, for example, certainly acquired a venerable if not indeed a sacral aura. The masters of the martial arts or *Go* or the Kabuki puppetry were more than merely artists. The honor one paid them reflected the conviction that what they were doing was a spiritual discipline. By working according to the ideals of their profession, they could expect to move forward toward enlightenment.

This conviction influenced the Japanese work ethic in that it gave a big boost to the notion that shoddy work was morally unacceptable. If one did not respect one's materials, take the time to fashion them well, and even strive to acquire the inner disposition from which alone, Japanese culture usually was convinced, the best art could derive, then one had defaulted on the vocation of potter or calligrapher or swordsmith.

The ceremonial arts may not have been so severely pressured, in that frequently they had amateur forms open to the masses, but graces such as floral arrangement, gardening, and executing the tea ceremony still were serious matters. The shrines that Buddhism, especially, developed were tended with a religious care. The skills of the dedicated geisha took her beyond mere entertainment, let alone courtesanship. Japan consistently was sufficiently this-worldly in its cultural ideals to demand good work of its citizens. Somewhat in contrast to Indian religion, which could find religious justification for neglecting this world and the body, Shinto and Japanese Buddhism gave believers few excuses for slovenliness.

A final component of the Japanese work ethic has been the collaborative nature of many Japanese enterprises. Recently this has intrigued American industrial psychologists and sociologists because of the dramatic successes that Japanese industry has achieved—above all the Japanese automobile industry, but also shipbuilding, electronics, and other industries. Whether or not Japanese methods of teamwork prove translatable into Western cultural terms, it seems that in most Japanese work the individual instinctively subordinates himself or herself to the group and the whole. If a mistake occurs, the etiquette requires that the individual accept responsibility for it and shield superiors from blame. If a success occurs, the individual whose idea led to it fades into the background, letting the group leader or the appropriate executive rake in the honors. No doubt everyone knows exactly who made what contribution, positive or negative, but the going rules stress the collective. Indeed, the going methods of many jobs themselves stress group meetings in which workers bounce ideas off one another and frequently experience that united they are much more insightful and productive than they could ever be apart.

The intense social interaction of traditional Japanese life, in which people regularly lived virtually on top of one another and so had to develop extraordinary sensitivity to one another's needs and moods, thus pays dividends on the production line. Communication often takes place almost instantly, as people intuitively sense what another is groping to say or is feeling as a problem in his or her part of the group project. We should not romanticize these Japanese skills, nor overlook the correlative liabilities that a less developed sense of individual responsibility, creativity, maverick protest, and the like can bring. But certainly we should give Japanese workers the credit their astounding achievements deserve, and we should as well examine very carefully the connections of the Japanese government with Japanese industry, the tax structure, the trade policies, the protectionism, the lack of military expenditures, and all the other components of today's Japanese economic life. Religiously, however, the main lesson is the simple one of efficacy: through Confucian shame, Buddhist concern for merit, samurai honor, and no doubt many other motivational keys, the Japanese have made themselves exceptionally intelligent and productive workers.

Social Justice

The Bushido code that flourished during the Tokugawa period integrated Shinto nationalism, Confucian integrity, and Zen Buddhist discipline. Originally it expressed the warrior's honorable way, but gradually it appealed to all the Japanese as an expression of the honor that the ethical person would rather die for than default upon. Prior to the modern period, when Japan was emerging as a world power and so was flexing its nationalistic muscles, honor no doubt pertained mainly to the Confucian relationships of lord and peasant, general and foot soldier, husband and wife, master and apprentice, or parent and child. Justice in any of these social relationships was the ideal balance that would obtain if each party was what it was supposed to be.

Prior to the intense modern nationalism, matters of charity and social service such as caring for the poor, the sick, and the disabled largely were worked out within the structure of the clan. That is, the first recourse that needy people had was their own extended family. The Buddhist monasteries sponsored charitable works, and the rural towns supported itinerant healers who offered relief to troubled souls as much as to troubled bodies. With the rise of the modern industrial Japan, many of these charitable and medical matters are attended to through the corporations in which people work.

In a Buddhist context, one's place in society and the relative justice or injustice that one receives relate to one's karma. In a Confucian context, old age is the time when one should receive the better portion in the division of goods, and the family or clan has the responsibility of making such an apportionment. Recently a few Japanese have espoused left-wing political views, trying to mount a radical challenge to the traditional hierarchization of Japanese social life, but they have had little overall influence. Indeed, commentators sometimes note with amusement that even student demonstrations against the construction of a new airport in a location the students consider undesirable, or against policies that they think would take Japan back into militarism, are carefully orchestrated, as though both protesters and police were following the script of an intricate ballet based on clearly defined social roles.

One modern document that often is cited as a good (if propagandistic) expression of the Japanese ethos is the Imperial Rescript on Education that was issued October 30, 1890. Certainly some of the ideas expressed in it have been challenged since the defeat of Japan in World War II, but the rescript expresses much of the traditional attitude that has set the Japanese sense of social order and responsibility down the centuries: "Our Imperial Ancestors have founded Our empire on a basis broad and everlasting and have deeply and firmly implanted virtue; Our subjects ever united in loyalty and filial piety have from generation to generation illustrated the beauty thereof. This is the glory of the fundamental character of Our Empire, and herein also lies the source of Our education. Ye, Our subjects, be filial to your parents, affectionate to your brothers and sisters; as husbands and wives be harmonious, as friends true; bear yourselves in modesty and moderation; extend your benevolence to all; pursue learning and cultivate arts, and thereby develop intellectual faculties and perfect moral powers; furthermore, advance public good and promote common interests; always respect the Constitution and observe the laws; should emergency arise, offer yourselves courageously to the State; and thus guard and maintain the prosperity of Our Imperial Throne coeval with heaven and earth. So shall ye not only be Our good and faithful subjects, but render illustrious the best traditions of your forefathers."[8]

The text makes clear the traditional Japanese conception that the imperial order was sacred. Indeed, as the capital letters of the translation suggest, the emperor was considered divine, while the imperial realm— the national social order—was considered to extend backwards to the founding of heaven and earth. To be sure, this sort of "divinity" is different from what the West, with its monotheism, instinctively pictures. If there could be 800,000 kami in Japan, certainly the emperor could be one of them. But one need only consider the willingness of the famous Japanese kamikaze pilots of World War II to die for the imperial realm to catch a glimpse of the power that this social myth held over the typical Japanese psyche.

Perhaps this psychological power helps to explain the militarism of Japan in some ages and also its current antimilitarism. One of the reasons that Zen Buddhism came to favor was the military suitability of its disciplines, while the Bushido amalgamation of Confucian, Shinto, and Buddhist elements could be considered a disciplining of energy and aggression so that they would serve Japanese honor. To marshal the Japanese fighting spirit, the local lord or national emperor needed only to portray the enemy as a threat to the things the Japanese held dear. In the years prior to World War II the Western enemy was, with some justice, portrayed as deliberately trying to thwart the rightful, fated expansion of the Japanese realm into the control of all Asia. One could be cruel, destructive, and monomaniacal in one's military efforts if one was serving the divine emperor and the sacral nation. No doubt all countries turn chauvinistic in time of war, but the Japanese sense of national honor made Japan's propaganda seem self-evidently true to most of its citizenry.

All the more shattering, therefore, was the defeat of this national expansionism, and all the more profound was the self-questioning that started to occur when intellectuals began to recover from their numbness. The atomic explosions at Hiroshima and Nagasaki offered all too concrete examples of what could go wrong when militarism considered any means to victory legitimate.

Ideas of social justice, we might here observe, vary dramatically with a people's world view. Certainly every people harbors a sense of fairness and instinctively is outraged when that sense appears violated. But how a people articulates its sense of fairness into social policies, both national and international, depends considerably on the fundamental assumptions or convictions at the roots of the people's culture. It depends, as well, on a reflectivity that few peoples produce in more than a small fraction of their population. These, the intellectuals and religious masters, have to go to the primal myths of the people's inheritance and then, ideally, move beyond to the basic mystery or nothingness that transcends all mythmaking. The Kyoto school of Buddhist philosophers, who have in the past few decades been concentrating on the traditional Mahayana Buddhist theme of nothingness or emptiness, suggests one of the resources that Japan is now trying to mine. Many of these philosophers engage in ecumenical discussions with other religious traditions, especially Christianity. Were they to make social justice a prime topic on their agenda, and try to correlate their sense of nothingness (which easily implies anti-idolatry and so moderation of all undue nationalism and militarism) with the present international crises, they might make a remarkable contribution to the new religious consensus that the twenty-first century appears to require.[9]

Nature

Taoism, Buddhism, and Shintoism all provided Japan stimuli to reverence nature, and for most of Japanese history the kami have been thought to inhabit all the striking phenomena of the landscape. The typical Japanese shrine is naturalistic, to the extent of downplaying humanistic or personalist overtones. The general sense has been that nature un-adorned, kept pristine, is the purest form of existence. Thus the national shrine at Ise at first may seem disappointing, because so much of it is given over to the nearly wild growth of trees and the simple flow of streams uncleansed of organisms. The buildings of the shrine are under-stated (Japan has had a tradition of rebuilding its shrines, which usually are made of wood, at regular intervals as a way of periodically renewing the vigor of the site), and nothing ostentatious intrudes. To be sure, at festivals there are colorful performances of ancient rituals, but the over-all tenor is reminiscent of Lao Tzu: things are best when they are far-thest from human artifice.

The folk tales that illustrate antique themes of Japanese religion often feature animal characters, suggesting the easy interaction of hu-man beings and other creatures that is a common feature of shamanistic cultures. For example, a tale about a serpent suitor tells of a mysterious nobleman who would visit the lovely daughter of a village headman each evening. The daughter grew frustrated because she could get no informa-tion from this nobleman about his origin or family. When she asked her maid how to solve this problem, the maid suggested pricking the skirt of the nobleman's gown with a threaded needle and then following the thread back to his home. The next night she did this, and when the nobleman departed she and the nurse followed the trail of the thread. This brought them to a big rock cave at the foot of Mount Uba. Leaning in they heard groaning, and on entering they saw a giant serpent writhing in pain, a needle thrust into its throat. The nurse fainted and died on the spot, and the serpent soon died also. The girl ran away terrified, and eventually the cave became a well-known shrine. Tradition has it that if one enters the shrine carrying any sort of metal, the spirit of the cave takes offense and causes a storm.[10]

The tale clearly is intended to explain the origin of the shrine at the foot of Mount Uba, as well as the custom that one must keep all metal away from the shrine. The motif of a serpent suitor occurs in other Shinto stories, and scholars usually point out the phallic overtones. For our purposes, the interesting elements are the interactions between human beings and animal forces that are assumed possible, and also the reference to the spirit of the cave. Just as the Jataka tales portray the Buddha as easily assuming an animal form to work on human beings' behalf, so this tale assumes that mysterious forces can assume many forms to influence human beings. This tale, like other tales featuring serpents, has the cautionary theme that human beings verge upon dis-aster when they are overly curious about the names and origins of things. It also shows the unquestioned assumption of traditional Japanese cul-ture that significant places such as shrines are inhabited by a local spirit, who might be considered its kami. In this case, the spirit could be natu-ralistic, deriving from the mythical serpent, or it might equally have derived from the nurse who died on the spot. Either way, the effect is to link human beings, nature, and animating forces—either benevolent spirits or harmful ghosts—in a single connected whole.

In technical terms, we have called this holism the cosmological myth, and it implies that a people 1) considers the many different beings of the cosmos to be but various expressions of a single elementary stuff, and 2) considers the divine or ultimate to lie within the cosmic orbit or be coextensive with it, but not to transcend it in the manner of the Western creator God. Certainly the Shinto tradition that has been at the center of Japanese religion and ethics accepted both of these propositions. Japanese Buddhism equally sacralized nature, and in fact came to an agreement with Shinto that the major Japanese spirits, natural or historical (gods or great religious saints) could be considered either kami or bodhisattvas.

Some of the heights of the Japanese appreciation of nature have been reached in the Japanese arts and folkcrafts. The discipline of the artist, as we have mentioned, has solicited a religious respect, and the goal of the artist frequently has been a union with the materials being used, to the end of presenting them with exquisite simplicity. Harmony ought to result, as well as a quality and timing that will please beholders. In her introductory history of Japanese art, Joan Stanley-Baker has described the relationship between the artistic worker and his or her work in this way: ". . . the key to understanding the relationship of the Japanese artist or craftsman to his work lies in one word: union. Whether it be the chopstick-rest one finds in a fish restaurant, or a signed painting, one sees a particularly developed artistic sensibility at work. Painters of old caught exactly this quality of creative absorption in their depictions of carpenters, tatami floor-mat and bamboo-blind makers and mounters of paintings. In literature, the perfection of *renga* or linked verse is believed to come only through repeated group practice among the poets. More than in any other culture, Japanese poets incorporate one another's essence; potters incorporate the essence of the potting process (including finger-prints and kiln accidents); woodworkers or print-makers incorporate woodgrain and chisel marks as an integral and essential part of the finished work."[11]

One might conjecture that behind this respect for the nicks and grains of one's materials lies the Shinto veneration of the kami, which served to dignify the face or plane of whatever natural object one was contemplating. Japanese society has not been uniformly gentle toward nature, as the smog of present-day Tokyo suggests, but many qualities or attitudes in the traditional Japanese ethos would seem to foster a positive and protective care of the environment. Indeed, the notion of care captures much of the distinctive quality of traditional Japanese art and work, as long as one does not sentimentalize this notion. The general regard that Japan has had for nature, despite the personifications of the folktales, has been impersonal: nature has been the realm where Buddha-nature appears blessedly free of human egocentricity, reflective complexity, emotional complication, and the like.

Probably this impersonalism is the source of much of the peace and pleasure that Japanese art offers, and perhaps it is the source as well of one of the major lessons that Japan has to contribute to the global environmental ethics now struggling to be born. As long as human beings grant rights or moral status only to other human beings, the environment stands little chance of surviving our industrial incursions. It is fine for environmentalists to make the valid point that our own sanity, as well as our physical survival and prosperity, depends on protecting the ecosystems that we inhabit, but even this point remains anthropocentric. Beyond anthropocentrism, Japanese views of nature suggest, lie a dignity and a right to exist that nature has on its own. The old debate about whether a tree that falls in a forest inhabited by no human beings makes a noise suggests some of what is at stake. As long as we define reality solely in terms of how things register in human consciousness or what they imply for human beings' welfare, we shall not have the epistemology or the ethics that our environmental problems now demand of us. The turn to the subject that has characterized modern philosophy in the West clearly was necessary, if we were to advance beyond premodern views that were simplistically objective. But now we have to develop a critically realistic epistemology and ethics that give nonhuman factors, as well as human factors, their due. Intuitively, Japanese religion has accomplished much of this program for centuries.

Models

The objectivity or impersonalism that appears to have been part of the Japanese aesthetic, religious, and ecological outlook somewhat complicates the question of ethical modeling. As we shall see, the Japanese certainly have followed other peoples in writing moralistic tales and honoring moral heroes, but their culture has also espoused a stratum in which nature or transhuman modes of existence were accounted superior modes of being. The poet Saigyo, as we mentioned, represents the school of naturalistic Buddhist poets who hymned the spontaneity and simplicity of animals and plants. For such poets, as we see in many haiku, enlightenment comes as a cherry blossom falls or as a leaf floats downstream. The great obstacle to enlightenment, and so to fulfillment, is the self-concern that afflicts human beings. Japan therefore developed its own version of the Western notion that to find one's life one had to lose it. The ethical person, in the sense of the person who reached the ideal of humanity, was one who had dropped human conflict (much of which focuses on questions of right and wrong) and lived integrally, with little energy dissipated on "questions not conducing to edification," as Buddhist piety might phrase it.

A further challenge to the notion of ethical models came in the Zen notion that the adept must "slay the Buddha." This was a cryptic way of saying that enlightenment is a matter of personal responsibility, and that when enlightenment comes the experience is its own validation. After enlightenment, one does not rely on the tradition, the example of the Buddha, or the advice of one's master. One relies on the time and place and nest of feelings that constituted the enlightenment experience itself (and, presumably, on their continued resonance in one's reconstituted consciousness and sense of reality). Indeed, one realizes that the tradition, the example of the Buddha, and the counsel or presence of the master can be impediments to spiritual progress. They are probably necessary in the first stages of one's journey, but with time they become distractions from the core of the task, which is personally realizing the truths of nondualism, the original purity of human nature, the emptiness of all beings, and the like.

Paradoxically, then, many of the Zen models showed an anti-authoritarian or anti-model aspect. In the crucial interview where the master would authenticate the disciple's claim to have received enlightenment, one of the key elements was the personal authority that the disciple displayed. A disciple who had in fact undergone the powerful experience of personal unification that "enlightenment" usually connoted would answer any question or challenge immediately, intuitively, thinking a gesture as good as a sentence. Such a disciple could solve any **koan** or riddle meant to exercise the forces of spiritual simplicity, which operates beyond or below either/or dichotomies. Such a disciple now lived at one with Buddha-nature or Suchness or Emptiness itself.

Still, even in this process of slaying the Buddha and demonstrating the self-sufficiency of the enlightenment process, the disciple would be following in the footsteps of previous adepts who had won the Zen victory. A certain sameness attends the stories of Zen enlightenment,[12] and these stories probably structure how Zen has come to understand and so to authenticate enlightenment. The great Zen masters, from Bodhidharma and the Sixth Patriarch, whom we have mentioned, to the founders of important schools or philosophical outlooks, such as Eisai and Dogen, were important models for their followers, and Zen has always at least implicitly conveyed that the doctrines it teaches are pale reflections of the full-bodied enlightenment lived by its greatest saints.

One could write a similar analysis for the other Japanese Buddhist schools, arguing that founders such as Shinran and Nichiren modeled the teachings and way of the more devotional Shin and Nichiren Buddhisms. In the case of Nichiren Buddhism, one could add the further wrinkle that the **Lotus Sutra** became the standard of faith, and so to some extent the picture of the Buddha displayed in the Lotus Sutra modeled the way or ethos that believers most treasured.

The Confucian cast of Japanese social thought and organization suggests that other influential ethical models have been the people who exemplified what fathers, princes, teachers, husbands, and elder sons were supposed to be. Thus many clans no doubt looked to their patriarch as the living embodiment of Japanese wisdom and honor. Many children looked to their parents for what masculine or feminine honor ought to entail. The subordinate in each of the five key Confucian relationships, too, would instinctively have looked to others—whether living people or literary figures—who were thought to have shown what a truly filial son, a truly loyal warrior, or a truly diligent student was like. The hortatory literature that we have mentioned as influential in fostering a strong work ethic in the Tokugawa era included exemplary tales. The folk literature handed down through the centuries included not only stories of how shrines got their peculiar customs and what false steps led to the deaths of nurses and serpent-men, but stories of people rewarded for their hospitality to strangers or honored for their defense of their sexual virtue.

An example of rewarded hospitality is found in the story of a girl who was at home alone doing her assigned task of weaving. An old man came staggering over the hill and asked her for a cup of water. She walked some distance to honor the man's request and fetched him the water. Pleased, he told her that as a reward he would free her from having to make such walks to the spring in the future. So he struck the ground with his cane, and immediately lovely spring water gushed forth. Tradition identified the old man as Kobo Daishi, the founder of Shingon Buddhism, and the courteous girl became an example of the kind people that the Buddhist saints always reward.[13]

A model of how to defend one's sexual virtue was Lady Kesa, whom the Bushido manuals regularly described for young girls. The wife of a samurai, she found herself the unwelcome object of the sexual advances of her husband's lord. Wanting neither to give in to these advances, and so compromise her virtue, nor to alienate the lord, and so compromise her husband's loyalty, she told the lord that she would submit on the condition that he first killed her husband. He agreed, and she instructed him to come to her room late at night, after she had gotten her husband to sleep. The lord needed only to kill the sleeper with the wet hair to have her for himself. When the appointed night came, Lady Kesa got her husband to sleep in her bed, rose to wash her hair, and then laid herself down beside her husband to await the death that would save the honor of them both.

Apart from the Buddha, then, Japanese ethics tended to have models that were illustrative more than normative. Moreover, the model of the

Buddha, as we have noted, was complicated by Zen notions of self-sufficiency, behind which lay the Mahayana stress on the metaphysical Buddha rather than the historical Gautama. Unlike Christianity, which had the model of Jesus, or Islam, which had the model of Muhammad, Japanese society had to work out its ethical ideals by constant reference to group consensus rather than by reference to a figure thought to be normative for all times and places. As one can see in the novels of Kawabata, this group consensus has recently broken down. A figure such as Shingo, who has many parallels in Kawabata's other novels, hankers after olden times, when social roles were more precise, yet he knows that such times have gone. He therefore waits between the times, feeling deracinated and alienated. By the very strength of its past customs, Japan holds important lessons for other contemporary nations, which also often seem deracinated and alienated.[14]

Summary

We began our historical orientation with the Jomon period, noting the evidence of a great concern for fertility. We then described the Shinto features that had arisen by the middle of the Yayoi period, when the imperial shrine at Ise was constructed. Primary among these features were the belief in the kami and the connection of the emperor with the sun goddess Amaterasu. We traced the advent of Confucian and Buddhist ideas, noting their rapid rise to prominence, and then we sketched the further development of Buddhism during Japan's medieval period. The modern period was dominated by the restrictions of the Tokugawa shoguns and the consequent control of religion by the state. We dealt with the opening of Japan in the mid-nineteenth century, the prelude and aftermath of World War II, and then such long-playing emphases as the significance of the clan and the blending of a naturalistic aesthetics with religion.

Concerning Japanese philosophy, we continued the theme of a love for natural beauty; then we added the notion of ethnocentrism and discussed Japan's borrowings from Chinese culture, especially the Confucian social thought. We reflected on the influence of the cosmological myth in Japan, the importance of loyalty to the clan, and the impact of Buddhist meditation. Finally, we considered the significance of the pleasurable and the painful in Japanese ethical evaluations.

To explain Japanese familial ethics we first focused on the predominant place accorded the husband and father. Then we noted the great influence of the corporation in recent Japanese family life. We described the usual situation of Japanese women and the significance that fertility traditionally has had, and we alluded to Japanese views concerning chastity, prostitution, homosexuality, erotic pleasure, and feminine beauty.

Then we returned to the family to discuss the unity between husband and wife that sociologists have observed, and the place of venerating the ancestors. Finally, we noted familial religious rites, clan shrines, and the new moral climate in which divorce, abortion, and euthanasia are more pressing concerns.

To describe Japanese views of work we first noted the general impact of Confucian mores and then the significance of Buddhist discipline and maxims. We considered the samurai sense of honor and its extension to women, and we discussed the honor accorded artists, craftsmen, and craftswomen, and the Japanese ideal of well-wrought work. Finally, we reflected on the collaborative nature of recent Japanese industrial work and the ethical implications of subordinating the individual to the group.

The topic of social justice first brought to mind the Bushido code and the Confucian ranking of social relationships. Next we considered the clan-context of traditional works of charity and of help for the disabled. We noted Buddhist influences in this area, and the relative impotence of recent left-wing views. As a specimen of the traditional social thought we considered an excerpt from the Imperial Rescript on Education of 1890; the excerpt stressed the holiness of the imperial rule that this Shintoist document assumes. We dealt with Japanese militarism in the years after the rescript, and then with the antimilitarism that has prevailed in the wake of World War II. Our last consideration was the great influence that any people's world view has on its articulation of its sense of fairness or social justice.

The first point we made when discussing Japanese ecological values was the naturalism of Shinto religious sensibilities. Next we noted the place of animals in traditional folktales, suggesting the power of the Japanese version of the cosmological myth. We discussed the naturalism featured in traditional Japanese arts and crafts, and finally we reflected on the impersonalism of Japanese art and religion, trying to link them with the sociological ethics needed in our present, global time.

The models of maturity or ethical achievement that we first considered came from Zen Buddhism, which perhaps paradoxically has harbored a strain of anti-model sentiment. Still, Zen has been shaped by the powerful personalities of sect founders, as have the other Japanese Buddhist schools. We speculated on the place of Confucian models in terms of the five directive relationships. Next we recalled the exhortations to hard work in the Buddhist literature of the Tokugawa period and then dealt with two exemplary tales from the folk tradition. Finally, we generalized that Japanese ethical models have seldom been normative, stressing the influence of group consensus and the lessons that the recent Japanese cultural crisis may contain for other cultures.

STUDY QUESTIONS

1. What does Susanoo suggest about Shinto tolerance for irrationality?
2. How does Japanese reverence for the kami dovetail with the Japanese aesthetic?
3. How does Kawabata's character Shingo epitomize Japanese familial values?
4. Explain the honor of the samurai warrior.
5. What understanding of social justice shapes the Imperial Rescript on Education of 1890?
6. What significance do you see in the impersonalism of Japanese views of nature?
7. Comment on the anti-modeling latent in the Buddhist counsel to "slay the Buddha."

NOTES

[1] See H. Byron Earhart, *Japanese Religion: Unity and Diversity.* 3d ed. (Belmont, Calif.: Wadsworth, 1982).

[2] Yasunari Kawabata, *The Sound of the Mountain* (Rutland, Vt.: Charles Tuttle, 1974), pp. 28–29.

[3] See Geoffrey Parrinder, *Sex in the World's Religions* (New York: Oxford University Press, 1980), pp. 106–8.

[4] Chie Nakatane, *Japanese Society* (Berkeley: University of California Press, 1972), p. 11.

[5] Earhart, *Japanese Religion*, p. 9.

[6] See *ibid.*, p. 206.

[7] Robert N. Bellah, *Tokugawa Religion* (Boston: Beacon, 1970), p. 119.

[8] Ninian Smart and Richard D. Hecht, eds., *Sacred Texts of the World: A Universal Anthology* (New York: Crossroad, 1982), p. 326.

[9] See Frederick Franck, ed., *The Buddha Eye* (New York: Crossroad, 1982).

[10] See H. Byron Earhart, ed., *Religion in the Japanese Experience* (Belmont, Calif.: Dickenson, 1974), pp. 101–2.

[11] Joan Stanley Baker, *Japanese Art* (New York: Thames and Hudson, 1984), pp. 13–14.

[12] See Philip Kapleau, ed., *The Three Pillars of Zen* (Boston: Beacon, 1967).

[13] See Earhart, ed., *Religion in the Japanese Experience*, p. 100.

[14] See Alasdair MacIntyre, *After Virtue* (Notre Dame, Ind.: University of Notre Dame Press, 1981), pp. 1–5.

8

Conclusion

Traditional Ethics
Transcendence
Mythology
Hope and Balance
Summary, Study Questions, Notes

Traditional Ethics

We have now surveyed the ethical views of seven major traditions. Occasionally we have noted how these traditions have changed recently, or how they stand in light of Western modernism. It may be helpful now, as the first of four retrospective considerations, to take up the notion of ethical traditionalism itself.

We may begin with a paragraph from Alasdair MacIntyre's well-received work *After Virtue,* to which we referred at the end of the previous chapter. There MacIntyre served as a source for the widespread opinion that contemporary Western culture has lost its ethical moorings. MacIntyre describes those moorings—the different conception of reality that premodern cultures have usually shared—as follows: "In many premodern, traditional societies it is through his or her membership of a variety of social groups that the individual identifies himself or herself and is identified by others. I am brother, cousin, and grandson, member of this household, that village, this tribe. These are not characteristics that belong to human beings accidentally, to be stripped away in order to discover 'the real me.' They are part of my substance, defining partially at least and sometimes wholly my obligations and my duties. Individuals inherit a particular space within an interlocking set of social relationships; lacking that space, they are nobody, or at best a stranger or an outcaste. To know oneself as such a social person is however not to occupy a static and fixed position. It is to find oneself placed at a certain

point on a journey with set goals; to move through life is to make progress—or to fail to make progress—toward a given end. Thus a completed
and fulfilled life is an achievement and death is the end at which someone can be judged happy or unhappy. Hence the ancient Greek proverb:
'Call no man happy until he is dead.'"[1]

The first part of the quotation calls to mind Japanese, Chinese, and
Hindu social stratifications. The clan, the Confucian household, and the
Indian caste all made the social definition of identity almost oppres-
sively strong. Buddhism offered the Indian, Chinese, and Japanese societies reasons for loosening their stranglehold on individual identity,
but on the whole tribal mores certainly were stronger than individual
liberties. Thus Chinese legal theory, as we saw, subordinated rights to
duties. One certainly can distinguish many different varieties of "traditional" culture, including most prominently the nonliterate and literate
cultures, but in all of them individuals have felt tradition to be a force
legitimating the ethos of their group.

Muslim, Christian, and Jewish ethics traditionally have had a stronger
role for the individual personality, insofar as that personality was thought
to come into sharpest relief when addressed by the transcendent and personal Creator. Thus Muhammad, Jesus, and Moses seem to press forward
toward filling out a recognizably historical identity. They are not time-
less avatars like Krishna. Muhammad and Moses, indeed, are not metaphysical principles like the Buddha, though as the Logos Jesus is. Nonetheless, the more scholars research the historical context in which
Moses, Jesus, and Muhammad came to prophetic authority, the more
they realize the influence of each prophet's social context. Despite the
legendary character of most of the primary materials bearing on all three
Western founders, it has become clear that each assumed a wealth of religious and cultural notions. Indeed, each fitted himself to a social role
recognizable to his people. To be sure, each also broke or greatly expanded that role, forcing people to think more deeply about what it
meant to be a prophet, a holy man, or a spokesman for God. And the
individuals who were later formed by the Jewish, Christian, and Muslim
traditions fitted themselves to both cultural and religious roles even
more closely than the founders of those traditions. So most of what Mac-
Intyre says of the social definition of personal identity holds for the history of Western ethics, as it does for the history of shamanic and Eastern
ethics.

The first implication of this fact is that prior to modernity it was
nearly impossible to feel alienated or deracinated, at least to the degree
that it has become not only possible but likely today. The negative side
of this fact is that traditionally one's freedom and range of self-definition
were considerably narrower, but the positive side was the certainty or
trust one enjoyed by living in a society and world whose basic mean-
ingfulness and orderliness were not questioned.

To imagine both this positivity and this negativity, we need only try to take personally the surahs of the Qur'an or the utterances of Confucius that we find in the *Analects*. The certitude they manifest is both attractive and repulsive. We would like to live alongside or apprenticed to people as sure of their values as Muhammad and Confucius seem to be. Yet we also fear that they would be tyrants, or suspect that huge tracts of knowledge and human self-perception that we have available to us were not available to them. The result is that we question their suitability as guides to the good life today, even as we wish they could be our directors.

The second part of the quotation from MacIntyre bears on the progressive aspect of traditional ethics—its connection with patterns of a life cycle thought to be headed toward a definite goal. Here the Hindu notion of the four stages of the ideal lifecycle certainly comes to mind, but we might consider other traditional schemata as well. For example, the Confucians spoke of three vices that beset the progress of the (male) personality. The first was lust, which threatened to derail young adulthood. The second was strife, which was the enemy of the prime of life. The third was greed, to which the elderly were considered especially prone. By the end of one's cycle, then, one was supposed to have successfully contended with three powerful forms of temptation or attachment and emerged able to move freely in the Way.

In the West, Christian masters spoke of three stages of the spiritual life. First was the purgative way, during which one had to scrape away vices and seriously work at the reformation of one's sinful character. Second was the illuminative way, when one started to realize, through the practice of contemplative prayer and the gifts of the Holy Spirit, how lovely and deep the truths one was professing actually were and how strong the forces of sin also were. Third was the unitive way, when one increasingly was able to find God in all things and feel the divine presence. This was a consummation in love, as the Creator's order for the world and the Redeemer's mercies made every being and happening appear a gift of grace.

Such traditional schemata made ethics a much different venture than it is today. As MacIntyre points out, in recent decades it has been characteristic of the dominant forms of ethical discourse virtually to ignore the social embodiment of the realities or norms that they have claimed to discover. By contrast, the entire weight of traditional evaluations went toward channeling actual behavior and so structuring social life. The notions of good and evil, desirability and undesirability, had no life apart from historical action: what people in fact were doing or judging. A purely academic discussion of how words functioned in a narrow enclave of worldwide society would have been shrugged off as trivial.

Once again, of course, there are pros and cons on both sides of the historical divide. Traditional, premodern ethics lacked the analytic precision that a detached academic approach can bring (though scholastics in many traditions—Jewish, Christian, Muslim, and Indian, certainly—pored over the varieties of ethical terms and judgments) and tended to fold the customary into the normative. On the other hand, it had a richer appreciation of the wholeness of human action and a praiseworthy insistence on taking guidance from the great, stubborn realities of cosmic nature, human mortality, and past tribal experience.

Transcendence

The holism of traditional ethics is now being retrieved somewhat, as social scientists win acceptance for their thesis that one cannot do justice to any cultural reality by considering only its notional aspects. Rather, one must take into account the density or richness of the concrete details that sociologists and anthropologists, at their best, render into discussable form. Thus everyday life has become the subject of numerous historical treatments, and more and more scholars are arguing against the disciplinary walls that have kept theologians and sociologists, anthropologists and philosophers, from dealing more holistically with what are in fact cultural wholes. Indeed, occasionally some startled humanist who has stumbled into a lecture on biological science comes away with the realization that natural reality itself is unremittingly ecological.

Nonetheless, holism is not the only characteristic separating traditional ethics from our present-day sensibilities. As we have regularly seen, the traditional convictions about right and wrong, in both the East and the West, have been integral to an assumption that reality has an order and depth not conferred at human beings' good pleasure. In other words, the religious traditions that we have studied have thought that the good human life was something objective: part of an order either created by a rational divinity or existent from time immemorial as a cosmological whole. One can speak of nature, human mortality, and past tribal experience as calling human beings to transcend simply commonsensical or everyday assumptions, but the heart of the traditional ethical systems has been the more radical transcendence of ultimate reality itself. In the West, this heart has been the expressed will of a Creator free of the world (not needing the world to be). In the East, the heart has been the beyond-going holiness of a moksha, nirvana, Tao, or Way of the kami. These Eastern notions, to be sure, have not separated the ultimate source of morality from the rhythms of the cosmos so clearly as the Western notions of religious Law have. Still, compared to the denial of transcendence or the disregard of human teleology (finality or ultimate goal) characterizing modern ethical systems, the traditional Eastern ethical systems have stood with the traditional Western systems as being based quite differently.

We shall not bother to elaborate the pros and cons of this distinction, except to note that the modern denials of transcendence and teleology, when seen in the concrete historical circumstances of their arising, had considerable justification. There can be a quite reasonable and morally defensible "atheism," as the higher traditions of both religious spheres, Eastern and Western, have allowed. The true God or Tao is not a thing that one can manipulate, let alone a guarantor of an unjust status quo. But more to our point is the deracination and alienation, as we have called it, that results when one's ethical system has no secure moorings. The short and too-brutal description of this state of affairs is Dostoevski's maxim that if God is dead everything is permitted. This would seem unbearably cynical had we not witnessed in the twentieth century systematic murder unprecedented in human history. The less **apocalyptic** observation is that our current meaninglessness, debilitating subjectivity, or emotivism (as analytical philosophers tend to call it: the divorce of reason and feeling in ethical life) is intimately connected with our loss of transcendence. We think we have no access to or guidance from an order or reality that transcends ourselves. We think we are alone in the universe, and we know all too well that human judgment and goodness are far too fragile a rudder to give us confidence that we can navigate successfully.

When we contrast this state of affairs with the disposition of premodern religious people, we should not exaggerate the tidiness of their ethical outlook. One has only to read the Hindu, Buddhist, or Confucian literature carefully to realize that our forebears were quite aware of the place of perspective, disposition, experience, and the rest in judgments about "reality." Still, they had sufficient experience of what they called the in-given order of the objective world to allow them to keep these intimations of chaos under control. Controlled, the intimations nourished humility and prudence but avoided hopelessness and relativism. Eric Voegelin has argued that the deculturation afflicting us today comes from our loss of such experiences of transcendence and in-given order. In his magnum opus, *Order and History*,[2] Voegelin indicates some of the crucial experiences that formed Western culture and now seem buried under a depressing weight of historical amnesia and impoverished education.

If one is to boil this thesis down, one could do worse than to say that we will not have the re-racinated, integral ethics we desire until we again make regular the disciplines through which past peoples experienced the transcendence that they made directive for their ethical action. Specifically, we need shamans, prophets, and sages—the people of experience upon whom past ethical systems depended. Through their ecstatic journeys, shamans contacted the realm of the gods who renewed their tribal mores. Through their encounters with God in prayer, prophets received the "Word of God" behind the ethical programs of Torah, Gospel, and Qur'an. The Eastern sages who begot or pondered the Vedas, the Upanishads, the Prajnaparamita literature, the *Analects*, the *Tao Te Ching*, and the other revered religious guides regularly took themselves to contemplation, peacefully pondering the problem they had to solve in light of ultimate reality.

As Voegelin and other analysts make plain, these experiential sources of the traditional ethical systems were considered available to any who felt inclined to follow their disciplines. Even today, the Jewish regime for studying Talmud, the Christian regime for praying the Scriptures, the exercises of Sufis pursuing the inner meaning of the names of Allah, and their analogues in the Eastern traditions remain in principle open to any who wish to try them. Indeed, many who have tried them in recent generations have come away convinced that they still can conduce to the experience of a transcendent reality that changes the context and significance of human time.

This is not to say that modernity has not made such ventures in the pursuit of transcendence more problematic. Our greater awareness of psychological motivation, sociological conditioning, and past oversights can be very helpful in controlling the excesses and imbalances to which such pursuits are prone (though, once again, we must add that the traditions themselves regularly provided cautions). Yet the final matter cannot be settled simply in academic or analytical terms. The final appeal is to the experience expressed in a Plato's description of the "in-between" (**metaxic**) character of human reason that sets the boundaries of our "reality," or in a **John of the Cross**'s description of how the purified personality has become convinced of the otherness and goodness of God.

By and large, modern proponents of anomie (normlessness) fail to contest the traditional ethical claims on this experiential ground. They prefer to rule such ventures, and the directives for the good life that they generate, irrational or ungrounded from the start. But of course this is a highly vulnerable form of refutation, and as the abuses of secularist culture have started to overshadow the abuses of the premodern religious or ecclesiastical cultures that first made secularism seem a liberation, it has become hard to respect people who try to dismiss experiences of transcendence without having tested the disciplines on which traditional ethical systems said such experiences depended.

Mythology

The meditational disciplines from which the traditional ethical masters derived their experience of transcendent reality were, it is true, somewhat elitist. That should not discourage our contemporary ethicists, who after all profess to be an intellectual elite, but if those disciplines had been the only means of forming a solid ethical outlook in people, premodern societies probably would have failed. As it was, the popular formation took place through myths and rituals in which all members of the tribe or larger culture could participate. We have seen specimens of folk literature that inculcated the responsibility to be hospitable to strangers. We have noted the ties between the Indian system of caste and the Indian mythology of creation. And we have mentioned the rituals, such as the habisha rites of middle-aged devotees of Krishna, that have given traditional people vehicles for expressing, very holistically, their needs and aspirations and beliefs. The point, clearly, is the important role that myth and ritual played in sustaining the traditional religio-ethical world view. Equally clearly, the implication is that our own poverty in this area is a large part of our present ethical crisis.

Let us take the example of death, which MacIntyre rightly indicated was the acme in the traditional views of the life cycle. One was to call no person happy until death, because prior to death tragedy could always strike. Moreover, death itself would be a final test. If one could die as Socrates had, in complete serenity of soul and self-possession, one would indeed merit being called happy. If one died shattered by physical or emotional suffering, one would have to be considered pitiable. And if this were true for people such as Socrates, who were quite untypical in their degree of wisdom (instructively, Socrates was the wisest man in Athens because he knew how much he didn't know), it was all the more true of common people who had not had Socrates' gifts of genes, history, and courage.

The upshot of such estimates of death, which all traditional peoples seem to have grasped with little trouble, was the need to ritualize people's "passing over" to whatever state they conjectured lay across the border of dying. Buddhism had much of its influence in East Asia because it solemnized that passage effectively. Confucianism made the passage of one's parents a major point of transition in one's own journey. Shinto rituals sought to ward off the pollution that Japanese instinct, like the instinct of many other peoples, associated with death. Jewish, Christian, and Muslim groups displayed similar patterns, sitting **shiva** with the corpse and family of the departed, or having "month's mind" masses to commemorate the first thirty days of separation.

Through such rituals, a people gave itself the chance to feel grief, express depression, and rouse its hopes that death was not the final word. All the senses and emotions were solicited by sights and sounds and symbols that might blunt the mind's trauma and heal the soul's cracks. Moreover, many of the ceremonies explicitly linked the fate of the person being buried or cremated with the condition of the person worshiping. Both were simply people whose lives were short, and neither had ever seen God. So both were pitiable—in need of compassion. Both had claims on the forgiveness of their fellow human beings for the defects in their imperfect lives. Both, indeed, had claims on God, the Buddha, or the kami—on the ultimate agency responsible for their having come into so fragile a body, so fearsome a psyche, so troubled and lethal a world.

Ironically enough, the myths and rituals that modern Western culture so often has mocked as superstitious and irrational regularly made traditional people absolutely realistic about their situation. Through their funerary rites, which usually were just the culmination of healing and pacifying rites afforded the dying person, traditional people could face death unblinkingly. People usually died at home, in the midst of even the smallest children. They died being prayed for by the community, who wished them a happy voyage to God or a better return in their future life. The typical traditional society did not display the denial of death that cultural analysts have come to decry in the West. There was not the relegation of the seriously ill to sterile hospitals that knew little about the spirit and considered each death a medical defect. So there was no need to rush about trying to develop a network of hospices in which people could die with dignity and meaning. Intuitively, from long years of participation in profound rituals and mythologies, traditional people knew that death was natural and always could be made meaningful, if not beautiful.

Mircea Eliade, the dean of American historians of religion, has been perhaps the foremost spokesman for our need to restore the mythological dimension to Western culture.[3] In widely ranging studies of archaic, Eastern, and Western religious phenomena, he has developed the thesis that all peoples are seeking transcendent meaning, regardless of how limited or bizarre their behavior may seem. Moreover, all peoples show a need to ritualize their passage from birth to death, and successful cultures are those that meet this need satisfactorily. Eliade would concede that the critical faculties sharpened in modernity have made myth and ritual more difficult to create. The rather ahistorical mentality in which mythology thrives is the antithesis of modern self-consciousness. But this may merely indicate that we have to become more sophisticated in our appreciation of symbolism, and more willing to situate our vaunted criticism in a context of genuine mystery. In other words, we may simply have to confess that reality indeed is too vast and rich for us to master, and that the honest response to this fact is reverence for reality and abandonment of our pretension to complete control.

An ethics linked to this sort of elementary religion would not only immediately become holistic, since the mystery acknowledged in such basic reverence and abandonment is relevant to every item and moment of our lives; it would also have restored to it the teleology whose present lack makes ethicists' prescriptions for human action vacuous. One cannot prescribe a way to maturity, nor discriminate good actions from bad, unless one has a clear sense of what end product the way and the actions ought to be creating. And one cannot tackle this question, obviously enough, as long as one avoids grappling with the significance of human death. Finally, one cannot mediate an effective ethics to ordinary people without telling stories and enacting ceremonies that make the ideal way of life dramatic, gripping, and persuasive.

On the other hand, today the charge to remythologize ethics does have to avoid the temptations to fundamentalism and simplism that modern gains in self-understanding reveal to be invitations to immaturity. The difference between a genuine mystagogy (education in the transcendent divine mystery) and a literalist attempt to manipulate a scripture or tradition is enormous. The latter is a form of magic, condemned by seers as diverse as the Upanishadic visionaries who ruthlessly criticized the Brahmanic ritualistic magicians and the Sufi masters who mocked the credulity of those who tried to possess and control the Qur'anic Word of God. And where fundamentalism has a natural affinity with puritanism, with a prideful sense of chosenness, and with a will to power if not to outright holy war, **mystagogy** of the type inculcated by the traditional meditational disciplines has a natural affinity with humility, universal love, and Socratic nescience (not knowing a lot of trivia, having certitude only that the divine is the sole master).

The Christian West once used the myths and rituals of two great cycles, that of Christmas and that of Easter, to foster in people a spiritual realism about birth and death. People once knew that the infant, the poor parents, and the crucified Master held secrets of everlasting value. Thus, people once could act freely and joyously, in view of a surpassingly valuable goal. The task of today's ethics is to fashion a path of action that will aim as high as this (and other such traditions) and be considerably more critical.

Hope and Balance

Our final conclusion about the ethics of the world religions is that they have consistently provided two things: hope and balance. The hope certainly came through most dramatically when people so ritualized death that even this apparent end of life became meaningful—indeed, became just a transition to a better set of possibilities. But such hope also bore on daily life in the time between birth and death. True, without an interpretation of death that took away some of its sting, a religion had little chance of illuminating daily life with hope. There is an intimate relation between **teleology** (final causality) and the other agencies, and this is why Aristotle made the end (*telos*) the first in the ordering of causes. But even without great stress on a death that was a transition to a heavenly afterlife, a religious tradition could draw on numerous resources for presenting life as good and making ethical effort seem worthwhile.

Few current writers do a better job of this than Grace Paley, whose own modern Jewish tradition has stressed radical politics more than blessed afterlife. In the following dialogue with her lover, Faith (Grace

Paley's alter ego) tries to make the case for bringing a new child into the world and raising it in hope:

"Listen. Listen, he said. Our old children are just about grown. Why do you want a new child? Haven't we agreed often, haven't we said that it had become noticeable that life is short and sorrowful? Haven't we said the words 'gone' and 'where'? Haven't we sometimes in the last few years used the word 'terrible' and we mean to include in it the word 'terror'? Everyone knows this about life. Though of course some fools never stop singing its praises.

"But they're right, I said in my turn. Yes, and this is in order to en-courage the young whom we have, after all, brought into the world—they must not be abandoned. We must, I said, continue pointing out simple and worthwhile sights such as—in the countryside—hills fold-ing into one another in light-green spring or white winter, the sky which is always astonishing either in its customary blueness or in the configu-ration of clouds—the way they're pushed in their softest parts by the air's breath and change shape and direction and density. Not to mention our own beloved city crowded with day and night workers, shoppers, walk-ers, the subway trains which many people fear but they're so hand-somely lined with pink to dark dark brown faces, golden tans and yel-lows scattered amongst them. It's very important to emphasize what is good or beautiful so as not to have a gloomy face when you meet some youngster who has begun to guess."[4]

The counsel is wonderful, and the rest of Grace Paley's stories make it plain that it is not a counsel sprung from naivete. Faith lives in the city, surrounded by the violence and despair of the city's many margin-alized people, so it seems fair to understand "some youngster who has begun to guess" in quite stark or radical terms. The youngster has begun to guess that life is not fair, people are not just, suffering is always just a hair's breadth away. Indeed, the youngster has begun to guess that parents are severely limited, teachers are less than wise, and governments often are dishonest. "Nonetheless," one can hear Faith say, "nonetheless." We must affirm life, must search out the marvels of nature and city and human being, because life does have beauty to balance its ugliness, life does provide goodness to balance its evil. Furthermore, unless we choose to stress the goodness, without closing our eyes to the evil, we will not have the courage we need to struggle on. It is all too easy to lose heart, feel betrayed, join all the naysayers and chiselers. That is why the ef-fective ethical systems have always reposed in a moksha that was ac-counted being, bliss, and awareness, or in a God in whom there was no darkness at all. Such systems went to the roots of reality and came up with positivity: being that predominates over nonbeing, light that pre-dominates over darkness, grace that predominates over sin.

We might call the hope sponsored by such systems **ontological.** What is or has being (on) can be thought of only in positive terms. But if this positive being is our being and the being of the world in which we live, then our action can be hopeful, and our ethics—the prescriptions for good action that we fashion—can be hopeful as well. We see an illustration of this viewpoint, and the consequent balance at which most religious traditions have aimed, in the protests of the ethically sensitive against the evils of their time. By the simple fact that they recognize such evils and speak out against them, the ethically sensitive reaffirm the canons of rightness and the protocols of decency that have always expressed human beings' better nature and possibility.

For example, religious people who have gotten involved in the sanctuary movement (a program designed to shield from deportation political refugees who face death if they are sent back to their [usually Latin American] homelands) have discovered to their disgust, if not outright horror, that their government has been trying to infiltrate paid informers into churches offering sanctuary. Such religious people take this effort as a sign of the extent to which their government will go to suppress opposition to its Latin American policies, many of which involve supporting the people who would murder the political refugees if they were returned. Moreover, such shocked religious people tend to confess their naivete and to repent of their previous assumption that such a system of informers was the mark only of depraved regimes like those that dominate eastern Europe and South Africa, and those that once dominated Nazi Germany.

Robert McAfee Brown, making such a confession and act of repentance, focuses on the corrosive effect that such a policy of infiltrating informers into the bosom of the churches—places where people used to think they could speak from the heart—has on church life, on the informers themselves, and ultimately on the government. In detailing some of the effects on the government, which after all is supposed to be of, by, and for the whole of us, Brown puts a sharp edge on what "some youngster" surely has begun to guess: "How does infiltration affect the initiating agent, the government? The answer is clear and painful: Our government becomes a government that honors deception, rewards acts of betrayal, gives bonus points for telling lies, and destroys the meaning of truth. Our government not only says that it intends to punish those who shelter people whose lives are endangered, but it also says that it will reward [pay] those who help it punish such people. Although the government may not say it explicitly, the government is acting out a belief that goes: We do not endorse saving people; we endorse (and reward) deceiving people. We do not endorse concern for friends in a prayer circle; we endorse (and reward) betraying the friend in the prayer circle by pretending to be a friend in order to become a more effective enemy."[5]

We have used this example not to raise hackles about the sanctuary movement or policies of the United States in Latin America so much as to make it clear that religious ethics is overwhelmingly concrete. Through history, people have died martyrs' deaths rather than violate their religious consciences, and sages have condemned—by declaring them to have no genuine authority—governments that tried to pervert human conscience. Today that process continues, as ethicists excoriate the Soviet Union for violations of basic human rights, pillory South Africa for its systemic racism, look back on Nazi Germany as a pathological regime, and, like Robert McAfee Brown, do not hesitate to draw the parallels at home.

Still, the final word, as Grace Paley indicates and Robert McAfee Brown would agree, is positive. We must stand in the middle if we are to be virtuous by traditional standards, but this does not mean a dualistic equation of evil and good. If we let ourselves be tutored by the world religions, Eastern and Western, our ethics will emerge as an affirmation of being, life, and love. We will say that these are the portion of "life," and that negativity, death, and hate are either the portion of failure or are things subsumed into a larger scheme (recall, for example, the necessary destructiveness symbolized by Shiva). Indeed, we will know, in our quiet times of midnight or dawn, why St. Augustine could summarize religious ethics as simply as he did. After years of wrestling with the problem of good and evil, of trying to get himself out of a Manichean **dualism** that pictured good and evil as equal, Augustine came to the faith that reality was thoroughly good and that evil was a mysterious though potent senselessness. Therefore he could say, trusting that those with religious experience would know what he meant and not abuse his counsel, "Love and do what you will." It's hard to think of a more provocative thought with which to conclude a work on ethics in the world religions.

Summary

Our first concluding reflection concerned the traditionalism of the systems of religious ethics that we have studied. Using a paragraph by Alasdair MacIntyre, we first stressed the social definition of identity that has prevailed in traditional societies, illustrating this in several of the world religions. We noted the contrast between such traditional meaning and modern deracination and alienation, and then we considered MacIntyre's idea that traditional cultures also sponsored a view of human life as having definite stages and a definite goal or term. This, too, we illustrated in Eastern and Western religions. In both cases we noted the pros and cons in both cultural situations, traditional and modern.

Our second reflection bore on transcendence, which we found even more crucial to traditionalism than its admirable holism. We alluded to the complexity of the modern rejection of transcendence (or disquiet about transcendence), considered the plight in which this rejection has left our ethical judgment, and then indicated the contrasting situation in several traditional religious world views. Our next topic was the meditational disciplines that the traditions fostered under the conviction that one had to experience transcendent divinity or ultimate reality to understand the tribal mores.

Our third concern was mythology (and ritual), which we considered to be the popular equivalent of the more elitist meditational regimes. Once again this traditional feature proved significantly lacking in modern culture, as our exploration of people's dealing with death illustrated. We noted the realism that the traditional ritualization of death and burial fostered, and then took up the difficult topic of how to remythologize death and other crucial experiences in a modern critical culture.

Finally, we dealt with the hope and balance that traditional ethical systems regularly have provided. We linked the hope with a solid teleology. Then we used an excerpt from a Grace Paley story to show how the ties between the generations also encourage hope and a positive emphasis. We balanced this with all the reasons for being sober about life's negative aspects, including such current practices of our own government as fostering informing. Our last reflections dealt with the ontological foundations for hope and ethics, and for a summary counsel such as Augustine's "Love and do what you will."

STUDY QUESTIONS

1. What place should death hold in a religious ethics?

2. How did traditional societies foster experiences of a transcendent ultimate reality?

3. What is the basis for claiming that the myths and rituals of traditional peoples made them realistic about death?

4. What have Robert McAfee Brown's churchpeople begun to guess about their government?

NOTES

[1] Alasdair MacIntyre, *After Virtue* (Notre Dame, Ind.: University of Notre Dame Press, 1981), p. 32.

[2] See especially Eric Voegelin, *Order and History*, vol. 4 (Baton Rouge: Louisiana State University Press, 1974).

[3] See Mircea Eliade, *A History of Religious Ideas* (Chicago: University of Chicago Press, 1978, 1982).

[4] Grace Paley, *Later the Same Day* (New York: Farrar, Straus, Giroux, 1985), p. 204.

[5] Robert McAfee Brown, "Paid Informers, Deception and Lies," *The Christian Century*, November 13, 1985, p. 1029.

Glossary

Agni: A major Vedic god associated with fire and the hearth.

Agnosticism: The position that one does not or cannot know anything determinative (about God, human destiny, and similarly crucial religious questions).

Ahimsa: An Indian term for noninjury, nonviolence, and respect for the sacredness of life.

Alchemy: Experimental studies seeking control over physical elements for wealth or spiritual power.

Anatman: The Buddhist term for no-self, for not having or being a subsistent, independent entity.

Animistic: Concerning souls or spirits, especially as forces divinized in popular religion.

Anthropocentric: Pivoted on human beings, making human beings the center of creation.

Apocalyptic: Concerning a divine disclosure about the pattern of the end of history, which is considered imminent.

Arabesque: Nonrepresentational patterns and swirls associated with the Islamic decorative arts.

Artha: The Hindu term for wealth, prosperity, good material fortune.

Ashram: The Hindu term for a religious community centered around a guru.

Atman: The Indian term for the ultimate principle of the living being (soul, self).

Avatar: The Hindu term for the embodiments of the deities that different historical eras enjoy. For example, Krishna is an avatar of Vishnu.

Bhaktas: Devotees of a Hindu god such as Krishna or Shiva who is to be worshiped emotionally as a lover or master.

Bhakti: The Hindu term for emotional, devotional love of God.

Bodhisattva: The saintly ideal of Mahayana Buddhism; a Buddha-to-be who postpones entry into nirvana in order to labor for the salvation of all living things.

Brahma Day: An Indian term for the positive phase of creation, when the universe is expanding and developing.

Brahma Night: An Indian term for the negative phase of creation, when the universe is contracting and resting.

Brahman: The Hindu term for the ultimate principle of the cosmos.

Brahmins (or Brahmans): Vedic priests; members of the first, most prestigious Indian caste.

Bushido: The Japanese ethical code that stressed honor and loyalty to one's superiors.

Cabalism: A medieval Jewish mystical movement that sought to allegorize Scripture and unlock both its secret directions for daily life and its descriptions of the emanations of God.

Caste: The stratification of Indian society into a hierarchy of distinct religiocultural groups.

Charismatic: Possessed of spiritual gifts giving energy and influence.

Conservative Judaism: A movement to accommodate traditional Jewish law without going as far as the radical shifts proposed by Reform Judaism.

Corporal works of mercy: A Christian term for practical acts of help and kindness such as visiting the sick and prisoners.

Cosmological myth: The story of the structure of the world that makes all beings part of a natural, living whole.

Covenant: A solemn compact pledging the partners to mutual rights and duties.

Creation: In the Christian view, God's having made the world, human beings, and angels from nothingness.

Creative fiat: The divine "let there be" that produced finite realities from nothingness.

Critical intelligence: Understanding that sifts sources and probes assumptions, ideally to issue solid, dispassionate judgments.

Cross of Christ: The instrument of the death of Jesus, raised to the status of a basic symbol for the sufferings caused by sins.

Dependent coarising: The Buddhist view of the interconnected character of all realities.

Descriptive ethics: Historical analysis of how people have in fact behaved and said one should live.

Dharma: Indian teaching, truth, wise analysis of reality, and prescription for successful living.

Dharmakaya: The body of the Buddha that identifies his enlighten-ment with the dharma (conceived as a cosmological principle and the essence of the Absolute).

Dhikr (pronounced "zicker"): The Muslim practice of trying regularly, even constantly, to remember the presence of God.

Distributive justice: Fair sharing of goods, based on the essential equal-ity of all human beings.

Diviner: One who discerns the future or the will of divinity.

Dualism: The position that two forces or realities divide the world, often competitively.

Ends: The goals, terminal results, or final products that an action or a proposal intends.

Eschatological: Concerning the end of history, the final things (death, judgment, heaven, and hell).

Eschaton: The final thing; consequently, the consummation of history, arrival of divine judgment, and commencement of heaven.

Exodus: The escape of the Hebrews from Egypt under the leadership of Moses.

Faith: Trust, holistic commitment, or doctrinal belief, usually as deter-mined by God or ultimate reality.

Fatalism: The position that things are determined and are out of hu-man beings' hands.

Five pillars: The main components of Islamic faith—creed, daily prayer, fasting during Ramadan, almsgiving, and pilgrimage to Mecca.

Geisha: A woman trained in Japanese arts of hospitality, entertainment, and comradeship.

Geomancer: A specialist in the significance of the forces of the earth (wind and water) for good fortune.

Habisha: A ritual used by contemporary Indian women of middle age to protect the health of their husbands and so avert widowhood.

Hasidic: Pertaining to the movement associated with the Baal Shem Tov, an eighteenth-century c.e. eastern European Jewish devotional leader.

Hermeneutics: The science of interpretation—how one should tease meaning from texts and other sources.

Hinayanists: Those Buddhists designated by their opponents, the Ma-hayanists, as followers of the smaller vehicle (raft) of salvation.

Hindu Vedas: The sacred traditions of the Aryans that have become the scriptural foundation of Hinduism.

Holy war: A military venture thought to be carried out by divine will and sanction, and sometimes carrying the obligation to exterminate one's (idolatrous) enemies.

Humanistic: Focused on human interests, resources, and possibilities, often to the exclusion of divine influences.

Iconic: Referring to an icon or sacramental representation of a divine reality, such that the representation itself deserves veneration.

Immanent: Within, present to; refers especially to the relation between God and creation.

Infidels: People not adhering to one's own faith.

Jen (pronounced "run"): A Chinese term for humaneness, goodness, benevolence.

Jesus Prayer: A form of devotion, dear to Eastern Christianity, in which one ceaselessly calls on Jesus and asks mercy for one's sins.

Jihad: The Muslim term for holy war—fighting to spread or defend the faith, with the assurance that death is a path to paradise.

John of the Cross: A sixteenth-century C.E. Spanish Christian mystic famous for his poems about the dark night of the soul and spiritual marriage of the soul to God.

Just war: In Christian teaching, armed conflicts that may be considered justifiable because undertaken in response to aggression and likely to achieve more good than harm.

Kali: A version of the Indian mother-goddess that stresses her dark, destructive side.

Kama: The Hindu term for sensual pleasure, physical and cultural enjoyment.

Kami: The Japanese term for naturalistic forces, spirits, great ancestors, and other numinous (divine) powers.

Karma: The Indian moral law of cause and effect, such that past unenlightened actions keep beings in samsara.

Karma-yoga: The Indian term for discipline that seeks to purify work (to render it neutral or positive in terms of karmic effect) by stressing detachment from concern about success or failure.

Koan: A paradoxical saying or riddle (for example, "the sound of one hand clapping") used by Zen Buddhist masters as a prod to enlightenment.

Kosher: What traditional Jewish legislation has deemed fitting, proper, or "clean," especially in diet.

Lao Tzu: The legendary founder of Taoism and author of the *Tao Te Ching*.

Li: The Chinese term for propriety, ritual etiquette, and due social form.

Liturgical year: In Christian usage, the annual cycle of festivals and days of penance, from Advent in the fall, through Christmas, Lent, Easter, and Pentecost, to the long summer period after Pentecost.

Lord Krishna: The most popular Hindu god, who is an avatar of Vishnu, the Preserver.

Lotus Sutra: A devotional scripture greatly venerated by Nichiren and other Buddhists.

Mahabharata: The most ambitious Indian epic poem, focused on an ancient war, in the midst of which occurs the Bhagavad Gita.

Mahatma: The Hindu term for a great soul or saint, applied most recently to Mohandas Gandhi, the twentieth-century liberator.

Mahayana: Referring to the branch of Buddhism that considers itself the great raft (more commodious vehicle) of salvation.

Mandate of heaven: The Chinese notion that political rule depended on a favor or license granted by the gods.

Mantras: An Indian term for sounds thought to have power and repeated as aids to meditation.

Maya: An Indian term for reality as perceived by the unenlightened—a realm of illusion and divine play.

Mediums: People serving as intermediaries between this world and the world of spirits.

Messiah: The anointed delegate of the biblical God, expected to bring a reign of peace and prosperity.

Metaethics: The point of view—deeper or higher than the horizon of specific ethical prescriptions—that provides an ethics its foundation and general orientation.

Metaxic: Concerning the Platonic teaching that the proper range of human understanding is between the divine One above and unbounded matter below.

Mishnah: A code of Jewish law, based on the opinions of the leading rabbis, as collected in the diaspora (dispersion from Jerusalem after the Roman destruction of the city in 70 C.E.) and promulgated around 200 C.E.

Modernity: The shifts away from medieval culture that became discernible by the sixteenth century in Europe and dovetailed with the new natural science, historiography, and philosophy of consciousness.

Moksha: The Hindu term for freedom, liberation from this-worldly constraints and sufferings.

Monotheistic: Concerning a God considered to be the sole deity, creator, savior, and ultimate good.

Mystagogy: Evocation of the divine mystery.

Mystics: Those favored with a direct, experiential knowledge of God or holy ultimacy.

Natural law: The view that God has encoded normative patterns in the makeup of both human beings and other creatures.

Nirvana: The Buddhist term for the state of fulfillment and release from the bondages of worldly existence.

Nuclear winter: The scenario according to which large-scale nuclear explosions would create dust blocking out the sun and so plunging the earth into lethal cold and darkness.

Ontological: Concerning being, existence.

Oracles: Expressions of the will of divinity, usually given through diviners, priests, or prophets.

Orthodox Judaism: Judaism that retains allegiance to the full sweep of traditional religious law (*Halakah*).

Orthodoxy: The position, regarding religious opinion or worship, that has come to be considered normative and representative of the traditional mainstream.

Orthopraxy: Right behavior, faith proven healthy by its producing the expected ethical fruits.

Phenomenology: The effort to let the data—the phenomena—of a given matter appear, so that one can describe them nonjudgmentally.

Pietists: Jewish groups (who had analogues in Christianity and other traditions) seeking an especially intense and regulated religious life.

Polluting: An action that renders one ritually unclean, in need of purification before reentering the presence of holy things.

Polytheistic: Having many divinities deserving allegiance.

Prajnaparamita: Buddhist literature supposedly written from the viewpoint of "the wisdom that has gone beyond" worldly ignorance.

Pre–Common Era (B.C.E. or B.C.): The time before Christ, who inaugurated an era (a history) common to both Christians and non-Christians.

Predestination: God's creative will that events in nature or human history and salvation follow a certain pattern.

Prescriptive ethics: Analysis and advice concerning what ought to be done, how people should behave.

Priestly legislation: Portions of the Hebrew Bible, such as Leviticus, that deal with the laws of ritual purity and the prescriptions for sacrifice.

Promised land: The land of Canaan, considered promised by God to Moses and entered under the leadership of Joshua.

Prophecy: Divine inspiration to discern the religious significance of one's times and proclaim its practical implications.

Providence: God's foresight and provision for the needs of creatures.

Puranas: A class of Hindu literature concerned with edifying tales about gods and heroes.

Purdah: The seclusion of Muslim women from public life, sometimes to a harem.

Ramayana: The Hindu epic poem influential for its many entertaining and edifying stories of gods and goddesses.

Rectification of names: The early Confucian reform that promoted political and ethical order by controlling terminology and thought.

Redemption: In Christianity, the notion that God has forgiven people their sins, covering their moral debts because of the work of Christ.

Reformed Judaism: A liberalizing response to modernity that proposed easing strict fidelity to the letter of the Talmudic laws and stressed general ethical uprightness.

Relativism: The ethical position that values are contextual, have no absolute or trans-contextual validity, and so vary from situation to situation.

Religion: The dimension of human life or the sort of human activity that deals with the ultimate and most important questions.

Revelation: The self-disclosure of the mysterious God, so that people may know the path to union with him or her.

Rg Veda: The most influential portion of the Vedas, composed of songs and prayers that best exemplify the ancient Aryan world view.

Rishis: The visionary poets and philosophers credited with producing the Vedas (Hindu scripture and revelation).

Sacramental: The use of a material thing as an effective means or channel of spiritual significance and divine grace.

Sacrifice: Offering something to divinity as a sign of one's devotion and petition.

Samadhi: The deepest state of trance or yogic self-possession.

Samsara: An Indian term for the cycle of deaths and rebirths causing cosmic suffering.

Sangha: The Buddhist term for the community of either monks and nuns or of monks, nuns, and laity.

Sannyasin: An Indian term for the sage or holy person who has gained enlightenment and wanders as an example and teacher.

Sanskrit: The Indo-European language in which many Hindu and Buddhist scriptures were composed.

Sati: The Hindu term for burning a (living) widow on the funeral pyre of her husband.

Satyagraha: Mahatma Gandhi's term for the force of truth and a righteous cause.

Sectarian: Pertaining to only a portion, a side-stream, of the tradition or community—often a portion or part dissenting from the majority.

Secular: Mainly concerned with this-worldly, nonheavenly matters.

Semantics: The study of meaning in language—how words and ideas convey significance.

Shakti: An Indian term for active, creative feminine power extrapolated into a cosmic principle.

Shamans: Specialists in archaic techniques of ecstasy.

Shankara: The ninth-century C.E. Indian philosopher who systematized the Upanishadic teachings in terms of nonduality.

Shariah: Muslim law, guidance, jurisprudence, ethics.

Shia: The group of Muslims ("Shiites") who believed the succession to rule of the community ought to have followed the bloodline of Muhammad.

Shinran (1163–1262 C.E.): The medieval founder of Shin Buddhism, one of the most influential devotional sects of Japanese Buddhism.

Shinto: The native, pre-Buddhist Japanese religiocultural traditions; the way of the kami.

Shirk: The Muslim term for idolatry—making anything a partaker with Allah of divinity.

Shiva: 1) The Hindu god of asceticism, eroticism, and destruction.
2) The Jewish ceremonies for honoring the dead.

Shogunate: The Japanese term for the rule exercised by nobles commanding strong armies.

Sikhs: Followers of the fifteenth-century C.E. Indian prophet Nanak, who tried to synthesize Hinduism and Islam.

Sila: The five basic ethical precepts—not to kill, steal, lie, be unchaste, or take intoxicants—incumbent on all Buddhists.

Soma: A ritual drink hymned in the Vedas as a source of visionary insight.

Starsy: Russian Christian spiritual guides celebrated for their holiness and wisdom.

Structuralism: The view that language and thought are informed by structures that lie below the levels of current culture and locale.

Sudras: The class of workers (laborers) that ranked lowest among the four official Hindu castes.

Sufism: A devotional movement in Islam seeking to supplement adherence to the law (Shariah) with interior prayer and asceticism.

Sunni: The majority party in Islam; it did not vest leadership in Muhammad's bloodline.

Sutras: Addresses of the Buddha; Buddhist texts attributed to the Buddha.

Talmud: The main collection of rabbinic teaching, comprised of the Mishnah and the Gemara (a commentary on the Mishnah) and promulgated around 500 C.E.

Tanak: The Hebrew acronym for Scripture, composed from the first letters of the names of each of the three main parts of the Hebrew Bible: Torah, Nevi'im (Prophets), and Kethuvim (Writings).

Tantra: Hindu and Buddhist use of imaginative and libidinal energies in the pursuit of salvation.

Tao (pronounced "dow"): The cosmic Way, which has been the Chinese equivalent of the Indian dharma.

Tao Te Ching **("The Way and Its Power"):** A work attributed to Lao Tzu that has been virtually scriptural for Taoism.

Teleology: Concern with ends, goals, final outcomes.

Theocentric: Pivoted on God, making God the center of life.

Theotokos: A Christian term for the Virgin Mary as the mother of God.

Theravadin Buddhists: Members of the more conservative, traditional branch of Buddhism (a remnant of Hinayana), which looks upon itself as the best preserver of the ancient teachings.

Torah: 1) Divine guidance, instruction, law;
2) The first five books of the Hebrew Bible (Pentateuch).

Transcendence: Going beyond this-worldly realities or present attainments, ultimately into the limitless mystery of God.

Trickster: A figure found in many tribal cultures who personifies irrational impulse and resistance to authority.

Unconditioned: Free of the constraints of space, time, ignorance, sin, mortality, and the like, which shape human existence.

Upanishads: The final writings of the Vedas, where the theme is the search for the ultimate principle explaining reality.

Utilitarian: Judged by usefulness or benefits rather than by intrinsic goodness or badness.

Vajrayana: The "thunderbolt vehicle," a branch of Buddhism developed in Tibet and owing much to Tantra.

Vinaya: The rules developed by the Buddhist Sangha to guide monks and nuns.

Vivekananda: A late-nineteenth- and early-twentieth-century C.E. Hindu swami (master) who urged social action as a form of religious living.

Vowed poverty: The first of the three commitments (to poverty, chastity, and obedience) constituting the life of Christian "religious"— monks, nuns, and members of other consecrated groups living a communal life.

Wahabism: A quite puritanical Muslim reform movement that gained dominance in twentieth-century Saudi Arabia.

Worship: Prayer that honors God as uniquely holy and worthy of praise.

Wu wei: The Taoist term signifying actionless action, positive not-doing.

Yin-yang: The basic duality of complementary forces that Chinese thought has postulated.

Yoga: Disciplinary exercises or regimens for the sake of interior freedom or overall health.

Zionism: The Jewish movement to reestablish a homeland centered on Zion, the hill in Jerusalem where the Temple of Solomon stood.

Bibliography

(Items marked with an asterisk [*] are suitable for undergraduates. Most of the items also offer further bibliographic leads.)

METHODOLOGY

* Green, Ronald M. "Morality and Religion." In *The Encyclopedia of Religion* [hereafter cited as *ER*], ed. Mircea Eliade, vol. 10, pp. 92–106. New York: 1987.

Green, Ronald M. *Religious Reason.* Oxford: 1978.

Little, David, and Twiss, Sumner B. *Comparative Religious Ethics.* San Francisco: 1978.

*Lovin, Robin W., and Reynolds, Frank E. "In the Beginning." In *Cosmogony and Ethical Order*, ed. Robin W. Lovin and Frank E. Reynolds, pp. 1–35. Chicago: 1985.

BUDDHISM
(see also *Chinese Religion* and *Japanese Religion*)

*Chen, K. K. S. "Buddhism." In *Abingdon Dictionary of Living Religions*, ed. Keith Crim, pp. 124–36. Nashville: 1981.

Dayal, Har. *The Bodhisattva Doctrine in Buddhist Literature.* Delhi: 1975.

Eberhard, Wolfram. *Guilt and Sin in Traditional China.* Berkeley: 1967.

*King, Winston. *In the Hope of Nibbana.* La Salle, Ill.: 1964.

*Rahula, Walpola. *What the Buddha Taught.* New York: 1974.

Reynolds, Frank E. "Buddhist Ethics: A Bibliographical Essay." *Religious Studies Review* 5 (January 1979): 40–48.

Reynolds, Frank E. "Multiple Cosmogonies and Ethics: The Case of Theravada Buddhism." In *Cosmogony and Ethical Order*, pp. 203–24.

*Reynolds, Frank E., and Campany, Robert. "Buddhist Ethics." *ER*, vol. 2, pp. 498–504.

*Reynolds, Frank E., and Hallisey, Charles. "Buddhism: An Overview." *ER*, vol. 2, pp. 334–51.

Saddhatissa, H. *Buddhist Ethics: Essence of Buddhism.* London: 1970.

Tachibana, Shundo. *The Ethics of Buddhism.* Delhi: 1975.

CHINESE RELIGION
(see also *Buddhism*)

Bodde, Derk. *Festivals in Classical China.* Princeton, N.J.: 1975.

*Chan, Wing-tsit. *A Sourcebook in Chinese Philosophy.* Princeton, N.J.: 1963.

*Chan, Wing-tsit. "Confucian Thought: Foundations of the Tradition." *ER,* vol. 4, pp. 15–24.

*Chan, Wing-tsit. "Confucian Thought: Neo-Confucianism." *ER,* vol. 4, pp. 24–36.

Ch'en, Kenneth K. S. *Buddhism in China: A Historical Survey.* Princeton, N.J.: 1964.

Ch'en, Kenneth K. S. *The Chinese Transformation of Buddhism.* Princeton, N.J.: 1973.

*Cohen, Alvin P. "Chinese Religion: Popular Religion." *ER,* vol. 3, pp. 289–96.

de Groot, J. J. M. *The Religious System of China.* 6 vols. Tapei: 1964.

*Gernet, Jacques. *Daily Life in China.* Stanford, Calif.: 1970.

Hsu, Francis L. K. *Under the Ancestors' Shadow: Chinese Culture and Personality.* New York: 1948.

Maspero, Henri. *Taoism and Chinese Religion.* Amherst, Mass.: 1981.

*Overmayer, Daniel L. "Chinese Religion: An Overview." *ER,* vol. 3, pp. 257–89.

*Thompson, Laurence G. *Chinese Religion: An Introduction.* Belmont, Calif.: 1979.

*Thompson, Laurence G. *The Chinese Way in Religion.* Belmont, Calif.: 1973.

Welch, Holmes, and Seidel, Anna, eds. *Facets of Taoism.* New Haven: 1979.

Wolf, Arthur P., ed. *Ritual and Religion in Chinese Society.* Stanford, Calif.: 1974.

*Yang, C. K. *Religion in Chinese Society.* Berkeley, Calif.: 1970.

CHRISTIANITY

*Beach, Waldo, and Niebuhr, H. Richard. *Christian Ethics: Sources of the Living Tradition.* New York: 1955.

Betz, Hans Dieter. "Cosmgony and Ethics in the Sermon on the Mount." In *Cosmogony and Ethical Order,* pp. 158–76.

*Bock, Paul. *In Search of a Responsible World Society.* Philadelphia: 1974.

*Carmody, John, Carmody, Denise Lardner, and Robbins, Gregory A. *Exploring the New Testament.* Englewood Cliffs, N.J.: 1986.

*Childress, James F., and Macquarrie, John, eds. *The Westminister Dictionary of Christian Ethics.* Philadelphia: 1986.

*Curran, Charles E. "Christian Ethics." *ER,* vol. 3, pp. 340–48.

Curran, Charles E., and McCormick, Richard A. *Readings in Moral Theology.* 4 vols. New York: 1977–1983.

Dorr, Donal. *Option For The Poor.* Maryknoll, N.Y.: 1983.

Forell, George W. *History of Christian Ethics.* Vol. 1. Minneapolis: 1983.

Gustafson, James M. *Protestant and Roman Catholic Ethics.* Chicago: 1978.

Harakas, Stanley S. *Toward Transfigured Life.* Minneapolis: 1983.

*Marty, M. E. "Christianity." In *Abingdon Dictionary of Living Religions,* pp. 169–77.

Meyendorff, John. *Byzantine Theology.* New York: 1979.

Niebuhr, H. Richard. *Christ and Culture.* New York: 1951.

*Pelikan, Jaroslav. "Christianity: An Overview." *ER,* vol. 3, pp. 340–48.

*Stoeckle, Bernard, ed. *The Concise Dictionary of Christian Ethics.* New York: 1979.

Troeltsch, Ernst. *The Social Teachings of the Christian Churches.* 2 vols. Chicago: 1981.

Hinduism

Amore, Roy C., and Shin, Larry D., eds. *Lustful Maidens and Ascetic Kings.* New York: 1981.

*Ashby, P. H. "Hinduism." In *Abingdon Dictionary of Living Religions,* pp. 306–18.

*Basham, A. L. *The Wonder That Was India.* New York: 1959.

Dasgupta, S. N. *Hindu Mysticism.* New York: 1959.

Dimock, Edward C., Jr., et al. *The Literature of India: An Introduction.* Chicago: 1978.

Dumont, Louis. *Homo Hierarchicus.* Chicago: 1970.

*Gonda, Jan. "Indian Religions: An Overview." *ER,* vol. 7, pp. 168–76.

*Hiltebeitel, Alf. "Hinduism." *ER,* vol. 6, pp. 336–60.

*Hopkins, Thomas J. *The Hindu Religious Tradition.* Encino, Calif.: Dickenson, 1971.

Kakar, Sudhir. *Shamans, Mystics, and Doctors.* New York: 1982.

Kane, Pandurong Varman. *A History of the Dharmashastra.* 5 vols. Poona: 1930–1962.

*Kinsley, David R. *Hinduism.* Englewood Cliffs, N.J.: 1982.

*Kinsley, David R. *The Sword and the Flute.* Berkeley, Calif.: 1975.

Lingat, Robert. *The Classical Law of India.* Berkeley, Calif.: 1973.

*Naipaul, V. S. *India: A Wounded Civilization.* New York: 1978.

O'Flaherty, Wendy Doniger. *The Origins of Evil in Hindu Mythology.* Berkeley, Calif.: 1980.

*O'Flaherty, Wendy Doniger. *Women, Androgynes, and Other Mythical Beasts.* Chicago: 1980.

*Organ, Troy Wilson. *Hinduism.* Woodbury, N.Y.: 1974.

*Radhakrishnan, Sarvepalli, and Moore, Charles A., eds. *A Sourcebook in Indian Philosophy.* Princeton, N.J.: 1957.

*Wood, Ernest. *Yoga.* Baltimore: 1962.

Zimmer, Heinrich. *Philosophies of India.* Princeton, N.J.: 1969.

ISLAM

Burkhalter, Sheryl L. "Completion in Continuity: Cosmogony and Ethics in Islam." In *Cosmogony and Ethical Order,* pp. 225–50.

Coulson, Noel J. *A History of Islamic Law.* Edinburgh: 1971.

Esposito, John L. *Women in Muslim Family Law.* Syracuse, N.Y.: 1982.

Grunebaum, G. E. von. *Modern Islam: The Search for Cultural Identity.* Los Angeles: 1962.

*Kamali, M. Hashim. "Islamic Law: Personal Law." *ER,* vol. 7, pp. 446–53.

Keddie, Nikki R., ed. *Religion and Politics in Iran.* New Haven: 1983.

*Lawrence, B. "Islam." In *Abingdon Dictionary of Living Religions,* pp. 345–58.

*Martin, Richard C. *Islam: A Cultural Perspective.* Englewood Cliffs, N.J.: 1982.

*Mayer, Ann Elizabeth. "Islamic Law: Shari'ah." *ER,* vol. 7, pp. 431–46.

Mulla, D. F. *Principles of Mahomedan Law.* Bombay: 1968.

*Rahman, Fazlur. "Islam: An Overview." *ER,* vol. 7, pp. 303–22.

*Rahman, Fazlur. *Major Themes of the Qur'an.* Chicago: 1980.

Rosenthal, E. I. J. *Political Thought in Medieval Islam.* Cambridge, England: 1958.

Schacht, Joseph. *An Introduction to Islamic Law.* Oxford: 1974.

Smith, Wilfred Cantwell. *Islam in Modern History.* Princeton, N.J.: 1957.

Trajabi, F. B. *Muslim Law: The Personal Law of Muslims in India and Pakistan.* Bombay: 1968.

Tritton, A. S., *Materials on Muslim Education in the Middle Ages.* London: 1957.

JAPANESE RELIGION
(see also *Buddhism*)

Blacker, Carmen. *The Catalpa Bow: A Study of Shamanistic Practices in Japan.* London: 1975.

*Benedict, Ruth. *The Chrysanthemum and the Sword.* Boston: 1946.

Casal, U. A. *The Five Sacred Festivals of Ancient Japan.* Tokyo: 1967.

*Earhart, H. Byron, ed. *Religion in the Japanese Experience.* Encino, Calif.: 1974.

Eliot, Sir Charles. *Japanese Buddhism.* London: 1959.

Ellwood, Robert S., Jr. *The Feast of Kingship.* Tokyo: 1973.

Herbert, Jean. *Shinto: At the Fountainhead of Japan.* London: 1967.

*Hori, Ichiro. *Folk Religion in Japan.* Chicago: 1968.

Hori, Ichiro. *Japanese Religion.* Palo Alto, Calif.: 1972.

Kidder, Jonathan Edward. *Japan before Buddhism.* New York: 1966.

*Kitagawa, Joseph M. "Japanese Religion: An Overview." *ER,* vol. 7, pp. 520–38.

Kitagawa, Joseph M. *Religion in Japanese History*. New York: 1966.

McFarland, H. Neill. *The Rush Hour of the Gods: A Study of the New Religious Movements in Japan*. New York: 1967.

*Miller, Alan C. "Japanese Religion: Popular Religion." *ER*, vol. 7, pp. 538–44.

Spae, Joseph John. *Japanese Religiosity*. Tokyo, 1971.

Smith, Robert J. *Ancestor Worship in Contemporary Japan*. Stanford, Calif.: 1974.

*Tsunoda, Ryusaku, et al. eds., *Sources of Japanese Tradition*. New York: 1958.

Watanabe, Shako. *Japanese Buddhism: A Critical Appraisal*. Tokyo: 1968.

JUDAISM

*Borowitz, Eugene B. "Judaism: An Overview." *ER*, vol. 8, pp. 127–49.

Borowitz, Eugene B. *Liberal Judaism*. New York: 1984.

Bulka, Reuven P. *Dimensions of Orthodox Judaism*. New York: 1983.

*Carmody, John, Carmody, Denise Lardner, and Cohn, Robert L. *Exploring the Hebrew Bible*. Englewood Cliffs, N.J.: 1988.

*Dan, Joseph. "Jewish Ethical Literature." *ER*, vol. 8, pp. 82–87.

Elon, Menachem. *The Principles of Jewish Law*. Jerusalem: 1975.

*Fishbane, M. "Judaism." In *Abingdon Dictionary of Living Religions*, pp. 385–92.

Ginzberg, Louis. *The Legends of the Jews*. 7 vols. Philadelphia: 1909–1938.

*Heilman, Samuel C. *Synagogue Life*. Chicago: 1976.

*Klein, Isaac. *A Guide to Jewish Religious Practice*. New York: 1979.

Knight, Douglas A. "Cosmogony and Order in the Hebrew Tradition." In *Cosmogony and Ethical Order*, pp. 133–57.

Knobel, Peter. *Gates of Seasons*. New York: 1983.

*Levenson, Jon D. *Sinai and Zion*. New York: 1985.

Maslin, Simeon J., ed. *Gates of Mitzvah*. New York: 1979.

Montefiore, C. G., and Loewe, Herbert, eds. *A Rabbinic Anthology*. Philadelphia: 1960.

Soloveitchik, Joseph B. *Halakhic Man*. Philadelphia: 1983.

*Zborowski, Mark, and Herzog, Elizabeth. *Life Is with People*. New York: 1962.

Index